God Has No Favourites

The New Testament on
First Century Religions

God Has No Favourites

The New Testament on
First Century Religions

Basil Scott

primalogue

GOD HAS NO FAVOURITES

The New Testament on First Century Religions

A PUBLICATION OF

PRIMALOGUE PUBLISHING MEDIA PRIVATE LIMITED

#32, 2nd Cross, Hutchins Road, St Thomas Town PO,

Bangalore 560 084, India.

COVER ART & TYPESETTING

George Korah

Primalogue Publishing

WWW.PRIMALOGUE.COM

ISBN/EAN: 978-93-82759-01-0

FIRST EDITION 2013

COPYRIGHT © 2013 *BASIL SCOTT*

The Cover Photo by Lucretious (www.sxc.hu/profile/Lucretious) shows the famous "Porch of the Maidens", six draped female figures (caryatids) as supporting columns to one of the porches to the Erechtheion, an ancient Greek temple on the north side of the Acropolis of Athens in Greece.

Printed by Brilliant Printers Pvt. Ltd, Bangalore, India

CONTENTS

Foreword

This is a very enlightening and helpful book on a subject that is relevant here in South Asia and makes for interesting reading. The author and his wife have not just spent 20 years in South Asia but have lived among South Asian immigrants in the UK since their return to the UK in 1983. Their interest in the South Asian religions, and their openness to dialogue and learn from their exponents comes through on every page.

In the first part of the book, the author examines biblical material – largely from the New Testament – on how the Christian faith relates to other faith systems and how Christians ought to relate to people of other faiths. Then, in the second part of the book, the author seeks to draw various conclusions from his study of the biblical material.

In his examination of the biblical material, the author first sets the material in the Jewish, Greek and Roman religious context of the first century CE, and the even-handed way in which he deals with various passages, some suggesting an exclusive understanding of Jesus as the only way to God and salvation, and others emphasising that God is the God of all people and desires that all should be saved, is a model of fair and wholistic [canonical] exegesis. He takes particular note of the fact that, although several New Testament texts categorically state that God has revealed himself in Jesus and is to be known through him, such statements are positive in tone and there is no condemnation of other religious systems or threats of judgment to come.

His understanding and interpretation of the material is particularly enlightening and helpful, for the author covers several texts and issues that are of current interest and some of them hotly debated – the texts on the uniqueness of Christ, the universal lordship of Christ, the implications of the mission imperatives in Scripture, Paul's holding up Abraham as a model of a 'believer' or one who puts his trust in God. Then, under the general overarching themes of the love command and the golden rule, the author identifies various areas within which Christians can love and work with people of other faiths. Also, he widens the discussion on mission to include much more than mere proclamation, and includes also the thorny issue of persecution and the reaction of Christians to opposition and hostility for the sake of Christ and the gospel.

All in all, this is a most valuable addition to the books already available on this subject. May the Lord bless this effort, and may many of those who read this book be encouraged as they seek to relate to those of other faiths in a way that glorifies the Lord Jesus and is a witness to his love and grace. If we faithfully uplift him in our lives and before others, he will draw men and women to himself.

Brian Wintle

Preface

In our pluralist world how should Christians view other religions and their followers? This has been a subject of debate for centuries, but now it has become a question that concerns Christians wherever they are, because few live in a society where all believe in Christ as they do.

Nowhere is this question more important than in India where a continual succession of writers has wrestled with this issue. Nineteenth century converts from Hinduism, such as Brahmabandhab Upadhyay and Narayan Vaman Tilak struggled to find their own solutions. Sadhu Sundar Singh refused to cut himself off from his Sikh and Hindu upbringing. Since Independence, Catholic writers, such as Raimon Pannikar and Swami Abhishiktananda have argued that Christ is at work in Hindu devotees.

Mahatma Gandhi reacted to Christian claims by saying that as all religions are rooted in faith in the same God, all are of equal value. He asserted a common Hindu belief that all religions are ways to the same end and that all are equal. Therefore preaching for conversion is seen as an affront, as are all exclusive claims to the knowledge of God. Many would argue that due to religious extremism cooperation among religions is the need of the hour not conversion.

How then should Christians evaluate other religions? Do some devout souls find salvation through Hinduism, Buddhism or Islam? Are founders of other faiths, like Guru Nanak, to be rejected because they did not know Jesus? Does Christ alone possess an exclusive knowledge of the truth? Whatever the answer to these questions, it must surely be agreed that Christians have often failed to treat the devotees of other ways with the love and respect Jesus showed to non-Jews in his lifetime. Is this due to a failure to understand the religions of the world as God views them?

What does the New Testament have to say about religions in the Greco-Roman world of the first century A.D.? Do these religions contain knowledge of the truth? Do they reveal anything about God? Is salvation only for those who have found their way to Christ? What should characterise Christian attitudes to other faiths?

When these questions are debated by Christians reference is usually made to a limited selection of well-known texts, such as Jesus' words: *I am the Way, the Truth and the Life, no one comes to the Father except by me* (John 14:6), and Peter's statement to the Jewish leaders: *Salvation is found in no one else, for there is no other name given to men by which we must be saved* (Acts 4:12). What is needed is a study of all the New Testament documents, not a discussion confined to a few texts. This book provides a survey of what the New Testament has to say about religions and how Christ's disciples should relate to the followers of other religious beliefs. The focus is on the books of the New Testament, not the Old Testament, because it was with Christ that the gospel began to be proclaimed to all nations. The relevant New Testament material will be examined, beginning with religious beliefs and practices in the Roman Empire. At the same time we cannot ignore the religion of the Jews, as the faith which Jesus practised, a religion that was based on the Old Testament, and yet one whose leaders opposed him and were also condemned by him.

Religion is not a biblical term. However the Bible does refer to what we commonly classify as religions, such as beliefs concerning God or gods and the supernatural realm, practices inspired by these beliefs, worldviews, and ways of worship. Biblical writers are acutely aware of the importance of such beliefs, worship and behaviour, and that these should conform to God's revelation. In this sense it is assumed in the Bible that all races and nations display religious characteristics. We can therefore examine how the New Testament views religion in both Jewish and non-Jewish contexts.

The New Testament does not give much detailed information about the religions of those who were not Jews. For such data we have to turn to reference books and commentaries. What the Gospels, Acts and Epistles do reveal is their attitude to contemporary religions. These are apparently treated as being of human not divine origin, though this is something we have to examine. This might seem to indicate that the New Testament is hostile to the peoples of the Greek and Roman world. That is far from being the case. Christ has embraced the nations on the cross. The evangelists have the great joy of presenting Christ as God's salvation for all people. If there is one word that sums up the attitude of the New Testament it is the word 'inclusive'. The Gospel is all-inclusive and so for all people, tribes, languages and nations. The marvel is that Christ has opened the door to all, irrespective of race, religion, language, gender, age, education, or social status. There is no difference, no distinction, no difficulty in allowing all, not only to come to Christ, but also to come into the church. For Christ there can be no favouritism and there are no favourites. No succeeding generation has ever proclaimed more enthusiastically than first century Christians, the universality of Christ, his gospel and his church.

In sharp contrast, in the Jerusalem temple, non-Jews were excluded. Even proselytes, who were converts to Judaism, were kept to the outer precincts and were unable to enter the temple proper. No wonder then that Paul considered the marvel of the Gospel to be the inclusion of all races at the appointed time of God's mercy. The transformation of God's people from being confined to Israel into a universal religion, not bound by birth or race or state decree, never ceased to amaze Paul, the one-time Pharisee.

The context in which the apostles went out to preach the Gospel was the plurality of religions in Palestine and the Roman Empire. This variety provides some analogies with world religions today. But the application of the New Testament teaching to the relations between Christians and world religions such as Hinduism, Islam, Buddhism, Judaism and African primal religions is a different topic. The purpose here is to identify the approach of the New Testament to the religions of its time, so that this understanding can be applied with due consideration to the contemporary scene and current questions.

Some will ask, why go back to the New Testament? Have we not learnt much through the experience of the last 2000 years about relating to other religions? The answer is that we have yet much to learn. In the global village east and west have been forced together and it is no longer possible to live in a cocoon where we only meet people of our own religious community. Nowhere is this more truly the case than in India, where, since Independence, authorities have had to wrestle with the competing interests of a plurality of faiths. Some Christians have reacted as if pluralism should be ignored or rejected. The reality is that the Bible took shape against a pluralist background. The Israelites were surrounded on every side by a bewildering variety of religions, including Egyptian sun gods, Baal cult temple prostitutes and Babylonian imperial religion. In the New Testament from the moment the apostolic mission got under way, the missioners of the Messiah were plunged into the pluralist environment of the Graeco-Roman world, which included monism, monotheism, asceticism, mysticism, gnosticism, polytheism, animism, agnosticism and atheism.

In the face of pluralism western Christians need to show a little humility and admit that they have much to learn from the orthodox churches of the east, which have always lived with religious diversity, and also from the wisdom of our scriptures. Some will still want to say that the New Testament has very little to say on this subject, which is relevant to the religions we are faced with. As we will see, despite the absence of a detailed critique of contemporary religions, there is a great deal in the New Testament that bears directly or indirectly on the Christian attitude to world religions. Consequently Christians ought to reflect on the implications of what the New Testament teaches for their relations with neighbours from many faiths.

If it is argued that there is little point in examining the New Testament references to religious beliefs and practices, because nothing new will emerge from such study, the same could be said about any aspect of biblical theology. Theologians do not neglect the study of scriptural material just because much has been written in the past 500 years on a particular doctrine, rather the more attention is paid to a subject the more debate is stimulated and the more is written. The approach to scripture taken here is to accept the canon of the New Testament as it stands and to study the teaching it provides.

In India the scandal of conversion has always been the chief cause for complaint levelled against Christians by other religious communities. Conversion to the Christian faith is also said to be the cause for attacks on churches and the persecution of Christians by zealous members of other faiths. Under pressure from critics the response of some Christians has been to deny the very foundations of their faith in favour of the notion that all faiths are equally ways to God. This egalitarian approach may be conducive to the demands of secular society and may appear at first hand to be fair to Asian religions, but can it commend itself to the followers of Christ, who want to remain true to their Lord? Christians have to respond to the challenge of being faithful to Christ and fair in treating people of other faiths with integrity, respect and love. This challenge forces us back to the Scriptures. How did the apostles treat their neighbours, whatever their race or religion? What did they think of them and their beliefs?

Chapter 1 surveys what the New Testament has to say about religions outside Palestine. In Acts Paul meets different religious cults and philosophies. Four of these encounters provide significant findings. The New Testament commends the faith of some outstanding people who were not Jews. We note the surprisingly positive attitude of the apostles to people outside Israel and the church.

In this survey we cannot ignore Judaism. In Chapter 2 we consider what Jesus had to say about the religion of his contemporaries. Jesus affirmed Israel's core beliefs, as coming from the revelation of God through the Torah and the prophets. But he was sharply critical of some aspects of what scholars refer to as Second Temple Judaism. What exactly did he criticise most sharply, and what relevance might that have for Christian relations with Semitic religions, such as Judaism and Islam?

The church has traditionally formed its view of other religions not on the basis of what the New Testaments says about other faiths but on what it says about Christ. In Chapter 3 we discuss texts such as John 14:6 and Acts 4:12 (quoted above), which are used to dismiss the faith of people who are not Christians. Is that fair, and is that legitimate? What deductions should we draw from the compelling passages that expound Christ's supremacy?

One of the most impressive features of the New Testament is the advice it gives to tiny Christian communities suffering persecution at the hands of their neighbours or the state. In Chapter 4 we look at the instructions given by the New Testament, beginning with the teaching and example of Jesus himself.

In Part 2 an attempt is made to piece together the evidence we have examined, in order to answer some of the questions with which we began. Is God guilty of favouritism? How does God view people outside the church? Does God use the world's religions in any way? Is there only one way of salvation? Are Christians guilty of arrogance when they engage in evangelism? Finally, in a concluding postscript we relate this survey of the New Testament to the modern debate concerning what should be the Christian view of world faiths. At the practical level of daily life we draw attention to the New Testament guidelines for Christian behaviour in our multi-faith world.

Far too much of the debate about the Christian view of world religions has taken place as an internal debate between Christians. What is needed is an understanding of Christian relations with other major world religions, which can be explained in the public arena of our multi-faith world, without giving unnecessary offence and without compromise. This may not be as impossible as it sounds, because Christ is held in respect by most religions despite his high claims. It is the church that has failed to come up to the standard set by her master. Here is another reason for returning to the New Testament, to see how Christ conducted himself, and to discover what clues he gives his followers concerning the way they should behave in our world of conflicting religions.

Part I : Examining the Data

Introduction

THIS BOOK CONCENTRATES ON THE WRITINGS OF THE NEW
Testament, but the context in which Jesus and his disciples lived and
taught was the Old Testament. The revelation of God to the patriarchs
and prophets was the foundation on which the mission of the church was
built. The call of Abraham epitomised the journey of faith, by which a
polytheist came to know the reality of the one true God. The deliverance
of Israel from slavery in Egypt not only gave birth to a new nation but
also disclosed the grace and goodness of Abraham's God. To Moses God
declared that he is Yahweh, the great 'I AM', the one who is and always
will be. At Sinai Yahweh entered into covenant with the people of Israel.
Through the ensuing history of Israel God revealed his character and his
being through his servants the prophets. Into that prophetic line came
Jesus, who said that he was sent to fulfil the Law and the prophets.

Christians need to be reminded of the significance that Jesus was a
Jew. He was born into a Jewish family. He grew up in the Jewish faith. He
worshipped in the synagogue and temple, not in a church. He arose out
of Judaism to fulfil the promises given to Israel of a Messiah who would
establish the kingdom of God on earth. As we now know, he fulfilled
the messianic vision in a way that no Jew expected. But what should not
be forgotten is that Jesus came to complete what God had begun in the
Old Testament era, and that without Abraham, Moses, David and the
prophets there would have been no Christ.

The creation narratives in the first chapters of Genesis are essential
reading for anyone who wishes to understand the message of Jesus.
These chapters present the biblical worldview concerning God, man
and the universe. Of particular importance for the relationship between

4 God Has No Favourites

the people of God and the devotees of other religious beliefs is the revelation of God as creator. On the one hand belief in God as creator logically leads to faith in one God or monotheism. There can be no room for other gods, hence the Old Testament rejection of polytheism and the worship of a multiplicity of idols. On the other hand, since God is not only One without a second but also the creator of all mankind, he cannot be restricted to one tribe. All nations must be invited to worship him.

With the birth of Jesus God's revelation to humanity moved from Judaism to the world. Strict monotheism led to incarnation. The ultimate, invisible God took flesh and blood in the person of Jesus the Messiah. Far from being only a saviour for the Jewish race, Jesus fulfilled God's intention of inviting all races to worship their creator. The particularity of Jesus' birth at Bethlehem blossomed into the inclusive gospel of grace for every human being.

How does this universal gospel of Jesus relate to the religions of the world? It should have been welcomed, but Paul tells us that the gospel was heresy to Jews and anathema to Greeks. Far from fulfilling what Jews longed for and what Greek philosophy thought reasonable, the incarnation, cross and resurrection of Jesus appeared foolish and were rejected with hostility and disdain.

The second chapter looks at Jesus' relationship with Judaism, the religion of his family and people. In the first chapter consideration is given to the encounter between the gospel of Jesus and the surrounding peoples of the Mediterranean region, as the church reached out to all nations.

Chapter One

Religions in the
Greek and Roman World

WHAT DOES THE NEW TESTAMENT TELL US ABOUT RELIGIONS outside Palestine and what is its approach to those who were Gentiles[1] (that is people who were racially and religiously not Jewish), and their beliefs and practices? Data concerning the religions prevalent in the world of the New Testament can be found in many reference works. What we focus attention on here is the evidence provided by the New Testament itself, and especially the attitude of its writers to contemporary religions.[2]

Gentiles

The English Bible uses the word 'Gentiles' to describe non-Jews. The Hebrew and Greek words in the original text of the Bible, which are translated 'Gentiles', literally mean 'nations'. In the Old Testament the Hebrew word for 'nations' is *goyim* and in the New Testament the Greek term is *ethne*, from which we get the English words 'ethnic' and 'ethnicity'. The word 'Gentile' comes from the Latin translation of the Bible, which was universally used in Europe until the Reformation, and

---

[1] Gentiles are usually referred to in the New Testament as *ta ethne* ('the nations'). The word *ethnikos* is also used 5 times with the negative connotations of the English word 'pagans'.

[2] As noted in the introduction I use 'religion' to refer to peoples' beliefs, ways of worship and practices. For further discussion on the use of the term 'religion' see Ida Glaser, *The Bible and Other Faiths*, Leicester, 2005, pp.16ff. and T.L. Tiessen, *Who Can Be Saved?*, Downers Grove, 2004, pp.297ff.

is derived from the Latin word *gens* meaning 'nation'. In Latin it was
an accurate and literal translation of the Hebrew and Greek words for
'nation', but that literal meaning is lost in modern English. Israel is one of
the nations, but Jews regarded Israel as different from all the surrounding
nations, because of God's dealings with them. They looked back to the
way God had rescued them from slavery through the Exodus from Egypt,
revealing his laws to them at Sinai, and how he had brought them into the
Promised Land of Canaan. By the time of Christ Jews had developed an
exclusive attitude to other nations and regarded them with opprobrium.

In this chapter we will sometimes use the word Gentile to refer to
non-Jews, not as a term of abuse but to mean those who were both racially
and religiously not Jewish. We will also use other terms to indicate that
Gentiles were people from other religions and races outside Judaism.

The church of today needs to remember that the New Testament is
a Jewish book. With the possible exception of Luke, all the writers were
Jews. From childhood Jews were brought up to view other races and
religions not only with suspicion but also with disdain. Since other races
were impure, any contact with them defiled a Jew. In Acts, Luke shows
the revolutionary impact on the Jewish church of God's command to take
the gospel to all the nations. The stories of Paul's commissioning as the
apostle to the Gentiles and Peter's encounter with the Roman soldier,
Cornelius, dominate Acts and show how the apostles' understanding of
mission was transformed by these events. How did this affect the way the
New Testament writers viewed other races and religions? The inclusion
of non-Jews in the church was a matter for debate and amazement in the
early decades of the new movement. It was difficult enough to accept
converted Gentiles. How then were Gentiles outside the church and their
religions to be regarded?

Encounters with Religion in the Roman Empire[3]

We look first at descriptions of religious practices and beliefs in the
Roman Empire, to discover the New Testament attitude to religious
practices in the ancient world. Then we review the positive records

---

[3] The Roman Empire included the whole of the Mediterranean and all the
provinces that bordered the Mediterranean, including north Africa. The territory
under the control of Rome stretched from Britain to Egypt and went as far north as
the Danube and the Rhine.

concerning some outstanding Gentiles who are mentioned mostly in the Gospels and Acts. We then summarise what the New Testament has to say about the achievements and conduct of religions in the Greek and Roman world.

In the Gospels we meet with Gentile individuals, but there is no description of any particular Gentile religion. When we move on to Acts the situation changes. From chapter 8 the church begins to move out from Jerusalem and Judaea into Samaria and then into the world beyond, to Phoenicia, Cyprus, Asia Minor, Greece and Italy. Not surprisingly then, it is in Acts that we get the first and clearest descriptions of encounters with Gentile religions in the New Testament. In the Epistles Paul does not describe any religious sect in detail. He has no interest in helping his readers to understand the religions practised in the cities he visited. Scholars have had to piece together data from non-biblical sources concerning the prevailing cults with their mixture of mysticism, gnosticism, asceticism, idolatry, divination and philosophy. The only aspect that Paul does give us any detail about is idolatry and his critique of it. In the remainder of the New Testament the only significant additional descriptions of religious practices occur in the book of Revelation, especially in its allusions to the worship of the Emperor.

The priest of Zeus   (Acts 14:8-20)

The visit of Paul and Barnabas to the Roman colony of Lystra provides a typical example of popular religion involving devotion to gods of Greek mythology. A similar incident could easily occur in parts of the Indian sub-continent today.[4]

The excitement of the Lycaonian crowd is aroused by Paul's healing of a man, who had been a cripple from birth.[5] The locals rightly attribute this miracle to divine power, but credit it to their gods not to God himself.

---

[4]   Anyone who has lived in a pluralist environment like India, where many gods are worshipped, will have no difficulty in identifying with this situation. The reaction of the crowd to the miracle in treating Barnabas and Paul as gods is just what might happen today in a similar situation. Scholars who think this story unlikely have probably never lived in such an environment for long.

[5]   Many commentators draw attention to the parallels with the healing of the cripple at Jerusalem's Beautiful Gate, e.g. F. Jackson & K. Lake, *The Beginnings of Christianity*, London 1933, I.4. p.163.

The gods (hoi theoi) have come down to us in human form (homoiothentes anthropois, v.11). The belief that gods can take human form is key to understanding their reactions to the healing.

Barnabas and Paul are taken to be Zeus and Hermes, the gods the crowd are devoted to.[6] Zeus, the chief god of the Greek pantheon, was the focus for their worship. Hermes, a son of Zeus, who was regarded as the messenger of the gods, is identified with Paul as the chief spokesman for the missionaries.

The temple of Zeus was located just outside, or in front of, the city.[7] The priest emerges from his temple and comes to meet the apostles at the city gates with bulls ready for sacrifice and with wreaths. The wreaths are probably to garland the bulls as sacrificial victims not to garland Barnabas and Paul as gods.[8]

Paul and Barnabas have to go to extreme lengths to stop the crowd carrying out their intentions and sacrificing the animals to them as gods. Only the most strenuous efforts of the apostles in tearing their clothing (indicating their horror at blasphemy) and rushing ungodlike into the crowd shouting, *Men, why are you doing this? We too are only human like you,* was in the end sufficient to stop their devotion. Later the frenzy of the crowd turned to anger and they stoned Paul unconscious (v.19).

The proclamation of the apostles (v.15-17), as they appealed to the crowd, is the centre-piece of this story.[9] Everything that precedes it from v.8 prepares for it and the verses that follow flow from it.[10]

Men, why are you doing this? We too are only men, human like you. We are bringing you good news, telling you to turn from these

---

⁶   According to local legend Zeus and Hermes had come down on earlier occasions in the guise of humans, cf. F.F. Bruce, *The Book of the Acts* (revised edition), Grand Rapids, 1988, p.274.

⁷   According to archaeological and historical evidence the temple of Zeus was located outside the city gates.

⁸   C.K. Barrett, *The Acts of the Apostles,* Vol. I, Edinburgh, 1994, p.678.

⁹   Some commentators point to the similarity between the speech at Lystra and Paul's preaching in 1 Thess. 1:9. Cf. I.H. Marshall *The Acts of the Apostles,* London, 1980, p.239 and F.F. Bruce *Commentary on the Book of the Acts,* London, 1954, p.277.

¹⁰   For a suggestive examination of the whole passage see M. Fournier, *The Episode at Lystra: A Rhetorical and Semiotic Analysis of Acts 14:7-20,* Peter Lang, New York, 1997.

worthless things to the living God, who made heaven and earth and sea and everything in them. In the past, he let all nations go their own way. Yet he has not left himself without testimony: He has shown kindness by giving you rain from heaven and crops in their seasons; he provides you with plenty of food and fills your hearts with joy.

This is the first speech in Acts directed to a polytheistic audience. What does it reveal about the apostles' attitude to Gentile religions?

Negatively Paul and Barnabas are horrified at being treated as gods in human likeness. *We are only human beings just like you*, they shout to the crowd. As Jews, brought up to believe in one God only and to reject all worship of other gods as blasphemy, their horror is understandable. They were also in an awkward predicament. The Lystrans believed the gods could disguise themselves as humans. This made it even more difficult for Paul and Barnabas to prove that they were not just pretending to be human, but really were ordinary people. To complicate matters further, they were foreigners and therefore different.

Paul does not approve of this religion, but on the other hand he does not condemn the people or their priest. Instead he remonstrates with them for worshipping the creature rather than the Creator and urges them to turn from worthless things to the living God.

The speech identifies the error of the Lystrans as belief in vain things (contrasted with faith in the 'living God'). They are urged to turn 'from these vain things' (v.15). What are these vain or futile things? The plural *ta mataia* may simply be equated with 'idols'.[11] They certainly include the idolatrous sacrifice of garlanded bulls, which the priest and people wanted to offer to Zeus and Hermes. They may also include the belief in many gods and in the manifestation of these gods in the guise of humans.

Positively, the apostles appeal to the people to put their faith in the 'living God'. God is referred to not as Yahweh or the Lord (Jesus) but as the one who is alive and active, in contrast to the dead gods of image worship and mythology. The good news is that the 'living God' is not someone they have never heard of and have no knowledge of, but someone who has been present in their past and is active in their present.

---

[11] Barrett, op.cit., p.680.

The apostles appeal to the Lystrans' experience of the creator God, who has revealed himself to them through creation, for the living God has *made heaven and earth and sea and everything in them* (v.15).[12] Rain, crops, seasons and harvests also point to him. These are a testimony not only to God's existence but also to his goodness and kindness, for he provides plenty of food and fills their hearts with joy (v.17). Though Paul did not refer to it, he knew the Lystrans were aware of monotheism through the teaching of some Greek philosophers and Jewish synagogues.

The Lystrans' ignorance of the living God is not condemned but explained by the fact that God permitted all the nations to worship ('to walk') in their own ways (v.16). There is no suggestion that the Gentiles have salvation, since they are ignorant of God and his ways. But God has forgiven their ignorance and included them in his new provision for the world. So they are invited to receive the good news and turn to God.

Luke portrays these worshippers of Greek gods as having the conditions for genuine faith. They recognise a work of divine healing when they see one. They are open to God coming among them and to appearing in human form. They were not blind to the evidence of God in creation, when it was pointed out to them. The door of faith is being opened to the Gentiles (v.27). Recognition and acknowledgment of the living God will be the faith that saves them. This will be the prelude to receiving the gospel of Jesus hinted at in the text by the word for 'preaching the good news' (v.7, 15, 21).[13] God cared for people who were not Jews and would continue to do so. The presentation is theocentric not Christocentric, which underlines the belief that Greek religion does not preclude faith in the one true God.[14]

Compared with modern world religions this cameo would fit most easily into a Hindu context.

---

[12]　14:15b contains a quote from the Septuagint of Ex. 20:11. Nevertheless God is not presented to the Lystrans as the God of judgment, justice and the Mosaic covenant, but as a provident and benevolent creator. Note that Acts substitutes *theon zonta* (living God) for *kurios* (Lord) in the Septuagint (Greek translation of the Old Testament).

[13]　See M. Fournier op.cit. The verb for preaching the good news, *euaggelizo*, is a keyword in this narrative and occurs in v.7, 15, 21.

[14]　Barrett calls it "an approach that owed so much to natural theology" (op. cit., p.665).

The Pythoness (Acts 16:16-21)

In Acts 16 Luke recalls Paul's visit to another Roman colony, this time Philippi in Macedonia. At first sight this reveals little of importance about religion in Greece. But the key words, *pneuma puthona* ('a python spirit'), translated by NIV as 'a spirit by which she predicted the future', open a window into a different cult. Here *puthona* refers to the mythological python or serpent, said to have been slain by Apollo, which guarded the Delphic oracle. Apollo was thought to be symbolised by the snake and to inspire his female devotees, or 'pythonesses'. The word *puthona* came to mean a person inspired by Apollo with a spirit of divination and associated with ventriloquism. The pythoness was a ventriloquist in the old sense of a spirit speaking from the belly ('venter'), usually with the mouth closed and uttering things beyond the person's control. These things included predictions and fortune telling. In the Septuagint (Greek translation of the Old Testament) the term for a ventriloquist (*eggastrimuthos*) is used of those who had an occult spirit, such as the witch at Endor.[15]

Luke regards the slave girl as being possessed with an evil spirit, which earned her owners a lot of money by fortune-telling.[16] We note that for many days the girl keeps crying out: *these men are servants of the Most High God*. The title 'Most High God' (*theos hupsistos*)[17] was used by both Jews and Greeks in referring to the supreme being, though Greeks might use it simply for Zeus. Nevertheless the name points to belief in a supreme deity. Luke attributes the girl's acknowledgment of the High God to the supernatural insight of the demon possessed. Compare this with what the possessed man said of Jesus in Mark 1:24: *you are the Holy One of God*. The girl adds that Paul and his followers were preaching 'a way of salvation', something that would have been of interest to both Greeks and Romans.

The fact that Paul finally exorcises the spirit from the girl demonstrates not only the demonic influence at work in the girl, but also the power of the name of Jesus Christ to liberate the possessed. In one sense casting out the Pythean spirit was an attack on the Delphic

---

[15] I Sam. 28:7ff.

[16] In v.16 Luke uses the term *manteuomai* ('give an oracle'), which is the technical term for ecstatic prophecy in the Hellenistic world and occurs nowhere else in the N.T.

[17] The corresponding title in Hebrew is *El Elyon*.

tradition. That may be hinted at in v. 20-21, where the owners of the slave girl complain that Paul and Silas were advocating unlawful customs. True, their main concern was the loss of their money-making fortune-teller, but in the process they could claim that Paul was undermining sacred traditions. There were in fact three charges lodged against Paul and Silas: that they were Jews, that they were disturbing the peace and that they were advocating unlawful customs. The third along with the first may simply have been an attack on the Jews and their foreign religious practices, such as circumcision, food laws and refusal to acknowledge the gods of Greece and Rome.

In the encounter with the slave girl Paul was concerned for three related issues: possession by an evil spirit, the exploitation of this girl's condition and fortune telling. Undoubtedly Paul attacked the use of psychic powers for fortune telling as demonic and the exploitation of the girl for motives of avarice. However this was not an attack on Greek religion as such but action in protest against debased forms of religion and the commercialisation of religion.

Fortune-telling and divination whilst in a trance state and the association of gods with the snake symbolism are commonly found in popular religion in both Asia and Africa. In Hindu mythology Shiva is usually pictured with a snake coiled around the upper half of his body and Nag, the snake god, is part of village folk lore. The similarities between Hindu and Greek mythology are striking, though the differences are also important.

Paul before the Areopagus   (Acts 17:16-34)

In Athens Paul met a sophisticated audience ready for philosophical discussion.[18] The trappings of popular religion were there, but within that setting there were intellectuals who despised idolatry and welcomed more refined debate.

---

[18] See C.K. Barrett, *The Acts of the Apostles*, Vol. II, Edinburgh, 1998, pp.824ff. for a discussion of whether the speech before the Areopagus court owes its origin to Paul or Luke. The contrast with Rom. 1:18-31 is misleading, for Paul's approach to Gentiles of a nobler sort is to be found in Rom. 2. To contrast the theocentric approach of Acts 17:22-31 with the Christocentric approach of Paul's epistles and to conclude that Paul could not have been the author of the Areopagus speech is to overstate the case. It can equally well be argued that Paul's approach in Athens articulated the theology of Romans 1-4 in a Gentile philosophical context.

The setting is outlined in v. 16-21. Paul was distressed by the plethora of idols in the city. Athens is said to have had 30,000 statues or idols, more than the rest of Greece put together. To be on the safe side, some Athenians had even erected an altar to an unknown god (v. 23). Paul debated with Jews and God-fearing Greeks in the synagogue. He also moved into the market-place (*agora*), where he met Epicurean and Stoic philosophers (v.18). It is these philosophers who took an interest in Paul and brought him to the court of Areopagus. This court was responsible for the corporate life of Athens, including matters of education, public morality and foreign cults. Therefore its members wanted to know why Paul was preaching two new gods, Jesus and *Anastasis* ('resurrection').

Both Epicureans and Stoics[19] disdained superstitious temple worship and devotion to idols. Epicureans theoretically opposed all forms of superstition. They would therefore have agreed with Paul that God does not live in temples made with human hands (v.24). They criticised the crass aspects of popular religion and ridiculed the idea of bringing God a sheep, as if he were hungry, or of supposing that he could be confined to a building. According to Epicurean teaching, the gods exist but live in tranquillity remote from the world. Man does not need to fear divine intervention in this life or punishment after death. The chief end of life is to live in undisturbed happiness.

Stoics, though believing in the one God, also recognised the gods of mythology. For them the terms 'God' and 'gods' were interchangeable, much as they often are in Hinduism today. They inclined to a pantheistic view that the soul of the cosmos is God and thought of God as impersonal. So providence tends to be impersonal too. The highest principle in nature is reason (*logos*), which was responsible for combining the elements to produce the world.

Reviewing this narrative, the following should be noted. Despite Paul's distress at seeing so many idols in Athens, he found common ground between himself and the philosophers at the Areopagus. He observed that the Athenians were very religious and found in the altar to an unknown god a point from which he could begin. What they

---

[19] See *The Oxford Classical Dictionary*, 3rd Ed., 1996, for articles on Stoicism and Epicurus.

were ignorant of he wanted to proclaim, moving from the known to the unknown (v.23). The God he knows is the creator of everything, who needs no temple to live in and no priests to feed him like a common idol (v.25). In v.26 Paul began to suggest some key principles for a theology of religions. He took a starting point outside Israel and before Abraham and began with Adam. God has created the diversity of nations (the Gentiles) with their differences of tribe, geography and history, but all descended from one ancestor.[20] There is no room for racism here, in fact Jews and Gentiles are brothers and sisters, part of the one human race. All human beings, whether Jews or Gentiles, are God's creatures, 'his offspring'. Paul then warmed to his theme, focusing on the human instinct to search for God (v.27). It is even possible that people will find God in response to his initiative, for God is not far from us and desires that man's search for him should not be fruitless. To press home his point he quoted from two Greek poet philosophers, Epimenides the Cretan and Aratus.[21] Paul argued that both Stoics and Epicureans were wrong to tolerate idolatry in practice, despite opposing it in theory (v.29). He went on to more controversial ground by declaring that God has proclaimed a day of judgment (rejected by Epicureans) and aroused the scorn of many in his audience, but not all, by talking of the resurrection. Such an 'unspiritual' concept was not to the liking of Greek philosophers. This proved too big a jump for most of his hearers.

What then did Paul think of Greek philosophical religion, of the Greeks' knowledge of God and of their standing before their creator?

How significant are Paul's quotes from Greek poets?[22] There is definitely one from the Stoic, Aratus, *we are his offspring*. But the first part of v.28 is not necessarily a quote from Epimenides and does not correspond exactly

[20]   For the significance of human diversity in the world God has created, see Jonathan Sacks, *The Dignity of Difference*, London and New York, 2002.

[21]   Epimenides the Cretan, is a somewhat mythical figure, said to be among the seven sages of Greece. A considerable amount of later literature was attributed to him, including a poem about Minos from which Paul's quotation may have been taken. Aratus was influenced by Zeno, the Stoic. He wrote a treatise in verse about astronomy titled *Phaenomeia*. It is from the beginning of this work that Paul quoted.

[22]   K. Lake, *The Beginnings of Christianity*, London, 1933, I.4. p.247, quotes the poetic verses concerned in Greek. F.F. Bruce, *The Book of Acts*, Grand Rapids, 1988, p.338f. quotes the verses in English translation.

with any known Greek text.[23] Aratus may have intended his words to have a pantheistic meaning, since for him God (Zeus) is the Logos who animates all things. However Paul did not endorse Stoic philosophy, but affirmed a truth the poet had expressed.[24] In v.29 he made it clear that he did not understand *we are his offspring* in a pantheistic sense, but in the biblical sense of human beings created in the likeness of their personal creator. Paul boldly used the words, because he wanted to persuade the Stoics, on their own premises, to refuse to tolerate the veneration of man-made images, however impressive (v.29). The phrase attributed to Epimenides, *in him we live and move and have our being*, recalls Stoic terms. Paul used the language of his audience to communicate new ideas. He wished to emphasise man's dependence on a personal creator. In using such language Paul was not only contextualising his message as an effective missionary,[25] but accepting the connection between the God he worshipped and the aspirations of the Greeks.

The citations of v.28 follow and were meant to support the statement in v.27, that God's purpose is that all should seek him, because he is near to all. Divine immanence was a Stoic concept, so Paul could reasonably appeal to this belief in the nearness of God, in contrast to the Epicurean notion that the gods are remote and have nothing to do with humanity. Paul saw the search for deity not as mankind's quest for God, but as God's desire that his creatures should find him. On this basis it would be surprising if God were to make the search an impossible task. It is true that Paul did not say that anyone who seeks will find, for he wanted to emphasise that both the search and the finding depend on God. Certainly Paul views the quest not as a philosophical pursuit based on the indwelling Logos, but as a seeking after God, to know and obey him, in the Old Testament Jewish sense, that is seeking a right relationship with God and not a merely intellectual knowledge of the divine.

---

[23] C.K. Barrett, op.cit. p. 848f.

[24] F.F. Bruce, op.cit., comments: "in both these poems Zeus is considered not as the ruler of the traditional pantheon of Greek mythology but as the supreme being of Greek, and especially Stoic, philosophy ... Even in their contexts, the words quoted ... could be taken as pointing to some recognition of the true nature of God."

[25] Paul's incarnational method is outlined in 1 Cor. 9:19ff. Note particularly the words: *To those not having the law I became like one not having the law ... I have become all things to all men so that by all possible means I might save some* (v. 21, 22).

What do v. 24-29 imply about the Greeks' knowledge of God? From classical literature we are aware that Greeks were familiar with the concept of God as the origin of the universe, but more as the prime mover or first cause than as the creator. The biblical understanding of creation *ex nihilo* and God as the personal creator is absent. But Greek philosophers were not gross idolaters, and thinkers like Plato demonstrated real insight into the transcendence of the Supreme Being. Paul's quote from Aratus implies an awareness of the divine presence. However, as Gartner[26] comments, "we rarely find any personal note in epithets applied to the All-God" of Stoic philosophy, which uses a neuter term for the deity. Paul was concerned to proclaim the character of God and to emphasise the need for relationship with him. He did not have to argue for the existence of God and could find Stoic and Epicurean support against gross superstition.

At Athens Paul did not put forward any argument for general revelation from creation, as he had done at Lystra and would do in Romans 1-2. On the other hand he appealed to the Stoic awareness of a divine being and argued that as they accepted belief in a Supreme Being, it was logical to reject image worship. In addition, since God himself *gives all men life and breath and everything else*, it is not surprising that Greek poets (whether Epimenides or someone else) recognised their dependence on God, *for in him we live and move and have our being*. Paul went a step further when he quoted the words of Aratus, *we are his offspring*, assuming that the Stoics had grasped from reflection on human nature a connection between us and God as our creator. If we are indeed his offspring, and therefore have a likeness to God, this link reveals clues about God's character, in particular that he is not inanimate and impersonal like *gold or silver or stone*, but alive, active and in control. So though Paul did not talk about the revelation of God's existence and attributes through creation, providence and the *imago dei*, he certainly implied it. At the same time it is true that Paul relied on the biblical revelation of God and his statements concerning God are drawn from the Old Testament, even though there are no scriptural quotations and the language used is influenced by Stoicism.

Why then did Paul accuse his hearers of ignorance both at the beginning and end of his speech (v.23, 30)? In both verses the ignorance that

---

[26] B. Gartner, *The Areopagus Speech and Natural Revelation*, Uppsala, 1955, p.185.

is rejected is the ignorance exhibited by idolatry. All Greeks had not fallen for superstitious practices and Paul could appeal to Stoics and Epicureans for support in decrying the worship of images. To them Paul wished to proclaim God's new way. The new way that Paul proclaimed was generous and universal, as well as demanding (v.30,31). As at Lystra, so here, Paul repeated that God did not hold people guilty for their ignorance in the past (v.30). In saying this Paul applied the principle enunciated by previous Jewish writers, as in the Wisdom of Solomon 11:23:

> But thou hast mercy on all men, because thou hast power to do all things, and thou overlookest the sins of men to the end they may repent.

Paul's vision is universalist in scope. There is one God, one human race and one mediator/judge. The thrust of the speech is to show God's concern for all his creatures. Note the frequent use of the word *all* (*pas* and its cognates occur 7 times in v. 22-31) and similar terms. None are beyond his reach or his concern. To this end God has announced a new epoch within which it will be possible for all to find him through the man whom he has raised from the dead.

Only at the very end did Paul lose the attention of his audience with mention of the resurrection (v.32). It should not be forgotten that when the Stoics and Epicureans came across Paul in the *agora*, they thought he was talking about two new gods, one of whom was *anastasis* ('resurrection', v.18). They therefore took him before the court of Areopagus to explain this foreign cult. Paul did not immediately respond, but he did not forget why he was standing before the Areopagites. In the end he wanted to talk to them about the resurrection of a man. Many commentators see it as a weak point that Paul did not refer to Jesus Christ but to a man. However, the miracle of the resurrection is the resurrection not of a god, for which there were mythical counterparts, but of a man. The reaction of the Athenians was understandable. N.T. Wright argues that: "Lots of things could happen to the dead in the beliefs of pagan antiquity, but resurrection was not among the available options."[27] That there were some, who wanted to give the new way more thought was commendable.

[27] N.T. Wright, *The Resurrection of the Son of God*, London, 2003, p.38. See the evidence he sets out in pp.32-84.

To sum up: Paul recognised Greek philosophers as those he could dialogue with concerning their approach to God. He did not condemn them or their poets. Seeing that the seeking after God in their religions could provide a basis for the gospel, he built a bridge toward the dominant culture of his time. His speech presents a positive evaluation of the best in Greek religious thought and offers a generous assessment of its achievements.[28]

The ideas of the Stoics and Epicureans resonate strongly with views held by the schools of Hindu philosophy and their rejection of Paul's gospel has points in common with the modern objections of Advaita Vedanta to Christian teaching.[29]

The Mother Goddess (Acts 19:23-41)

From mainland Greece we turn to Ephesus, one of the great cities of Asia Minor. The temple dedicated to Artemis is well known due to the outcry of the silversmiths complaining against Paul (v.23ff.). The temple was one of the seven wonders of the world. The image of Artemis was housed there, as it was said to have fallen from heaven (possibly a meteorite).[30]

Artemis of Ephesus was the great mother goddess of Asia Minor, worshipped as Demetrius claims, *throughout the province of Asia and the world*. Originally a fertility goddess, linked with child birth and also with hunting, she resembles the mother goddess Cybele. The main role of Artemis was that of protectress for the city and for those who fled to her, especially young women (also young men).[31]

Not only did the Ephesians visit the temple of Artemis, they also bought silver shrines[32] of the goddess for use in their homes. It was this trade in shrines that suffered, as did the trade in occult scrolls mentioned

[28] S.G. Wilson, *The Gentiles and the Gentile Mission in Luke-Acts*, Cambridge, 1973, p.217.

[29] For an Indian viewpoint see Prema Vakayil, *Paul's dialogue with the Athenian intellectuals Acts 17:16-30* in Indian Theological Studies, 45. 2008, 4. – pp. 449-459.

[30] For a study of Acts 19:23-41, see Rick Strelan, *Paul, Artemis and the Jews in Ephesus*, Berlin & New York, 1996.

[31] Strelan op.cit. p.52.

[32] Miniature silver niches containing an image of the goddess were bought by devotees and blessed in the temple.

in v. 18-20, as a result of Paul's preaching. Demetrius complains that Paul spread the word that *man-made gods are no gods at all* (v.26).

Addressing the hostile Ephesian crowd, the city clerk acknowledges that Paul and his followers had not blasphemed their goddess or robbed their temple. It is worth noting that Paul like Philo and Josephus did not believe in denigrating local deities.[33] The clerk rejected the claim of the guild craftsmen to business protection on the ground that the Artemis image and temple would survive the new teaching, and ruled that for their business concerns they should go to the courts. Once again Paul avoids wholesale condemnation of a Gentile religion and concentrates on presenting the word of the Lord (v. 20) in convincing fashion. However Acts 19 does show that Paul was critical of 'man-made gods', but in this he was not alone. Others such as Heraclitus and the Epicureans had also attacked image worship. Again in this narrative, as in Acts 16:16-24, there is an implied criticism of those who commercialise religion.

Here we have another familiar figure in the world of popular religion, the mother goddess. Compare and contrast this figure with the Hindu cults devoted to the mother goddess, such as Durga, Kali and many others, to draw out the differences and similarities.

Idol worship

Gentile religion is most often characterised in the New Testament as idolatry, and not without reason, for the worship of images was the most common ingredient in popular cults. Paul's encounters with some of the religions of the Roman Empire in Acts illustrate the point. Elsewhere in the New Testament the most extended reference to the practice of idolatry is to be found in 1 Corinthians 8 and 10, where Paul discusses the issue of meat offered to idols.

In the New Testament the word for idol (*eidolon*) is used for heathen gods and their images. The idols are usually images of the gods of mythology, made of gold, silver, bronze, stone or wood (Rev. 9:20). Jose Faur explains the significance of the connection between the idol and its god. "The identification of a god with an idol was......effected by a

---

[33] Strelan op. cit. p.151 quotes Philo and Josephus advising Jews not to blaspheme pagan deities. Cf. Rom. 2:22.

special ritual of consecration ..."[34] The god infused his spirit into the idol. This took place at the ritual of consecration. Before that the idol was lifeless. Through consecration the image was thought to acquire all the senses of a living being. Therefore sacrifices of food and drink were given to the idol (cf. 1 Cor. 8:4-10; 10:21). Idols needed to be housed and clothed (cf. Acts 17:24f.).

The New Testament attitude to idolatry can best be seen from Romans 1:18-32. Here Paul finds the root of evil in the world to be idolatry. This is not a condemnation of the Gentile world alone, for Israel in the past had been guilty of falling back into idolatry many times. However as a Jew, who had been brought up from childhood to recite the Shema - *Hear O Israel: the Lord our God is one Lord*[35] - Paul instinctively recoiled from any hint of idolatry. The pluralism of his surroundings was a constant threat to monotheism. His response was to proclaim the one against the many, to preach one God and one Lord Jesus Christ against the many so-called 'gods' and 'lords' of the Gentile world (1 Cor. 8:4, 5). Paul was distressed to find Athens full of idols (Acts 17:16) and urged both Athenians and Lystrans to *turn from these worthless things to the living God* (Acts 14:15; cf. 17:29f.). He congratulated the Thessalonian believers on doing just that, rejoicing that they had *turned to God from idols to serve the living and true God* (1 Thess. 1:9).

The New Testament criticism of idolatry is based on the Old Testament analysis. "The biblical injunction against idolatry rests on two different premises: it violates the Covenant and it is useless", says Faur.[36] To this the New Testament adds that idolatry is dangerous.

The fundamental point is that idol worship violates the bond between God and his creatures. This was particularly serious for the Jews, who were favoured by God's covenant, but it also applies to every human being. Idolatry substitutes something or someone else in place of God. It is the supreme act of treachery. Whatever claims the loyalty that belongs to God alone is idolatry (cf. 1 John 5:19-21). It is not possible to have fellowship with God and with his opponents (1 Cor. 10:21).

[34] Jose Faur, *The Biblical Idea of Idolatry*, Jewish Quarterly Review, 1978, pp.1-15.
[35] Deut. 6:4.
[36] J. Faur, op. cit. p.9.

The Old Testament had derided the powerlessness of idols. The New Testament continues to repeat the same theme. Paul derides 'dumb idols' (1 Cor. 12:2). *We know,* he says, *that an idol is nothing at all in the world.* As for the many 'so-called gods', whether they are said to be in heaven or on earth, they are false and have no meaning for us, who know only one God, the Father, and one Lord, Jesus Christ (1 Cor. 8:4-6). Elsewhere, the author of Revelation describes idols as useless – *they cannot see or hear or walk* (Rev. 9:20).

However, though the idols are 'nothing' and the gods are 'no gods' (Gal. 4:8), to worship them is dangerous. Paul identifies two dangers in 1 Corinthians. First idol worship leads to immorality, as it did in Israel's history at Peor (1 Cor. 10:7, 8; cf. Rom. 1:22-25). Second, *the sacrifices of pagans are offered to demons, not to God, and I do not want you to be participants with demons* (1 Cor. 10:20). Paul seems to be saying that a demonic spiritual force operates behind the deceptive mask of images dedicated to counterfeit gods. Probably he has in mind the Song of Moses in Deuteronomy 32, where Israel is accused of sacrificing to demons by their idolatry (Deut. 32:17). Although he denied the real existence of pagan gods, Paul acknowledged the presence of evil spiritual powers, which are associated with pagan cult practices. In Romans 1:18-32 Paul goes further and argues that the distortion of worship (bowing down to the creature not the creator) results not only in immorality (1:26f.), but in the perversion of the whole of life (1:28-32). It affects the mind, the emotions, personal relations, ambition, family life and society. It is the source from which spring sins of every kind. It results in the reversal of moral values, turning good into evil and evil into good.

This does not mean that all Greek and Roman religion had to be rejected as idolatrous and of the devil. Some Greeks poured scorn on the worship of images[37] and some like the God-fearers, whom Paul met on his journeys, were monotheists.[38]

Emperor worship

A religion of a different kind, found throughout the Greco-Roman world, was the veneration of the Roman emperor as supreme terrestrial Lord.

---

[37] Such as Euripides, Heraclitus and the Epicureans quoted above.
[38] God-fearing Gentiles are mentioned in Acts 10:2, 22:13:26, 50; 17:4, 17.

The imperial cult was the one religion that covered the whole Roman Empire and grew in the importance given to it as the first century drew to a close. If a late date for Revelation is accepted, it would coincide with the reign of Domitian (A.D. 81-96), who took his pretensions to divinity seriously and demanded worship, inflicting death on those who refused. Compare this with Jesus' advice: *Give to Caesar what is Caesar's and to God what is God's* (Mark 12:17), which reflected the less aggressive stance of emperors earlier in the first century.

By the end of the century, once a year, everyone in the empire was expected to demonstrate their loyalty to Caesar by burning incense to the divine emperor and confessing, 'Caesar is Lord'. If they complied, citizens could follow any religion they liked and worship any god or goddess.

In Revelation chapters 13-20 there are numerous references to emperor worship and to the seductive power of Rome symbolised as Babylon (Rev. 17:9). Revelation 13:7-17 provides illuminating references to this cult, especially in the context of Asia Minor.[39] The first beast from the sea symbolises the Roman Empire and the second beast represents the local power of the imperial cult to enforce the worship of the first beast.[40] Note the following points:

All inhabitants must worship the beast (13:12). The imperial cult required that images of the emperors be made and venerated. The emperor was honoured alongside the gods, though on a lesser level. Sacrifices of incense, ritual cakes, wine or animals were offered for the emperor. Domitian went further than any of his predecessors in calling himself 'Lord and God'.[41]

Those who refuse to worship will be killed (13:15). Some years later, about A.D.112, Pliny wrote to the emperor Trajan that he compelled

[39] The Letters of Revelation chapters 2-3 were addressed to the Seven Churches of Asia and John was himself arrested in the province and imprisoned off its coast at Patmos. The first temple dedicated to the imperial cult was built at Pergamum in 29 B.C.

[40] S.R.F. Price suggests that this local authority is the priesthood of the imperial cult in the province of Asia. See his *Rituals and Power: The Roman imperial cult in Asia Minor*, 1984, Cambridge. p.197.

[41] D. Fishwick's standard work on *The Imperial Cult in the Latin West*, Leiden, 1987-1992, details the way worship was carried out and distinguishes this from the worship of the gods.

those who were accused of being Christians to do homage with incense and wine to the emperor's image, and if they refused, he ordered them to be executed.[42]

Images were set up in honour of the beast (13:14). Images were often busts of emperors, but they could be made of any size or substance. Reverence offered to these images was basic to the practice of the cult. A colossal cult statue was set up during Domitian's reign at Ephesus and it may have been this statue that the writer had in mind.[43]

Signs and wonders, such as fire from heaven and an image that spoke, were produced to make people believe (13:15). These signs and wonders were performed by the false prophet (Rev. 19:20). John does not dismiss these miraculous events as trickery, but believes these were real demonstrations of demonic power designed to coerce people into worshipping the emperor. Supernatural power was habitually attributed to the images and statues of imperial worship in the first three centuries of the Christian era.[44]

If a Christian did not have the mark of the beast, he could not buy or sell in the market place (13:17). The mark of the beast may well have been the certificate issued by the magistrates to show that the recipient had burnt incense to the emperor and called him Lord. Once a year the citizens of the Roman empire were expected to offer incense before the image of the emperor. When this had been done people were issued with a certificate. William Barclay cites the wording of one such certificate: "We, the representatives of the emperor, Serenos and Hermas, have seen you sacrificing."[45] Although participation in the imperial cult was not strictly enforced, Christians aroused suspicion and were isolated if they did not produce the annual certificate.

The number of the beast, 666, may have represented Nero, standing for Nero redivivus (13:18).

But this may not be what John had in mind. All he says is that the number of the beast is the number *of man* or *of a man* (*anthropou*),

---

[42]   Pliny, *Epp.* 10.96.
[43]   S.R.F. Price, op.cit., p.197.
[44]   S.R.F. Price, op.cit., pp.196ff.
[45]   W. Barclay, *The Revelation of John*, Vol.2, Edinburgh, 1960, p.113f.

emphasising that the beast is only human and falls far short of Christ, the one and only begotten of the Father.

Faced with this stark challenge, no one who belonged to Christ could say anything other than 'Jesus is Lord', not Caesar. The book of Revelation was written to encourage the tiny church to stand firm and claim the glories of martyrdom in heaven (Rev. 15:2). They and not the empire were the victors.

Emperor worship was not confined to Rome and has had many successors since then. For an example from the Old Testament see Daniel 3 and the gripping story of Shadrach, Meshach and Abednego.[46] Confronted with the command to worship the image Nebuchadnezzar had set up, the three Jews reply defiantly that they will not worship the image of gold. God vindicates them and the king is forced to confess that their God has rescued them from the fiery furnace and '*no other god can save in this way*' (Dan. 7:29). Such a happy ending in this life has not been the lot of many Christians, who have always been called to follow the way of the cross to martyrdom, if need be, rather than compromise in worshipping a totalitarian regime and its god. Communism provided an example of this perversion of worship, especially in the devotion demanded of Mao Tse-tung, the great helmsman and lord of the little red book. Every totalitarian regime, whether religious or secular, demands subservience and worship of its ideological symbols.

Non-Jews who are commended for their faith

In the New Testament period Jews not only sharply distinguished themselves from Gentiles[47] as non-Jews and foreigners, but also looked down on other nations as people who were enemies of God and ignorant of him. In the Jerusalem temple Gentile worshippers were excluded from all but the outer court. A barrier surrounded the inner sanctuary, beyond

---

[46]   Three paintings in the catacombs at Rome show the three young men in the fiery furnace refusing to worship the image set up by Nebuchadnezzar. S.R.F. Price, op.cit., p.199.

[47]   In the Greek New Testament the term most commonly used for Gentiles is *ta ethne*, meaning 'the peoples' or 'the nations'. Paul also uses the word 'Greek(s)' as a synonym for Gentiles, e.g. in Rom. 1:16.

which people of other religions were not permitted. On the low parapet that marked the barrier were notices warning foreigners to keep out. One of these notices, dating from the first century or earlier, was found in 1871. It reads: "No foreigner is to enter within the forecourt and the balustrade around the sanctuary. Whoever is caught will have himself to blame for his subsequent death."[48]

Negative comment on people who were not Jews is reflected in some of the New Testament references, for example in the Synoptic Gospels. In the Sermon on the Mount, Jesus says: *when you pray do not keep on babbling like the Gentiles* (Matt. 6:7; see also 6:32). But Jesus also cites individual Gentiles or Gentile cities and peoples as examples, which provide a warning to his own people (Matt 8:10; 11:20-24; 12:41f.). The Synoptic Gospels assume that the good news of the kingdom is for all peoples and indicate that Jesus Christ has come to be a light to all nations, as well as to be the Saviour of his own people (Matt. 4:15f.; Luke 2:32).

Although negative references to Gentiles can still be found in Acts and the Epistles, the conversion of Paul and his calling to take the gospel to the nations of the Roman world changed the church's approach to non-Jews. Paul recognised that God treats all humanity as one. Therefore there is no separation in God's sight between Jew and Gentile, for in Christ there is neither Jew nor Gentile (Gal. 3:28). In Christ the temple's middle wall of partition has been broken down (Eph. 2:14). The barriers of race and nationality have been overcome. Abraham is to be thought of not only as the father of the Jewish nation but as the father of all believers and the one through whom all nations including Israel are to be blessed (Rom. 4:16-17).

The change in the attitude of the Jewish writers of the New Testament can be seen in the accounts concerning certain foreigners who are praised for their faith.

Outstanding examples of the faith of people who were not Jews that are mentioned in the New Testament include the following: the Magi from the east, who came to worship Jesus (Matt. 2:1-12); the centurion at Capernaum, who asked Jesus to heal his servant (Matt. 8:5-13); the

[48]   E. Schurer, *The History of the Jewish People in the Age of Jesus Christ*, Edinburgh 1979, 2.222 n.85.

Syro-Phoenician woman, who begged Jesus to heal her daughter (Mark 7:24-30); the centurion at the Cross, who said, *Surely this man was the Son of God!* (Mark 15:39); Cornelius, the centurion of the Italian Regiment, who called Peter to his house (Acts 10); and Lydia, a woman of high standing, who became the leader of a church (Acts 16:13-15). There are also references to some Old Testament characters, such as the Queen of Sheba and the people of Nineveh (Luke 11:31-32) and Melchizedek (Heb. 7:1-10).

In addition to these individuals there are references to the God-fearers. These God-fearers, though not Jews, were drawn to and influenced by Judaism. Many city dwellers in the Roman Empire, whilst unwilling to accept the stringent requirements for becoming a proselyte, were attracted by the monotheism of synagogue worship and by Jewish ethical standards. It was to such God-fearing people that Paul appealed on his missionary journeys (e.g. Acts 13:16, 26, 50). They often formed the nucleus of the churches Paul founded (cf. Acts 17:4, 18:7) and among their number were Cornelius and Lydia.

The Magi

The Magi were unusual and of exceptional interest. They were the first to worship Jesus, despite being foreigners. Also despite the warnings against astrology in the Old Testament, their knowledge of the stars was put to good use.

The word *magos* has several meanings,[49] but the one that seems to fit the Magi in Matthew 2:1-12 indicates a scholar or wise man, who interpreted dreams and predicted the future, e.g. by astrology. Originally magi were linked with Persia, but Matthew only says they were from the east. It was to these easterners that God revealed the birth of Jesus, the royal Messiah of the Jews.

In v.2 the Magi are quoted as saying: *We saw his star in the east.* Their quest began with the observation of a star. From this and other clues given to them, they concluded that this star indicated the birth of one born to be king of the Jews. It would be wrong to conclude that their knowledge of astrology alone provided them with this information, for

---

[49] See the article on *Magos* in the *Theological Dictionary of the New Testament (TDNT)*, ed. G. Kittel and G. Friedrich, Grand Rapids, 1964-76.

astrological systems are flexible and any prediction arrived at depends on the astrologer. But it is significant that it is to observers of the stars and to Gentiles known as astrologers that God chose to reveal the birth of Jesus, as king of the Jews, and led them to him. So God was able to speak to those who were not Jews through the religious knowledge that they had at that time. The revelation to astrologers is even more remarkable when we note the Jewish Rabbis' hostility to magi. One of their sayings was: "Whoever learns a single word from a magus deserves death."[50]

Throughout the story in Matthew, the obedience of the Magi to the truth they received is striking. They took the long journey from the east to Palestine. They followed the star to the place where Jesus was born. It is true that the Old Testament prophecy about Bethlehem told them where to go, and Herod sent them there, but the appearance of the star confirmed their destination and filled them with joy. And when told in a dream to go back by a different route they obeyed without equivocation.

Even more astonishing is the account of the Magi's worship of the child Jesus (v.11). Matthew, with his concern for Messianic prophecies and their fulfilment, saw this as a dramatic fulfilment of the prophecy in Isaiah 60:3: *Nations will come to your light, and kings to the brightness of your dawn.* Throughout the Gospels the word *proskuneo*[51] is used for those who fall down and worship Jesus or for the worship of God. Whatever the Magi meant by their actions, their obeisance to the Christ child was pregnant with meaning for the future, and an example of the way God would use people of different races and religions for his glory.

Most important of all, however, for our study is the light this story sheds on the question of how much Gentiles knew about God and what were their sources of knowledge. God chose to use the Magi's religious training as astrologers, by which they were skilled to interpret dreams and to observe the stars. From v.12 we learn that God was able to warn them in a dream that they should not go back to Herod but should return home another way. This implies that they acknowledged the one God, that they were able to receive a specific message from him, that they responded to him and that dreams were a means by which

---

[50]   Op.cit., TDNT, *Magos.*
[51]   'Proskuneo' meaning 'worship', used in v.11.

God could communicate with non-Jews (just as he had done in the Old Testament, e.g. Gen. 20:6). The rest of the story shows that God was able to communicate quite specific information to these Gentile worshippers. They concluded rightly that an unusual baby was to be born king of the Jews, that they were to go and worship him, and that they would be guided to him.

How should God's dealings with the Magi be applied to Christian understanding of God's interaction with the followers of world religions today? If God could use astrology could he not also choose to use yoga or Sufi meditation? If God could use the Magi can he not also use religious leaders, such as imams, acharayas, lamas or rabbis, and communicate with them, whether they become followers of Christ or not? What then should be said about the use of dreams? Nowadays many western Christians do not expect to receive spiritual revelation from dreams, but Muslims, Hindus, Sikhs and others do. Like the Magi they may be more open to God and more sensitive to spiritual reality than many who call themselves Christians. In the case of the Magi the striking fact is that God communicated to them important knowledge that even his own people did not have. They were exceptional, but who can say that God cannot multiply exceptions, for he is always the God of surprises.

The Centurion at Capernaum

The centurion mentioned in Matthew 8:5-13 (cf. Luke 7:1-10) was recognised by Jesus as a man of outstanding faith: *I tell you the truth, I have not found anyone in Israel with such great faith* (v.10).

It seems likely from Luke's account that the centurion was a God-fearer, a believer in the one true God, for he had built a synagogue and impressed the Jewish religious leaders with his love for their nation (Luke 7:4-5). He certainly showed cultural sensitivity and ability to cross racial barriers, making friends with Jews. So according to Luke, he sent Jewish elders not soldiers to Jesus to plead for him.

The officer's humility as well as his faith is apparent from the narrative. The elders say he is worthy (Luke 7:4). The centurion says, *I did not even consider myself worthy to come to you* (7:7). When we put ourselves into the cultural situation, his humility is even more striking.

As a Gentile he realised that a Jew would not enter his house lest he be contaminated. As an Italian cohort commander he could have brushed this aside and bent his pride enough to ask for a favour. But instead he accepted the status of being unworthy and as a human being begged for compassion on his servant. Imagine an officer in the days of the British Raj coming to a Hindu guru and saying, 'I know you despise us British and I am not fit to make this request of you, but please do what you can for my batman, who is desperately ill.' This Roman officer went further and said, *I did not even consider that I am worthy to come to you…* It is an extraordinary thing for him to have said, and reminds us of another Gentile in the Gospels who humbled herself because of faith in Jesus. That was the Syro-Phoenician woman.[52]

However, it was the centurion's faith that caused Jesus to marvel. Only twice in the Gospels is it recorded that Jesus marvelled at people, once here because of faith and once at Nazareth because of unbelief (Mark 6:6). He not only marvelled but turned to the crowd and said, *I say unto you …* (*lego humin*), drawing attention to his comments. Why was Jesus so impressed?

There may have been more than one reason. For example, the Roman did not require Jesus to see the sick man or even to touch him. He had seen none of Jesus' healing miracles, as the crowds had done. He had none of the advantages of a Jew, who had been brought up to believe in one God and look forward to the coming of his Messiah. But the most important reason is given in the story itself in the words of the centurion.

"Just say the word, and my servant will be healed. For I myself am a man under authority, with soldiers under me. I tell this one 'Go', and he goes; and that one, 'Come', and he comes. I say to my servant, 'Do this', and he does it" (Luke 7:7-8).

The centurion compares himself to Jesus in respect of authority. He has authority because he is under the emperor. Jesus is invested with divine authority because he is under God. So the officer's faith is in God, whose servant Jesus is, not in his healing reputation. Jesus was not simply impressed by the man's unhesitating faith in his ability to heal immediately and completely, but by his recognition of who he was.

---

[52] See next section for an analysis of her story.

In other words the centurion recognised more than the crowds, who pressed around Jesus seeking healing for their suffering relatives. This was a man with more than a charismatic gift of healing, here was a divine person whom he was not worthy to entertain and yet one he could rely on absolutely to do whatever he said. Even among Jesus' own people few had understood what this centurion saw with startling clarity.

Jesus' comment that follows in Matthew 8:11-12 widens the implications of the centurion's example. Though Jesus' ministry was confined to Israel, he predicts that one day the kingdom of God will be thrown open to people of every race and nationality. 'From the east and the west' indicates the whole of the then known world. Gentiles like this man will not only inherit the blessings of the patriarchs, but also displace those who have been privileged to be born Jews, presumably because of the latter's lack of faith and obedience. Race will no longer be a barrier, instead the faith in God that understands his Son and relies on his word will be the one requirement, which opens the kingdom to all believers.

The Centurion at the Cross

The other centurion noted in the Gospels is the one who is moved at the foot of the cross to say: *Surely this man was the Son of God!* (Mark 15:39).

Here again there is a marked contrast between unbelieving Jews and a hard nosed captain of the occupying power, who despite his race, religion, culture and profession, recognised Jesus for who he was. Mark's comment is that when the tough Roman centurion saw how Jesus died and heard his cry, he gave this unsolicited testimony, that Jesus was no criminal, no poor Jew deserving death, but that he was rightly called Son of God. Although the definite article is missing in the Greek and the centurion's words could literally mean 'a son of God' (*huios theou*), the words echo the first verse of Mark's Gospel, where Jesus Christ is given exactly the same title, 'Son of God' (*huios theou*). Time has shown that whatever the Roman soldier meant his words have a greater significance than he could have dreamt of. The author of Mark's Gospel acknowledges that people from non-Jewish religious backgrounds are capable of spiritual insight.

The Syro-Phoenician woman

The context of Jesus' encounter with the Syro-Phoenician woman (Mark 7:24-30; Matt. 15:21-28) is important and is often ignored. Both Mark and Matthew place their accounts after Jesus' teaching on what makes a person clean or unclean (Mark 7:1-23; Matt. 15:1-20). This provides a clue to the exegesis of the narrative. Far from being shocked by contact with non-Jews, Jesus disregarded the idea of defilement by association with those the Pharisees regarded as unclean. He headed straight for Gentile territory and there conversed with a Gentile woman. Compare this with Peter's attitude to clean and unclean people in Acts 10 and God's difficulty in getting him to change his ideas and treat Cornelius with impartiality. Jesus' response to the Syro-Phoenician woman has to be judged against this background.

The story would have reminded Matthew's readers of Elijah's visit to the widow at Zarephath (I Kings 17), referred to by Jesus when he shocked his own townsfolk at the beginning of his ministry by recalling God's care for a Sidonian woman (Luke 4:25f.). Kenneth Bailey suggests that Jesus used this occasion to build on his manifesto at Nazareth, where he had cited the example of Elijah's care for the widow of Zarephath. He aimed to teach his disciples a lesson about racial prejudice. They are mistaken if they think that Jesus will drive the woman away. Far from colluding with their prejudices, he takes time to expose their thoughts and to confound them by honouring the woman and healing her daughter.[53]

We are told that this woman was a Greek, a description, which must be understood religiously not racially. She is described as Syro-Phoenician, Phoenicia being part of the province of Syria. The district of Tyre was about 20 miles north-west of Capernaum. Jesus' journey to the area is his only recorded excursion outside Jewish territory. According to Matthew he did not go to preach to Gentiles (15:24). Mark tells us that he did not want anyone to know he was there. Apparently Christ took this diversion, in order to get some peace away from the Galilean crowds.

Jesus had already had contact with people (Jews?) from Tyre and Sidon (Mark 3:8). Probably from them the woman had heard news about

---

[53] K. Bailey, *Jesus Through Middle Eastern Eyes*, London 2008, pp. 217ff.

Jesus and his unexpected arrival in their village. Desperate for healing for her daughter the woman came to the house where the Lord had found lodging. She must have known that she was breaking the rules of cultural sensitivity in approaching a Jewish rabbi, but her daughter's need drove her on. She fell at his feet and asked him to exorcise the 'unclean'[54] (that word again) spirit from her child.

The woman crosses religious, racial and cultural boundaries to claim by faith Jesus' attention and healing powers. Like the centurion at Capernaum she is not seeking healing for herself but deliverance for a beloved member of her family. She recognises Jesus' power over evil spirits (demons). She begs him to use his power to deliver her daughter and exorcise the demon. But she has to get over another hurdle. For Jesus the timing is not right to launch into Gentile ministry on Gentile territory.

What was Jesus to do? Clearly he was reluctant to get involved, as Matthew makes plain (Matt. 15:23f.). The time had not yet come for him to inaugurate the mission to the world beyond Israel. His reply to the woman's pleas recalls other hard words to women, such as those to his mother: *woman, why do you involve me? … my time has not yet come* (John 2:4).

Whatever Jesus' intentions may have been he gave this desperate mother a severe threefold test, responding to her cries first with silent indifference, then with apparent rejection, followed by a painful insult. He was reluctant to make an exception in her case. No doubt he did not want to give a signal to Phoenecians that would cause crowds of their sick to flood the streets around the house where he was lodging. His words seem hard, but the word 'first' (Mark 7:27) gives the woman hope. 'First let the children of Israel hear God's word ('bread') and be satisfied,' he seems to say, 'for it is not right now for me to give up my ministry to Israel and give it to Gentiles.'

The woman responds by fastening on to Jesus' simile of parents feeding their children and not the dogs nearby. She sees the dogs as household pets waiting under the dining table for crumbs and argues that the dogs (puppies) eat at the same time as the children from the scraps that fall their way. There is no need for Jesus to delay and no need to deny mere crumbs to the waiting Gentiles in the house (v.28).

---

[54] Mark 7:25. The Greek for 'evil spirit' is 'unclean spirit'.

As with the centurion, so here, Jesus is immensely impressed by the woman's grasp of the truth. She had risen to his challenge, first with humility. She humbly accepted her unworthiness, as a foreigner outside the household of Israel, to ask him for anything. She was not worthy to be called a child, but only a despised dog.[55] She had nothing to offer Jesus, but cast herself wholly on his mercy and appealed to his grace alone, for she had faith in Jesus and calls him 'Lord'. He praised her, *Woman, you have great faith!* (Matt. 15:28). Here was a foreigner who did not treat him just as a faith healer who could help her out, but acknowledged that salvation came from the Jews and Jesus was its bearer.

Jeremias puts it this way: "The key to the meaning of Jesus' words to the woman who sought his help lies in the fact that she understood that Jesus was speaking of the Messianic banquet. Her 'great faith' (Matt. 15:28) consisted in her recognition, as shown by her words about the crumbs that the little dogs might venture to eat, that Jesus was the giver of the Bread of Life." [56]

The whole story confirms the principle, 'to the Jew first, and also to the Greek' (Rom 1:16). Jesus' ministry was to the Jews. But here is a sign of things to come. Like the story of the prodigal son, the incident reveals the way to God's heart. In both cases the plaintiffs accept that they are unworthy and come with nothing to commend them or to offer to God. They cast themselves on the mercy of God and both receive the status of children in the Father's family. This is the good news: the puppy becomes a child.[57]

Racial origins are no barrier to God for those who humbly rely on his grace. People of all races are as capable as Jews of rising to the heights of faith. Like the story of the Capernaum centurion this is an example of a Gentile recognising divine authority in Jesus. It is also an acknowledgment of this woman's innate wisdom and courage,[58] and her reply becomes a proverbial part of scriptural wisdom.

---

[55] The associations with the Hebrew term for Gentiles, as dogs, cannot be avoided.

[56] J. Jeremias, *Parables*, London, 1955, p.118 n.14.

[57] J. Pokorny, *New Testament Studies*, 1995 pp.321-337.

[58] See Aruna Gnanadason, *Jesus and the Asian woman: a post-colonial look at the Syro-Phoenician woman from an Indian perspective* in Studies in World Christianity, 7.2001, 2., pp. 162-177.

Cornelius

Peter's encounter with Cornelius is one of the crucial turning points in Acts and few incidents are given as much space as this one, running as it does from Acts 10:1 to Acts 11:18 with a further reference in Acts 15:7-11. At stake was the attitude of the church to Gentiles and whether the gospel was to be shared with them or kept exclusively for Jews and proselytes.

The narrative shows that prior to meeting Cornelius, Peter had no desire to talk to Gentiles and no intention of preaching the gospel to them. In fact he thought them unclean and unfit for the kingdom of heaven. Fortunately for us God had different ideas and the story is a revelation of his attitude to those who are outside the circle of the baptised people of God.

To understand the implications of what happened in Acts 10 it is important to understand Cornelius in his setting and to identify whom he represents. He is described as a centurion of the Roman army of occupation in the Italian cohort. This suggests he would have been from Italy, though we cannot be sure. As for religion he is said to be a Gentile, who was *pious and God-fearing* (v.2), *respected by all the Jewish people* (v.22). Like other God-fearing Gentiles mentioned in Acts,[59] it appears that Cornelius had not been circumcised as a full proselyte.[60]

God-fearing Gentiles worshipped Yahweh only, attended the synagogue and observed Jewish food laws.[61] Among these foreigners, attracted by Judaism, Cornelius was outstanding. The Gentile mission did not begin with the conversion of reluctant pagans but with the response of prepared souls. God had already been at work in Cornelius before he was introduced to Peter and the gospel.

We note the following positive things that are said about Cornelius:

- Like other God-fearers, he only worshipped the one creator God and had given up belief in other gods (vv. 2, 22, 35).

- Following the example of Jews his piety was expressed in action: *he*

[59] God-fearers are variously called *phoboumenos ton theon* (Acts 10:2,22 etc), *sebomenos ton theon* (Acts 18:14, cf. 16:14), or simply *sebomenoi* (Acts 17:4,17; cf.13:50).
[60] See Acts 11:3, where Peter is accused of visiting the house of uncircumcised men; cf. Acts 2:11 for mention of proselytes in the company of Jews in Jerusalem.
[61] See the next section on Lydia and the footnote on God-fearers.

gave generously to those in need (v.2). Later he is commended by the Lord for his godly deeds of almsgiving (v.4, 31).

- He is commended for his prayers. He followed the Jewish hours of prayer (v. 3)[62] and his prayers are said to have ascended to God as a burnt offering (v. 4, 31; cf. Ps. 141:2).

- When God wished to speak to him, he was able to communicate with him through an angel and to give a detailed message telling him to send men to Simon Peter at an address in the distant town of Joppa (v.5, 6, 32).

- Unlike Peter he obeyed immediately after receiving his vision (v.7, 8).

- In v. 22 he is called 'righteous' and this was confirmed by God in v.35, as he is referred to as one who does 'what is right'.

- No wonder he was *respected by all the Jewish people* (v.22).

- When Peter began to speak he was ready to hear all that God had to say. It also seems from Peter's summary of the gospel that he had already heard something about Jesus of Nazareth (v. 36, 37).

- He had taught his family and household to worship Yahweh and one of his soldiers is described as 'devout' (v. 2, 7, 33).

Above all Cornelius was a man of faith, who had shown his reliance on God alone for his spiritual welfare. His example showed that all non-Jews could not be dismissed as idolaters. By the same reckoning all religious Gentiles cannot be treated as if they were like Cornelius. He was an unusual person and therefore we need to be cautious in drawing parallels between his case and that of the followers of world faiths today. For instance it would be wrong to conclude from Acts 10 that the religious practices of all devout persons from whatever religion are acceptable to God, for Cornelius modelled his worship and his prayers on Jewish practice and the Old Testament. Nor would it be true to conclude that his knowledge of God came solely from his own religion, for he was manifestly greatly influenced by biblical revelation.

---

[62] The ninth hour or 3pm was the time of the evening oblation, see Acts 3:1. The set times for Jewish prayer were the early morning, the ninth hour and at sunset. See F.F. Bruce *The Acts of the Apostles: the Greek Text with Introduction and Commentary*, London, 1951, p.103.

It is the principles revealed by God on this occasion and expressed by Peter in Acts 10:34-35 and 15:7-11, that are of universal relevance. To these we now turn.

Peter learnt that just as God is not racially biased, so Christ's followers must not be racist either. Before God we all stand equally in need of his grace, his salvation and his Spirit. He does not make his judgments on the basis of our distinctions, whether these are affinities of race or religion, and neither should we. Fortunately for all of us God shows no favouritism or partiality towards his creatures, wherever they come from (10:34).

> "But he accepts men from every nation who fear him and do what is right" (10:35).

What did Peter mean by saying that God 'accepts' (*dektos*) people from every nation? The word *dektos* means 'acceptable', 'welcome', 'pleasing'.[63] In what sense were Cornelius and his family and friends pleasing to God? Some think that they were accepted by God and so already saved before they heard the gospel. This is possible, but unlikely considering what the angel says to Cornelius in Acts 11:14, *(Peter) will bring you a message through which you and all your household will be saved.* The conclusion drawn in Acts 11:18 after the baptism of Cornelius and household is that *God has granted even the Gentiles repentance unto life.* According to these two verses the centurion and his household needed to hear the gospel so as to repent and be saved. Another explanation is that *dektos* means that God is pleased by the faith and deeds of people like Cornelius and will therefore provide them with a means of hearing the gospel. That is to say, God notices such people, and acts to lead them to the knowledge of himself.[64]

This does not always happen as it did in the case of Cornelius, nor does Acts 10:35 say that it will happen.

---

[63] *Dektos* occurs 5 times in the NT, 3 of the occurrences being in Luke-Acts. Usually it is used of something or someone acceptable to God. The dominant idea is that of welcome, as in welcoming a guest to one's home. Compare this with the rejection experienced by Jesus in Nazareth, and his saying: *"No prophet is accepted (dektos) in his home town"* (Luke 4:24).

[64] For a discussion of this verse see J.R.W. Stott, *The Message of Acts*, Leicester, 1990, p.198f.

We are left with a further possibility, that God can accept people who have not encountered Christ and that this acceptance is prior to and apart form the experience of salvation and new birth through the gospel. On the one hand this indicates that the accepted still need the benefits of the gospel, and on the other hand God's acceptance is real and those he accepts will not be rejected at the last judgement. Their experience is paralleled by Jewish believers before Christ, who despite their partial knowledge of God, needed the liberation of being transformed by Christ. By the cross and resurrection of the Messiah they have been saved and given what they missed in this life. Similarly genuine God-fearers, whatever their religious community, are known by the Lord and will be given that full experience of knowing God for which they longed.[65]

On what basis does God accept people, whatever their religious affiliation may be? The ones who are commended are those who 'fear him' (*phoboumenos auton*) and 'do what is right' (*ergazomenos dikaiosune*). Cornelius was a God-fearing man in the sense that he acknowledged the God of Israel, but more than that he was a man of faith in God. His fear of the one true God was one of reverence, worship, belief and dependence. That is why he and his whole family gave themselves to prayer and waiting upon God. God is also pleased by those who do righteousness (*dikaiosune*). This is a strong commendation and in the case of Cornelius refers to his almsgiving and other good deeds, which were born of obedience to whatever he knew of God's commands. It would be wrong to draw the conclusion that Peter meant that godly people are justified by their piety and good deeds. He emphatically rejects this view in Acts 15:7-11, by saying that believers are saved through faith by the grace of Jesus Christ alone. But it is true that Cornelius was singled out to be the first Gentile to have the good news preached to him and to be given the Holy Spirit, because of his godly prayers and actions (v. 4, 31).

That both Jews and Gentiles need to encounter Christ for salvation is confirmed by Peter in Acts 15. Peter reveals in Acts 15:7-11 that through his meeting with Cornelius and all that God did in the course of it, he learnt the great lesson, that God makes *no distinction between us and them*, Jew and Gentile (15:9). The fact that Cornelius and his household needed the gospel of forgiveness and the gift of the Holy Spirit did not place

---

[65] Rowan Williams, *The Dwelling of the Light*, Norwich, 2003, p.27, 28.

them on a lower level than the Jews, but on the same level. Just as pious Jews needed to believe the gospel, so did devout Romans. Peter drew the following parallels between believing Jews and Gentiles, when he addressed the Jerusalem Council (Acts 15:7-11):

1. *God ... accepted them by giving the Holy Spirit to them, just as he did to us* (v.8).

2. *(God) made no distinction between us and them, for he purified their hearts by faith* (v.9).

3. If we Jews could not bear the yoke of the law, why should we put that yoke on believing Gentiles and require them to bear and obey the law of Moses (v.10)?

4. Gentiles are saved *through the grace of our Lord Jesus ...just as* (we) *are* (v.11).[66]

The first two points indicate that religious people, whether Jews or Gentiles, need the gift of the Holy Spirit and purification of heart, which includes forgiveness of sin and inner cleansing.[67] The second two points show that Gentiles, like Jews, are not saved by their own godliness and morality or by their own knowledge of God. Salvation is a free gift bequeathed through faith to all races alike and is not a reward for a futile attempt to attain God's standards by keeping the law in its entirety.

What conclusions should be drawn from this story concerning the biblical view of God-fearing non-Christians? Cornelius represents those non-Jewish monotheists, who have been greatly influenced by the Old Testament. Today these include some Muslims, who are truly devoted to God in prayer and almsgiving and are open to new revelations from God, which point them to *Al Masih Isa ibn Maryam*.[68] It is also important to recognise, that Acts 10:34, 35 states a general principle, of which Cornelius was one example. It does not say that God accepts people like Cornelius, nor does it say that only God-fearers in contact with the Jewish faith can be accepted, instead it is said that God accepts anyone

[66] Peter states the point the other way round: Jews are saved through grace just as Gentiles are.

[67] The word for cleansing, *katharizo*, only occurs in Acts here and 10:15; 11:9, in connection with the Cornelius story.

[68] The Qur'an refers to Jesus as *Isa ibn Maryam*, meaning 'Jesus son of Mary'. One of the titles given to Jesus is *Al Masih*, that is 'the Messiah'.

from any nation who fears him and does what is right. The story makes an important distinction between being accepted by God and being saved. Not only Cornelius but also all his family and household were first accepted and then saved, experiencing new birth in Christ by the Spirit. God accepts people of other faiths, who trust solely in him and show by their actions the genuineness of their faith. To them he will send messengers of the gospel, but if the messengers refuse to go or are not available, as has happened for many centuries in many parts of the world, God's acceptance is not cancelled. The fact that God-fearers, who have not known Christ, have not had the experience of salvation through new birth does not mean that they will not be accepted by God and received into heaven. What it does mean is that, like believers before Christ, they have not been privileged to experience the transforming power of Christ in this life. What implications this has for the Christian view of people of other faiths will need to be considered later.

Lydia

Paul's first convert in Europe, Lydia, is an example of all those God-fearers who formed together with their Jewish brethren the core of believers in the multi-racial churches that Paul founded on his missionary journeys (Acts 16:13-15).

Lydia may not have been her personal name, but simply mean 'the Lydian woman', as she was from the district of Lydia in western Asia Minor, the most highly cultivated area of the province. She belonged to the city of Thyatira, a commercial centre on the trade routes to the interior of Asia Minor with connections to Macedonia. A woman of wealth and rank, she traded in the purple dye for which her district was famous. Since she appears to have been the head of her household (Acts 16:15), it is thought that she must have been a widow or unmarried.

Of particular importance were her Jewish connections. She is said to have been at a Jewish place of prayer[69] on the Sabbath and to have been

---

[69] The word used is *proseuche*, which can be a synonym for a synagogue, but here probably means a place of prayer, as only women are mentioned and at least ten men were needed for a synagogue. See F.F. Bruce, *The Acts of the Apostles, the Greek Text with Introduction & Commentary*, London, 1951, p.314.

a worshipper[70] of the God of the Jews. Thyatira had a Jewish colony and she may have learnt about Jewish religion there.

In Acts two words, *phoboumenos*[71] and *sebomenos*,[72] are used to describe those people of other religions in the Roman Empire, who worshipped the God of Israel and were sympathetic to Judaism. *Sebomenos* meaning 'worshipper' is the term applied to Lydia (16:14). It was not unusual for women as well as men to be followers of Jewish beliefs and practices. Acts mentions women of high social standing like Lydia who were God-fearers (17:4, 12). The terms when applied to sympathetic Gentiles are used by Luke to refer to non-Jews who venerated the God of the Jews. The term *sebomenos*, in particular, would have been understood by Luke's readers as a 'semi-technical' designation for Gentiles, who sympathised with Judaism.[73]

It should also be remembered that Luke-Acts is dedicated to Theophilus, 'friend of God'. Whether Theophilus was the name of a real person or a code name, Luke-Acts was written with a strong bias in favour of God-fearing Greeks and Romans.

Melchizedek, the Queen of Sheba and the people of Nineveh

The New Testament contains significant references to some people who were not descendants of Abraham. Melchizedek is particularly important. But first we will look at the Gospels and at Christ's references to the Queen of Sheba and the Ninevites (Luke 11:29-32).

The Queen of Sheba is commended for the arduous pilgrimage she undertook to visit Solomon and listen to the wisdom God had given him. As with the centurion at Capernaum, what is commended is her recognition of God at work. She would have condemned the Jews for failing to listen to Jesus and failing to recognise his greatness. What is particularly interesting is the statement: *The Queen of the South will rise at the judgment with the men of this generation and condemn them* (v. 31). It

---

[70] The word is *sebomene*.

[71] See Acts 10:2, 22, 35; 13:16, 26.

[72] See Acts 16:14; 17:4, 17; 13:50; 18:7.

[73] M.C. de Boer, 'God-Fearers in Luke-Acts' in *Luke's Literary Achievement*, ed. C.M.Tuckett, Sheffield, 1995, pp. 64-65.

suggests that God will acquit the Queen of Sheba on the day of judgment on account of her search for God's wisdom.

Similarly the men of Nineveh are held up for their example in repenting at the preaching of Jonah and contrasted unfavourably with Jesus' contemporaries who failed to repent at the preaching of the Son of Man. Again it is said that, *The men of Nineveh will stand up at the judgment with this generation and condemn it; for they repented at the preaching of Jonah...* *(v.32).* The inference is that they will be acquitted at the day of judgment, because they repented when they heard God's message through Jonah.

What is said about Melchizedek in Hebrews 7 is of an altogether different order.[74] Although a Semite, Melchizedek was not part of the family of Abraham and was not related to him. A Canaanite king of Jerusalem, he appears suddenly when Abraham returns triumphant after rescuing Lot (Genesis 14:18-20). No one in Scripture apart from Jesus is accorded the status given to Melchizedek. The writer to the Hebrews expands on what is said in the Old Testament to portray Melchizedek as superior even to Abraham. The reason for this is not simply that Abraham gave him a tithe, but that he was a priest of God Most High. Even Abraham is not called a priest. As TK Thomas notes: "It is interesting that the very first priest who appears in the pages of the Bible is neither a Jew nor a Christian."[75] Here is a non-Israelite, who like Christ is both king and priest and is described as 'king of righteousness' and 'king of peace' (7:2). Psalm 110:4 is quoted to show that with Melchizedek began a new order, which is not contained in the Aaronic priesthood. Hebrews does not hesitate to draw the conclusion that he must then be like Christ (7:3). The Greek word aphomoiomenos means 'resembles'. Melchizedek is a reflection of the Son of God. He is also a prototype of Christ in that he was without beginning or ending and remains for ever (v.3).[76] In rabbinic fashion, the writer of Hebrews

[74] For a survey of interpretations concerning Melchizedek, see P.E.Hughes, 'Excursus I: The significance of Melchizedek' in *A Commentary on the Epistle to the Hebrews*, Grand Rapids, 1979, pp. 237 –245.

[75] TK Thomas, *Melchizedek, king and priest: an ecumenical paradigm?* The Ecumenical Review, 52. 2000, 3. pp. 403-409 and Bangalore Theological Forum, Vol.31, No.2, Dec. 1999.

[76] See J.H. Neyrey, *Without Beginning of Days or End of Life (Hebrews 7:3): 'Topos' for a True Deity*, in the Catholic Biblical Quarterly, 1991, pp. 439-455.

deduces from the absence of any recorded genealogy for Melchizedek that since he is without ancestors or descendants, he is without birth or death. Not only did Melchizedek precede Abraham but he also went beyond the Jewish priesthood in anticipating the new covenant with all humanity inaugurated by Jesus. For us Melchizedek represents the possibility that a person who is neither a Jew nor a Christian may know God intimately and may play a prominent role in God's economy outside the church or the people of God.[77]

Awareness of God outside Judaism

We can now review what we have noted about outstanding examples of the faith of people who were not Jews and about religions in the Roman Empire and can begin to answer some questions. Although the New Testament is critical of some religious practices such as idol worship, there are indications that both Jesus and Paul found many positive aspects in the spiritual awareness of peoples outside Israel and the church.

Spiritual Qualities

Before we consider how much people of other nations knew about God, it is worth noting that they were credited with some impressive spiritual qualities.

Recognition of the divine presence at work was not limited to a few outstanding individuals. At Lystra the crowd attributed the healing of the cripple to divine intervention. The slave girl at Philippi was quick to see that Paul and Silas were servants of the supreme God. In a highly religious society the quest for God, for knowledge of the spiritual world and for salvation were everywhere evident. It was not only in Athens that Paul observed people who were very religious, but there he did perceive that the quest was inspired by God and that God did not intend the desire he had implanted to remain unfulfilled.

---

[77] Some Reformed theologians try to argue that Melchizedek was not a Gentile outsider but a Semite and recipient of special revelation like Abraham. Others like Bruce Demarest admit that Melchizedek is an example of *God's activity outside of the usual vehicles of his saving purpose* (Bruce A. Demarest, *General Revelation*, Grand Rapids, 1982, p.261)

In the Gospels' account of Jesus' encounter with a wide variety of people, the capacity for spiritual discernment was not limited to Jews. Among the Gentiles Jesus met, there were two he singled out for special praise. As we have seen the Capernaum centurion saw clearly what others had missed, that the reason for Jesus' power was his direct connection to God. Similarly the Syro-Phoenician woman perceived Jesus to be Messiah and Lord. The tough centurion at the Cross, in charge of the execution squad, saw in his dying victim the one who is Son of God. We should not then be surprised to find among Greeks and Romans examples of outstanding faith. Jesus commended the centurion and the woman from Tyre not for their belief in his power to heal or for their moral excellence but for their unhesitating and unflinching faith. Their humility in approaching Jesus and casting themselves wholly on his mercy won his admiration.

In the examples of the Magi and Cornelius we noted that their unquestioning obedience to the directions God gave them contrasted sharply with the reluctance even of apostles like Peter to obey what God had told them. The Magi were the first to worship Jesus. Cornelius was commended for his worship, for his life of prayer and for his almsgiving. Such people were as ready to repent for their sins as were the citizens of Nineveh when convicted by the Spirit of God. No wonder then that Paul acknowledges that people of other nations, despite not knowing the law, are capable of doing what the law requires and of living lives that are remarkable for their moral and ethical standards.

Knowledge of God

In the rich variety of religious cults in the Roman Empire many deities were worshipped. But apart from these gods and goddesses of popular devotion there was consciousness of a supreme power. The cries of the fortune telling slave girl in Philippi expressed a common belief in 'the Most High God'. To this Paul appealed in Athens when he spoke of 'the Lord of heaven and earth' (Acts 17:24). Though the Stoics thought of this High God as impersonal, there were others who believed in a creator God. The Magi may have been among these, though nothing is said about their beliefs concerning God, only that he was able to communicate with them. In the Gospels the outstanding Gentiles whom Jesus met may have been influenced by Jewish monotheism. It was also true that idolatry was rejected by some of the philosophical elite in Athens. Paul's appeal to the Epicurean disdain for superstition provided him with a base from which to praise the attributes of the creator.

In Romans 1:18 – 2:15 Paul set out the theology on which his preaching at Athens was based.

First he argues that everyone, the Gentile included, knows about God as creator, because God has made this knowledge plain to all (v. 19). Through creation they know not only that God exists, but they also know something of his power and divine nature (*theiotes*). Though invisible, God has made himself known by the visible evidence of creation and providence. Second Paul acknowledged that Gentiles know what they should not do (v.32) and also what they should do (2:14-15). Therefore despite being ignorant of the Mosaic law, they know through conscience (*suneidesis*) the substance of God's moral law. They know perfectly well what is evil, as is spelt out in v.29-31, and conversely they know what is good. Therefore we should not be surprised if they commend what is true and good in their scriptures. This is a point that Paul used to good effect in Athens.

The immanence of God seems to have been appreciated more readily by the Greeks than the transcendental glory of the creator. The quote Paul used from Aratus and the one attributed to Epimenides bear this out. The citation *for in him we live and move and have our being* expresses the Stoic concept of divine immanence. Here and elsewhere there is also an awareness of the possibility of incarnation. That was evident in a polytheistic form at Lystra, where Paul and Barnabas were idolised as Hermes and Zeus. But it was also a possibility assumed by the Magi when they knelt before the baby Jesus and worshipped him. Since God is not only present in human life but also the one who has made us like him (*his offspring*), it was reasonable to believe that God could assume a human form without contradiction to his nature.

Worship of the living God

Do Gentiles worship the living God? Yes, some do. It is true that Paul's complaint is that many, despite knowing about their creator, have chosen to worship created things and have made images to look like them. But others have proved themselves exceptions to the rule of idolatry.

The God-fearers are the main group mentioned in Acts, who worship the one true God. But they are not the only ones. The first to worship Jesus in Matthew's Gospel were the Magi from the east. The centurion at Capernaum and the Syro-Phoenican woman impressed Jesus more than his own people by their faith.

Cornelius devoutly worshipped the one true God. As a result Peter realised that God was not limited to Israel, but is worshipped and obeyed by people from the nations, however few or many they may be.[78]

To these true worshippers we may add a long line of examples in the Old Testament, some of whom are quoted in the New, of whom Melchizedek was the greatest. The example of Melchizedek was regarded as particularly significant by the author of Hebrews. Paul describes Abraham as *the father of all who believe but have not been circumcised* (Rom. 4:11). Yet Abraham was blessed by Melchizedek, so he who had no known father and mother became like a spiritual father to Abraham. Now Melchizedek was a Canaanite priest, a devotee of El Elyon. Scripture accepts that despite the Canaanite name for God, he was a true servant and priest of the living God, whose sacrifices were acceptable to Yahweh. Hebrews goes on to describe Jesus as a priest in the order of Melchizedek (not Aaron). We can, therefore, say that there is a line of priests and worship, which existed outside Israel and may continue through Christ outside the church. Of this possibility Melchizedek remains a sign.[79]

The sources of religious knowledge

Theologians draw a distinction between general and special revelation. General revelation is available to everyone. Special revelation is a fuller revelation given to God's people through the patriarchs and prophets of Israel and through the coming of Christ. The purpose of special

---

[78] For an exposition of the passages concerning the Gentiles mentioned in this paragraph, see the previous section on 'Gentiles who are Commended for their Faith'.

[79] Wootton comments: "We may conclude therefore that though God chose Israel ... he still had his faithful ones in other nations, men and women enlightened by his wisdom, conscious of his majesty and offering acceptable worship to him, though continuing in the traditions of their own people ..." (R.W.F. Wootton, *Christianity and Other Faiths*, Exeter, 1983, p.19).

revelation is to give the knowledge of God by which mankind can be saved. Consequently general revelation is thought to be inadequate for salvation. However the range of means by which God could communicate with people outside the covenant as mentioned in the New Testament is impressive and shows the potential for Gentiles to move close to God.

Creation. Paul believed that everyone, whatever their religion, knows about God as creator, because God has made this knowledge plain to all (Rom. 1:19). Through creation they know not only that God exists but also about his power and deity. *Since the creation of the world God's invisible qualities - his eternal power and divine nature - have been clearly seen, being understood from what has been made* (Rom. 1:20).

Those who draw a sharp distinction between general and special revelation usually assume that the created order gives human beings some knowledge **about** God but not direct knowledge **of** God. However the word Paul used for knowledge, *ginosko*, can refer to experiential knowledge. So it could be that Paul wanted to make the point that everyone can come to know God personally through the revelation of creation.[80] The importance of revelation through creation, as Tiessen points out, is "that creation is a mediatory work of the Son".[81] It follows that the Son reveals the Father not only through his incarnation but also by his work of bringing the world into being (John 1:3).

Providence. God maintains the ongoing life of the universe he has created. His presence is revealed by the way in which he provides all that his creatures need for life and well being. Paul and Barnabas relied on the argument from providence to convince the Lystrans that they should worship the living God who gave them life. God *has not left himself without testimony. He has shown kindness by giving you rain from heaven and crops in their seasons, he provides you with plenty of food and fills your hearts with joy* (Acts 14:17).

Conscience. The fact that moral consciousness is part of human nature explains why Gentiles, who were ignorant of the Mosaic law, knew what God required of them. Everyone has a sense of right and wrong. The Gentiles knew what was wrong (Rom. 1:21-31). Paul concluded that they also knew

[80] T.L. Tiessen, *Who Can Be Saved?* Downers Grove, Leicester, 2004, p. 106f.
[81] op.cit. p. 107.

what was right, as shown by their actions. *When Gentiles, who do not have the law, do by nature things required by the law, they are a law for themselves, even though they do not have the law, since they show that the requirements of the law are written on their hearts, their consciences also bearing witness, and their thoughts now accusing, now even defending them* (Rom. 2:14-15).

Although human moral judgement has been affected by the Fall, God expects everyone to follow the dictates of their conscience. Religions bear witness to the universality of the ethical imperative through the many similarities contained in their moral teaching.

The Logos. The Logos is the light of men, *the true light that gives light to every man* (John 1:9). Exposition of this verse and its implications for Christology will be dealt with later in the section on the uniqueness of Christ. Here we note that taken in connection with John 1:3-4, this verse shows that as creator Christ has given all men life and light. John 1:1 recalls creation with its repetition of the opening words of Genesis – *In the beginning God*. In this context John 1:9 is the New Testament equivalent of the Genesis statement that *God created man in his own image*, with divine potential (Gen. 1:27). However, John is quick to point out that, *though the world was made through him, the world did not recognise him* (John 1:10). Despite this blindness the God-given potential in human beings creates the possibility for spiritual discernment and for the longing for God, which Paul saw evidence of in Athens (Acts 17:22, 23 & 27). God communicates through his Word (*Logos*), who has been operative in the world both before and after the incarnation. Through the Logos God speaks to those who have never heard the name of Jesus.

The work of the Spirit. The Spirit of God is not in everything as pantheists believe, but is present everywhere. As the agent of God in creation, he is not part of this material world. But he is omnipresent and also active in all human beings. Through his Spirit God is ceaselessly at work in all his creatures, though many are unaware of his presence (1 Cor. 2:14). But occasionally even Greek philosophers acknowledged the activity of the Spirit of God and articulated their awareness that *in him we live and move and have our being* (Acts 17:28).[82] The Spirit influences the

---

[82] For a creative discussion of the work of the Holy Spirit in the world's religions, see Amos Yong, *Beyond the Impasse : Towards a Pneumatological Theology of Religions*, Grand Rapids, 2003.

God Has No Favourites

hearts and minds of those who have never heard the gospel, and inspires those who are open to his promptings to search for God.

Intuition. In several of the stories of Gentile believers we have examined in the previous section, their intuitive grasp of spiritual reality is remarkable. For example, the Capernaum centurion and the Syro-Phoenician woman recognise who Jesus is much more readily and with profounder insight than the Jews with all their covenantal advantages. In biblical terms this intuition is attributable to the *imago dei* in man. Human beings not only long for God, they can also sense his presence.

Religious Experience. What humanity knows about God is reflected in religious language, which represents a storehouse of knowledge from human experience. The use of the word *logos* reminds us of a surprising and often overlooked fact, that the New Testament was written in Greek, despite the fact that all the authors were Jews, except Luke. Considering that God revealed his word to Moses in Hebrew and through Jesus in Aramaic, it is amazing that the words of God were written down in the New Testament in a language that was the mother tongue of people whom the Jews regarded as pagans. Buddhists preserved the words of Buddha in the sacred language of Pali, Hindu texts are only authoritative in Sanskrit, and the only God-given language for Muslims is the Arabic of the Qur'an. But Jewish Christians deliberately chose to forego Hebrew and recorded the Gospel in the common language of foreigners.[83] This at the very least indicates that the disciples of Christ not only wanted to communicate the gospel to Gentiles, but also believed that the language of their pagan neighbours witnessed to a shared religious experience, which could be used and built upon in declaring the revelation of God. Language reflects what people have learnt through human experience and human experience has taught people about God. The languages of the ancient world are full of religious vocabulary, including words for God, prayer, worship, forgiveness, holiness and much more. These languages witness to the desire for God as well as to the experience of God far beyond the confines of the Jewish people. The term *logos* is just one example of a linguistic vehicle that could be used to convey enhanced

---

[83] Lamin Sanneh points out that Christianity, in fact, "seems unique in being the only world religion that is transmitted without the language or originating culture of its founder" (*Whose Religion is Christianity?*, Grand Rapids, 2003, p. 98).

understanding of Christ as the eternal Word. Language is a repository of human knowledge based on the experience and discoveries of previous generations. The Bible views this process as going back to our primordial ancestors, Adam and Eve. Therefore some theologians argue that there is a residual knowledge of the revelation given to the antediluvian patriarchs that has persisted in the traditions of some ancient cultures.

God's revelation to Israel. The God-fearers, like Cornelius, were attracted and influenced by synagogue worship. It was through the teaching of the Hebrew scriptures that they came to believe in one creator God and to understand the ethical demands of a holy Lord. We cannot tell how widely known was the teaching of the Pentateuch and the prophets. But Paul's experience in Athens shows that God-fearing Greeks as well as Jews were to be found worshipping in synagogues (Acts 17:17).

Dreams and visions. The Magi and Cornelius were all guided by remarkable acts of God. The Magi are said to have been directed by a dream, as well as being guided through a star. Cornelius had a vision of a messenger from God. Through this vision he was given very specific information. Not only was he told specific details of a man and an address in a town more than 30 miles away, he distinctly saw an angel of God. From the angel he learnt that God approved of him and his prayers and his giving to the poor. He also learnt that Peter would give him a message of critical importance for his own salvation.

Specific individual revelation. In the case of Melchizedek there is no reference to him having a dream or a vision. We are not told how he came to be so close to God as to be accepted by him and treated as a genuine believer in Yahweh, who was instrumental in blessing Abraham. From the New Testament point of view, Hebrews treats him as a type of Christ, who had been taught to be a priest of the Most High. From this we understand that God had revealed himself to this remarkable priest-king of Canaan.

The Magi may also be examples of specific revelation, which they received apart from the directions they were given through a dream and the guidance of a star. We are not told how they came to know the identity of Jesus. The fact that they worshipped Jesus and the symbolism of the gifts they gave indicates that God did reveal important truths to them. They became part of God's revelation to Israel concerning the child Jesus.

The New Testament critique of religion
in the Greco-Roman world

In the Gospels and Acts there is forthright commendation of some Gentiles. There is no such assessment, either positive or negative, of any Greek or Roman religion. Many have thought that the New Testament is wholly negative to the religions of the nations, but its writers never say so. There are critical comments but there are also some indications of more positive appreciation than we might expect. Here we look at a variety of different pointers.

No condemnation

The apostles and New Testament writers did not condemn non-Jewish religions. We noted in the stories of Paul's encounters with religions in Acts how he very carefully refrained from launching into any assault on the cults around him. At Lystra the apostles did not denounce the priest of the temple of Zeus nor did they lecture the locals on the folly of believing in Greek mythology. At Philippi Paul said nothing about the Delphic oracle. At Athens, despite being distressed at the sight of so many idols, Paul spoke with great courtesy and did not despise Greek philosophy. At Ephesus the town clerk specifically exonerated Paul of the charge of blaspheming against their goddess. Unfortunately many missionaries in the past two hundred years have attacked the religions they met and have poured scorn on the beliefs of their adherents.

We can only speculate on the reasons why Paul refrained from criticising religions. He may have been influenced by Jewish practice in the Hellenistic world. He may have wished to avoid stirring up trouble, but he was not known for avoiding controversy. He may have preferred to deal with specific errors like idolatry rather than making sweeping generalisations. Whatever the reasons may have been for Paul's restraint, we would do well to follow the apostolic example, because there is good as well as error in all religions. Religions are much too complex to be divided into 'good' and 'bad'. There is also the danger of writing people off, just because they were born into a religious community, whose beliefs we disagree with. Paul had been commissioned by God to embrace the Gentiles, peoples he had previously despised. So his approach is always positive, combining both exposition of the gospel and the identification of specific errors that deflected his hearers from the truth, so that all might be welcomed into God's kingdom.

Identifying errors

Some of the errors that Paul dealt with can be summed up as false worship, false wisdom and false ethics.

False worship. Despite knowing that there is one supreme being, the Most High God (Acts 16:17), the creator of all (Acts 17:28), religions have either tolerated (Stoics and Epicureans) or promoted the worship of the creature rather than the creator (Romans 1:23). Instead of worshipping the one true God, who has made himself known to all through the evidence of creation (Romans 1:19-21) and providence (Acts 14:17), men have made images and idols and worshipped them. Despite knowing about God, they have neither glorified him for his greatness nor thanked him for his goodness (Rom. 1:21). Paul defines the heart of idolatry as the worship of something God has made in place of God himself. Idolaters have *exchanged the glory of the immortal God for images (eikonos) made to look like mortal man and birds and animals and reptiles* (Rom. 1:23). The glory of gold, silver or stone is nothing compared to the glory of God. The fact that these images owe their existence to *man's design and skill* (Acts 17:29) only compounds the folly of idol worship. How can man-made gods be any gods at all (Acts 19:26)?

False worship leads to further errors. Paul and Barnabas protested at being treated like gods, for the people had made the serious error of deifying humans (Acts 14:15). Worse still, though idols are nothing, the reality behind them is demonic, for sacrifices offered to idols are *offered to demons (daimonioi), not to God* (1 Cor. 10:20). This results in slavery to the gods of mythology, who are by nature no gods at all (Gal. 4:8). Paul thus defines not only the idols but also the gods, which they represent, as illusory. He is however aware that demonic activity may be associated with them, as in the case of the slave girl, dedicated to the Apollo cult, whose spirit he exorcised (Acts 16:16-18). Paul also describes this slavery as subjection to 'the basic principles of this world' (Gal. 4:3; Col.2:8, 20; cf. Eph. 2:2), which may refer to the spiritual powers apart from God that are at work in the universe.

It would be no surprise to find that such worship can lead to superstition and may corrupt prayer into mere repetition of many words. At Athens Paul appears to be saying that he found the Athenians superstitious (Acts 17:22 & 16). He certainly encountered superstitious practices throughout his journeys and some of these are recorded for us in Acts (e.g. 14:11 & 28:6). As for prayer, Jesus' comment to his disciples is still relevant today: *When you pray, do not keep on babbling like pagans, for they think they will be heard because of their many words* (Matt. 6:7).

False wisdom. Paul expounds this theme in 1 Corinthians 1:20-29. The Greeks were proud of their intellectual heritage. The names in their past and present that mattered most to them were the names of their philosophers. They worshipped at their shrines and despised other races as barbarians, who were unacquainted with their learning and sophistication. So they looked down on Paul, sneering at him when he spoke of the resurrection of Christ from the dead (Acts 17:32). But writing to Christians at Corinth in the light of his debates in Athens, Paul observed that all this wisdom had failed to bring the wise to the knowledge of the living God. Although the wisdom of the Greeks sounds clever, it fails to deliver and fails to save. Greeks considered the gospel of a crucified Messiah to be foolishness. But God's apparent foolishness confounds the wisdom of the philosophers, for what is of God is wise and what is purely human is no match for God. True wisdom begins with God and is given to those who are in the habit of believing (1 Cor. 1:21).

In Colossians Paul identifies the source of this false wisdom as 'human traditions' (Col. 2:8, 22). Such philosophy is deceptively impressive, but empty of true content. Its dogmas appear to be wise (Col. 2:23), but in fact they are not from God. They will not last for eternity. In Romans Paul emphasises that this false wisdom springs from and results in futile thinking. As a result of human refusal to give the glory to God, *their thinking became futile and their foolish hearts were darkened* (Rom. 1:22). The result of promoting false wisdom is blindness to the truth (2 Cor. 4:3, 4; Eph. 4:17, 18) and ignorance of God (Acts 17:23; Eph. 4:18).

False ethics. The New Testament makes a strong connection between idolatry and sensuality (Rom 1:24, 25; 1 Cor. 10:7, 8; Eph. 4:19). "A false image of God leads to a false understanding of sex", comments

John Stott.[84] In Romans Paul widens this charge to include other evils, saying that idolaters not only engage in the evils listed in 1:29-31, they also defend these practices.

In Acts on at least two occasions false worship opened the way for people to make money out of religion. At Philippi the owners of the slave girl made money out of her by using her trance states for fortune telling. When she was delivered, far from being glad for her, they were furious that they had lost their means of making easy money. At Ephesus the riot led by Demetrius was fanned into flame by his appeal to the silversmiths to be wary of the threat to their business: *Men, you know we receive a good income from this business* (Acts 19:25).

Something less gross and more subtle in its appeal was the asceticism which Paul complained about to the Colossians. His rejection of ascetic arguments, that religion depends on what you wear, what you eat and what you touch, is interesting. He argues that however impressive this strict lifestyle may appear, its harsh treatment of the body has no power to restrain sensual indulgence (Col. 2:21-23). Compare this with Jesus' comments on pagan lifestyle in Matthew 6:31-32.

God's attitude

Despite errors in mankind's religions God cares for all. The New Testament witnesses to the inclusive action of God to draw all persons to himself from all religions. In this process God deliberately embraced all nations in the full knowledge of their religious upbringing, allegiances and practices.

No favouritism. At Lystra the apostles spoke of the good news that God is kind to all. They pointed to God's provision of food for all through the earth's consistent seasons. He not only provides plenty of food, he also fills men's hearts with joy. At Athens Paul told his audience that God *himself gives all men life and breath and everything else* (Acts 17:25). God's new way is designed to be universal, for all the nations. All are included. God has no favourites. All are precious to him. For Jesus this was a foundation truth that should govern the lives of his followers. For just as our *Father in heaven ... causes his sun to rise on the evil and the good, and sends rain on the righteous*

---

[84]   J.R.W. Stott commenting on Rom. 1:24 in *The Message of Romans*, Leicester, 1994, p.76.

and the unrighteous, so should the love of his disciples include everyone, whatever their religion. Therefore whatever a person's religious label, if he or she is a God-fearer and does what is right in God's eyes, they are welcomed by God. To say this does not imply that God approves of the religion of the one he accepts, but it also does not imply that the person could not have received anything good from their religion.

No racism. God is the author of diversity. Paul drew attention to this feature of God's economy at Athens (Acts 17:26). As a Jew he was acutely aware that God was the one who had divided humanity into many races. These diverse races were not an accident, nor were these races the authors of their own identity, as if they had no common ancestry and were answerable to no one but themselves. God determined their boundaries and their history. God's plan is not limited to one nation, it extends to all, for all are part of God's one human family. Diversity and difference are God's variety. There is therefore no justification for racism in religion or anywhere else. No community should be ostracised because of their religion.

Tolerance. God is amazingly tolerant. Paul drew attention to this both at Lystra and Athens.

At Lystra the apostles affirmed that, *in the past (God) let all nations go their own way* (Acts 14:16). At Athens Paul, commenting on the tradition of making images for worship, said: *In the past God overlooked such ignorance, but now he commands all people everywhere to repent* (Acts 17:30). God accounts for ignorance in religion. He recognises that there are those who have not known what he requires, because they have not been informed. Similarly in the Gospels Jesus is quoted as saying that Tyre and Sidon will be judged more leniently than Galilean towns like Capernaum, who had seen his miracles (Luke 10:13ff.). Or again the inhabitants of Nineveh and the Queen of Sheba will be preferred to Jesus' contemporaries, because they responded to what they were told (Matt. 12:41f.).

What are the implications of these statements of God's tolerance for scripture's view of other religions? First, the followers of religions were not blamed for their ignorance. Second, this does not mean that the religions were satisfactory, for God has proclaimed his way of salvation through Jesus for all to follow. Third, God holds people responsible not for what they do not know but for what they would have done if they had received the revelation of Christ. Religions may be used in this process, because despite ignorance of Christ they may inspire search for and faith in God. God's desire is that people should be saved, not damned (1 Tim. 2:4).

Theocentric approach. God's purpose is to bring humanity back to himself, for it is faith in God that saves. In his preaching to Greeks Paul took a theocentric approach. He called on his hearers to have faith in God. Only later after fully explaining the gospel did he ask Gentiles to believe in Jesus. He did not separate faith in God from faith in Jesus Christ, as if faith in Jesus is superior to faith in God, as some seem to suggest. The truth that Jesus Christ is the one and only saviour of the world should not be construed to mean, that faith in Christ saves, but faith in God without the knowledge of Christ does not. This would be to divide the persons of the Trinity. A christocentric approach must always be theocentric, otherwise it ceases to be true and becomes divisive. Put differently, the Christian view of religions and their followers must be trinitarian, if it is to be balanced. People may be divided by their knowledge of Christ but brought together by their love for God. A trinitarian approach embraces the world. The Father is the creator to whom people turn in faith; the Son is the pre-existent Logos who is universally at work to reveal the Father; and the Spirit is present everywhere to convict and convert.

Religions as means of salvation

Does God use the world's religions to save some? There is nothing to suggest that the New Testament sees religions as salvific, for Jesus Christ is God's plan for the salvation of all people everywhere, not some people somewhere. But this does not mean either, that God cannot use religions if and when he chooses, or that religions may not play a useful role. The Magi are an example of God using the knowledge cultivated by a religion for his purposes. Melchizedek is a sign of the great things God can do through the leader of a religion, who would otherwise have been thought to belong to a polytheistic cult. Religions are ambiguous and complex combinations of ideas and practices, insights and delusions. They reflect and commend elements of truth received from the revelation that God has made available to all, apart from Christ and the Bible. As seen above these sources of revelation are not confined to creation and conscience. The New Testament does not attack other religions as such, since it sees that everything has been replaced by the one way, which God has authorised through Jesus Christ. Nevertheless God uses all means to call people to himself and accepts all whatever their religious training, if they have faith in him alone and obey him by doing what is right (Acts 10:35).

Chapter Two

Jewish Religion

Introduction

SO FAR WE HAVE CONSIDERED WHAT THE NEW TESTAMENT
has to say about religions in the countries bordering the Mediterranean.
What then of the main religion which Jesus faced, the religion he was
born into, the religion of the Jews? This should not be identified with
the Judaism, which took its distinctive shape after the destruction of the
Temple in 70 AD and after the Jewish followers of Christ had left the
rabbinic fold.

Any discussion of Christ's encounter with the religion of his people
is complicated by the tension between God's revelation to Israel through
the Law and the Prophets, which Jesus came to fulfil, and the religious
practices of his Jewish contemporaries, which he criticised on various
counts. It is also complicated by the variety of sects and religious
groupings within Israel during Christ's lifetime. The tendency to identify
Pharisaism as the religion of the Jews must be resisted. Jesus met not
only Pharisees, but also Sadducees, Herodians, Zealots, the followers of
John the Baptist and probably Essenes as well. In addition the Gospels
mention the following groups: the crowds, the tax collectors and sinners,
the chief priests and scribes and elders, and the priests and Levites.

However critical Jesus was of contemporary religious leaders, he
remained a Jew, prayed as a Jew, worshipped as a Jew in synagogue and
Temple, and obeyed the Law of Moses.

Judaism in the New Testament period

The religion of Jesus' Jewish contemporaries is often referred to by
scholars as Second Temple Judaism. This has the benefit of distinguishing
it from Judaism as it developed in the centuries after the destruction of
the Temple in 70 AD. But it should not conceal the fact that there was
considerable diversity in the Judaism of the first century AD. Josephus
distinguished four sects: Pharisees, Sadducees, Essenes and Zealots. In
addition there were two large groups, the priests, and ordinary Jews,
who did not belong to any of Josephus' parties.

The Priests

From the Gospels it might be thought that the Pharisees were far more
numerous and ubiquitous than the priests, but that was not the case.
According to Josephus there were four priestly clans, each with more
than 5,000 members, totalling at least 20,000.[85] In comparison he estimates
there were about 6,000 Pharisees. The priests mostly lived outside
Jerusalem, only going up to the holy city to perform their duties in the
Temple, when their time for service was due. At home they were not idle,
they were the teachers of the law on whom Jews depended for religious
direction and judgement. The priests were the religious authorities to
whom the populace turned, because they had studied the Torah and
officiated at the Temple. The importance of their local role can be seen
from the incident in Matthew 8:4ff., where Jesus told the cleansed leper
to show himself to the priest and be declared 'clean' by him.

The Pharisees

The Jewish scholar, Jacob Neusner, states that the dominant trait of
Pharisaism before 70 AD was, "as depicted both in the rabbinic traditions
about the Pharisees and in the Gospels, concern for certain matters of rite,
in particular, eating one's meals in a state of ritual purity as if one were
a Temple priest, and carefully giving the required tithes and offerings
due to the priesthood."[86] Loyalty to God's covenant with Israel was the
great concern of Jewish sects reacting against Roman rule and the defiling

---

[85] Josephus, *Against Apion* 2.108.
[86] J. Neusner, *Early Rabbinic Judaism*, Leiden, 1975, p.43.

presence of pagans in Jerusalem; hence the Pharisees' insistence on purity. Tom Wright puts the point this way: "faced with social, political and cultural 'pollution' at the level of national life as a whole", the Pharisees reacted by concentrating on "personal cleanness, to cleanse and purify an area over which one did have control as a compensation for the impossibility of cleansing or purifying an area – the outward and visible political one – over which one had none."[87] Pharisees sought to protect themselves from defilement by maintaining strict rules of purity. They were determined to practise a level of holiness similar to that required of priests in the Temple. The biblical injunction in Exodus 19:5-6 expressed their intent: *You shall be a kingdom of priests and a holy nation.* Pharisees are thought to have been laymen not priests, but as scholars they were concerned to apply rules of purity to everyday life, especially to the meal table. Everyday food should be served and eaten, as if they were priests serving in the Temple. Therefore utensils used must be pure, the food eaten must be from agricultural produce properly tithed and companions at the meal table could not include the 'unclean', such as the maimed, the sick and 'sinners'. They were also concerned more widely for the study and practice of the Torah.

The Essenes

Unlike the Pharisees, the Essene community at Qumran withdrew into the desert to await God's judgement on all his enemies. Calling themselves the 'Sons of Light', they regarded everyone else, both Jews and pagans, as 'Sons of Darkness'. In their view they were the remnant, waiting to return from exile. God would send his king to remove the apostate high priest running the Temple and install a true priest in a new and purified Temple. Their communal life was their chief preoccupation. The daily meal, according to Josephus, was very important for them. No one but the initiated could attend. Entering the dining area was like entering a sacred shrine: special clothes had to be worn like 'holy vestments', the meal began and ended with prayer, a priest blessed the bread and wine, and the food was eaten in silence. Levitical laws for priests (Lev. 2:17-21) were applied to the Qumran community, so no one who was ill or injured or deformed could enter, including the lame,

[87] N.T. Wright, op.cit., p.187.

blind, deaf and paralysed. Philo and Josephus estimated that the Essenes numbered 4,000 or more, and that they lived in many Judaean towns, not only at the strict community of Qumran.

The Sadducees

The chief priests of the Jerusalem Temple mostly belonged to the aristocratic party of the Sadducees. Rejected by the Essenes and often criticized by the Pharisees, they were concerned with the politics of leading the nation and dealing with the Romans. They believed in the permanent validity of the written Torah of the Pentateuch and placed no reliance on the oral law, so greatly valued by the Pharisees. As the New Testament makes clear, they did not believe in the resurrection or after life.

The Zealots

The mention in Luke 6:15 of 'Simon, called the Zealot', as one of the twelve, indicates that Zealots were known to Jesus. The noun 'zeal' and the adjective 'zealous' were used widely to refer to anti-Roman attitudes and activities. A Zealot party came into being at the start of the war with Rome in 66 AD. Whether or not there was a party called the Zealots at the time of Jesus is uncertain. What the Zealots stood for, however, is clear, that is resistance to Rome.

Ordinary Jews

The great bulk of the population of Judaea and Galilee were not priests or Pharisees, Zealots or Essenes. Despite the disparaging use of the term 'the people of the land' (*amme ha-arets*) in later rabbinic literature, ordinary Jews were not to be equated with prostitutes and collaborators with Rome. The Jews Jesus met in Galilee and Jerusalem were brought up to pray, to fast, to attend the synagogue and to go on pilgrimage at festival seasons to the Temple. They kept the Sabbath, circumcised their babies and were careful not to eat unclean food. Notice how Peter, brought up as a fisherman, could say in later life: *I have never eaten anything impure or unclean* (Acts 10:14). There speaks an ordinary Jew, not a Pharisee. Note also that the same Peter shared the common Jewish concern for purity from contamination by association with unclean people. *You are well aware*, he told the Gentile household of Cornelius, *that it is against our law for a Jew to* **associate** *with a Gentile or visit him* (Acts 10:28). Besides all this, Jewish families believed in one God, Yahweh, the God of Israel, in the Torah, the Temple and the election of Israel as God's chosen people. Most significantly they shared a common longing, that God would intervene to liberate their land from oppression and restore his rule over his people and his holy place, the Temple.

What is commended in Judaism ?

Jesus affirmed the fundamental beliefs of the faith of Israel and their divine origin. The pillars of second Temple Judaism are generally acknowledged to include monotheism, the Torah, the Temple, election and the covenant. These can be summarised as Holy God, Holy People, Holy Land, Holy Book and Holy Temple.[88]

One God

Every Jew was taught to say every day the Shema: *Hear, O Israel: The Lord our God, the Lord is one;* or, *...The Lord our God is one Lord* (Deut. 6:4). In replying to the question of a teacher of the Torah, Jesus repeats the Shema and insists that the most important of all commandments is love and obedience for the one and only God.[89] Throughout the New Testament it is taken for granted that there is only one creator God, who alone is worthy of worship. Therefore the worship of many gods is not merely wrong, it is also blasphemous and the worst form of treachery.[90]

The Chosen People

Intrinsic to the Old and New Testaments is the conviction that God chose Israel to be his people and bound Israel to himself by divine covenant. Israel's history shows how God called Abraham and promised to bless his descendants with the land he had given them. This promise was fulfilled through Moses and Joshua, and subsequently by the return of the exiles from near extinction in Babylon.

---

[88] See S. Nigosian, *Judaism: The Way of Holiness*, Bath, 1986.
[89] Mark 12:28ff.
[90] See Chapter One above on Idol Worship.

Jesus reflects this belief when he says to the woman of Samaria: *You Samaritans worship what you do not know; we worship what we do know, for salvation is from the Jews* (John 4:22). It also lies behind the priority Jesus gave to ministry to Israel prior to his resurrection. *Do not go among the Gentiles or enter any town of the Samaritans,* he told his disciples. *Go rather to the lost sheep of Israel* (Matt.10:5f.; cf. Matt.15:24). This priority was crystallised in Paul's formula: *first for the Jew, then for the Gentile* (Rom. 1:16; 2:9). Every Jew was the inheritor of God's promises, therefore the wayward should be reclaimed and the deformed transformed. So Jesus said of Zacchaeus: *Today salvation has come to this house, because this man, too, is a son of Abraham.* He also said of the crippled woman: *should not this woman, a daughter of Abraham, whom Satan has kept bound for eighteen long years, be set free on the Sabbath day from what bound her?* (Luke 19:9; 13:16).

The rest of the New Testament expresses the same Jewish assurance of their national identity under God. Stephen's speech in Acts 7 rehearses the Jewish view of Israel's history. From first to last it is a history of God's initiative in calling and recalling his people to himself. Paul affirms most emphatically in Romans 9 – 11, that whatever might be the errors of his Jewish compatriots: *Theirs is the adoption as sons; theirs the divine glory, the covenants, the receiving of the law, the temple worship and the promises.* Election is irreversible: *as far as election is concerned, they are loved on account of the patriarchs, for God's gifts and his call are irrevocable* (Rom. 9:4f.; 11:28f.).

The Scriptures

Although the Sadducees regarded the Pentateuch alone as their final authority, most Jews, like the Pharisees, regarded Scripture as comprising the Law, the Prophets and the Wisdom literature. Jesus consistently appealed to Scripture. During the temptations in the wilderness he refuted the devil by quoting from Deuteronomy.[91] At the beginning of his ministry, in the Nazareth synagogue, he took the scroll of the prophet Isaiah and, reading Isaiah 61:1,2, told the people that this prophecy had been fulfilled in their hearing (Luke 4:18ff.). He went on to refer to

[91] Deuteronomy 8:3; 6:16; 6:13.

the records of the prophetic actions of Elijah and Elisha in support of his ministry (I Kings 17; II Kings 5). In his debates with the Pharisees he argued that the Scriptures pointed to him. After his resurrection he upheld the authority of the Law, the Prophets, and the Psalms and rebuked the disciples for their failure to believe all that the prophets had spoken (John 5:39; Luke 24:25-27, 44).

The rest of the New Testament relies on the authority of the Old Testament, referring directly and indirectly, especially to the Pentateuch, the major prophets and the Psalms, and teaching the divine origin of Scripture (e.g. 1 Cor. 15:3f.; 2 Tim. 3:14-17; 2 Pet. 1:19-21).

The Law

Fundamental to Jewish religious practice was the law (Torah) given by God to Moses. Deuteronomy is the classic statement of this law, with its repeated injunction, which could be summarised in Jesus' words, *Do this and you will live.* The post-exilic reforms of Ezra put the Torah at the centre of Jewish life. 'Zeal for the law' was quickened by the Maccabean revolt and became a common characteristic of second Temple Judaism. Jews took it for granted that God had made a special covenant with Israel and had therefore given them the law to define what God expected of them, a law which they were bound to keep. Particularly important were circumcision, the food laws and the Sabbath, which marked Jews out as different from the nations around them.

The Jewishness of Jesus is nowhere more obvious than in his loyalty to the Torah. In his Sermon on the Mount, he repudiates the suspicion that he might contemplate using his authority to rewrite the law: *Do not think that I have come to abolish the Law or the Prophets; I have not come to abolish them but to fulfil them* (Matt. 5:17). Despite criticising the Pharisees he tells his hearers: *The teachers of the law and the Pharisees sit in Moses' seat. So you must obey them and do everything they tell you* (Matt. 23:2f.). The law should be practised in all its details, as well as in its great principles (Matt. 23:23). We should not be surprised that he sent the cleansed leper to the priest to offer the sacrifices the law commanded (Mark 1:44; cf. Luke 17:14).

Similarly Paul upheld the law, despite his re-evaluation of its place in the history of salvation. In Romans 7 he affirms the importance of the law: *So then, the law is holy, and the commandment is holy, righteous and good...We know that the law is spiritual* (Rom.7:12, 14). The law was given to bring us to Christ (Gal. 3:19-24).

The Temple

At the heart of Judaism was the Temple , the centre of Israel's national and religious life. The Temple was the holy place, sanctified by God's Shekinah glory, in the holy city, in the holy land. The Temple was the symbol of God's presence and God's ownership of his people.

Jesus came to the Temple at significant points in his life: at his dedication, when he was twelve years old, when his ministry began and in the week before his death (Luke 2:22, 42; John 2:13ff.; Mark 11:11ff.). Zeal for his father's house burned within him and he wept when he thought of the destruction that would later overwhelm it (John 2:17; Luke 19:41ff.). He called it the house of God and taught that everything in it was holy, because God dwelt there (Matt.12:4; 23:21). Similarly he was much at home in the context of synagogue worship. Here he read the scriptures in public worship and expounded the word of God. His first recorded sermon in Luke took place in the synagogue at Nazareth. Much of his teaching ministry took place in the synagogues of Galilee and Judaea.

Considering that Jesus upheld the fundamentals of Judaism, how was it that there was such a division between himself and the Jewish leaders, which led first to his crucifixion and then to the break between church and synagogue? What was it that Jesus found lacking or amiss in the religion of his contemporaries? We should not forget that Jesus and the first apostles were all Jews and that the division between Jew and Christian, which we take for granted, would not have occurred to them. Jesus and the New Testament writers criticised the faith of their fellow countrymen, not because they were Jews, but for other reasons. What these reasons were must now be examined.

The New Testament Critique of Second Temple Judaism

Despite the common ground of belief in the fundamentals of Judaism, Jesus clashed with the Jews. The division sharpened when the Gentile mission began after Pentecost. Later the church sought to show the inadequacies of the old covenant. The New Testament critique of Judaism is to be found in the Gospels, Paul's letters and the Letter to the Hebrews. We will look at these in turn.

The Gospels

Jesus clashed with the Pharisees and other Jewish leaders over a number of issues. These included Sabbath observance, purity rituals, association with defiled people, fasting, exorcisms, the cleansing of the Temple and the authority of Jesus. What were the underlying reasons for these clashes? How did Jesus' viewpoint diverge from that of Jewish religious authorities? In particular, what did Jesus find deficient in Jewish religion?

Following the Prophets

"Jesus stood, and was conscious of standing, in the long tradition of the Hebrew prophets," comments Tom Wright.[92] Like them he was concerned for heart obedience to God, not for the mere performance of religious acts. Jesus must have meditated deeply on Isaiah 40-66, because his own words and works resonate with Isaiah's themes. The prophets condemned religiosity unaccompanied by repentance, obedience, justice and heart loyalty to God. They reserved some of their harshest words for meaningless sacrifices offered to Yahweh. Even the sanctity of temple worship did not escape their invective.[93]

The only verse Jesus is recorded as quoting twice in the Gospels, Hosea 6:6, calls for mercy and not sacrifice. In the first instance Jesus responds to the Pharisees' objection: *Why does your teacher eat with tax collectors and 'sinners'?* (Matt.9:11). As we have noted above the Pharisees were careful to avoid association with impure people especially at the meal table.[94] So this was no idle question out of social prejudice. Jesus' reply takes issue with their priorities. God, he says, is concerned to show mercy to 'sinners', even at the expense of his holiness, if by doing so he can bring them back to himself and make them whole (Matt. 9:12-13). In the second instance the question is about the Sabbath. Jesus implies that the Pharisees' interpretation of Scripture is faulty, bound more

[92] N.T. Wright, *Jesus and the Victory of God*, London, 1996.
[93] See for example, Isaiah 1, Jeremiah 7, Amos 5 and Hosea 6.
[94] See the Section on the Pharisees.

by concern that the law is kept than by concern for the purpose of the Sabbath. The Sabbath is meant for the good of man not as a rod for his back, so God has mercy on the hungry and the maimed, even on the Sabbath day (Matt. 12:1-14).

Jesus calls on his contemporaries to major on mercy whilst not ignoring the details of the law. *"Woe to you, teachers of the law and Pharisees, you hypocrites! You give a tenth of your spices -- mint, dill and cummin. But you have neglected the more important matters of the law -- justice, mercy and faithfulness. You should have practised the latter, without neglecting the former. You blind guides! You strain out a gnat but swallow a camel* (Matt. 23:23f.).

Surprisingly, he found the righteousness of the Pharisees lacking (Matt. 5:20), despite all their strict rules and insistence on purity and holiness. What Jesus required is not mere outward observance of the law, but right inner attitudes, reflected in compassionate action for others. In requiring a righteousness greater than that of the Pharisees, Jesus did not abrogate the law but demanded a deeper obedience to its spirit.[95] In the six examples, which follow, Jesus extends the meaning of the law and rejects interpretations, which would restrict it to the letter only. What was commonly taught Jesus said was that murder, adultery, failure to give a certificate of divorce, breaking oaths, unjust punishment and lack of love for your kith and kin are acts that break God's commands. Jesus went much further. He said that anger, lust, divorce except for adultery, swearing any oaths, resisting violence and failure to love your enemies are equally sinful. In the kingdom of heaven such high standards are possible, because the prophesy of Jeremiah will be fulfilled: *I will put my law within them, and I will write it upon their hearts* (Jer.31:33).

In the Sermon on the Mount Jesus criticizes public displays of almsgiving, prayer and fasting (Matt.6:1-18). 'Acts of righteousness' done for public show, do not win God's approval. He specifically singles out the Pharisees for doing everything 'for men to see' and gives examples: *They make their phylacteries wide and the tassels on their garments long; they love the place of honour at banquets and the most important seats in the*

---

[95] For a clear restatement of the view that Jesus did not contradict the law of Moses, but explained "the true meaning of the moral law with all its uncomfortable implications", see J.R.W. Stott, *Christian Counter-Culture*, Leicester, 1978, pp.74-81.

synagogues; they love to be greeted in the market-places and to have men call them 'Rabbi' (Matt.23:5-7).

The Pharisees set high standards for themselves. They aimed to fulfil Exodus 19:5-6, maintaining in ordinary life the purity required of a priest in the Temple. Neusner estimates that of the material in the Mishnah which can be attributed to the period before 70 A.D. two-thirds deal with dietary laws covering the fitness of food to be eaten and ritual purity for meals.[96] Jesus did not deny the value of these regulations in themselves, but he did condemn the preoccupation of the Pharisees with externals. It is good to clean the cup, but not to ignore its contents. The contents are more important: *You clean the outside of the cup and dish, but inside they are full of greed and self-indulgence. Blind Pharisee! First clean the inside of the cup and dish, and then the outside also will be clean* (Matt. 23:25f.).

What exactly lay behind this contrast between 'inside' and 'outside' becomes apparent from Mark 7:1-23. Here the topic of discussion is purity, the focus of Pharisaic effort. What precisely makes things 'clean' or 'unclean'? 'Why don't Jesus' disciples keep the traditions and eat without cleansing their hands with a ceremonial washing?' ask the Pharisees. Jesus responds by quoting the prophet Isaiah: *These people honour me with their lips, but their hearts are far from me. They worship me in vain; their teachings are but rules taught by men* (Isa.29:13). The Pharisees are guilty of giving priority to the 'the traditions of men' at the expense of God's specific commands. But what is even more important is the inconsistency between the inside and the outside, between their lips and their hearts. They define what is clean by externals: how you eat, with whom you eat, what you eat. That, says Jesus, is irrelevant, because evil comes from the inside, from the evil desires of the heart, and they are what make a person 'unclean'. It is no good having the outside right and the inside wrong.

Another theme voiced by the prophets and repeated by Jesus was the error of relying on the presence of the Temple in Jerusalem as a permanent guarantee of God's favour. There is no security in relying on Temple worship, if the Temple is defiled by injustice. The most outspoken

---

[96]   See for example the summary of Prof. Jacob Neusner's views in his article, *Mr Sanders' Pharisees and Mine*, Scottish Journal of Theology, 1991, Vol. 44, pp. 73-95.

attack in the Old Testament on those who go to worship in the Jerusalem Temple occurs in Jeremiah 7. The prophet does not mince his words: *Do not trust in deceptive words and say, 'This is the temple of the Lord' ...Will you steal and murder, commit adultery and perjury, burn incense to Baal and follow other gods you have not known, and then come and stand before me in this house, which bears my Name, and say, 'We are safe'... Has this house, which bears my Name, become a den of robbers to you?* (Jer.7:4, 9-11). By the phrase 'den of robbers' Jeremiah clearly meant the use of the temple as a place of retreat after crimes and acts of violence.

In quoting this verse Jesus may have been attacking not so much the corruption and commercialisation of the traders, as the crime of robbing God's temple of his glory by focus on the means of worship and not the ends. Sanders rightly points out that the doves and moneychangers were all needed for the provision of sacrifices and the payment of the temple tax. Jesus did not stop the trade for long and the traders would have been back within hours. Jesus also quoted Isaiah 56:7, and by doing so may have included criticism of the way the court of the Gentiles was misused for trade.[97] He wanted the Temple to be inclusive and used equally by Gentiles as well as by Jews.

The cleansing of the Temple was a symbolic action,[98] which struck at the heart of Israel's claim to God's favour. God was not pleased with the purity even of the Temple worship. Taken together with the acted parable of the cursing of the barren fig-tree, which brackets the driving out of the moneychangers in Mark, the Temple cleansing indicated a sign of God's judgment not only on the Temple but on Israel as a whole. Jesus' prophesy of the Temple's destruction (Mark 13:2) only reinforced this prediction, for God would not allow the Temple to be demolished stone by stone, unless there was something radically wrong with its worship.

The Temple was not inviolable. God alone is the Rock to rely on. Israel's privileges as God's chosen people did not guarantee that all Jews would be saved. God is not mocked; only those who cast themselves on

---

[97]   H.D. Betz believes most scholars opt for the court of the Gentiles as the place where Jesus expelled the merchants. See his article in the Journal of Biblical Literature, 1997, pp.455ff.

[98]   Matt. 21:10-11 puts the action in the context of Jesus entering Jerusalem as a prophet, suggesting the cleansing of the Temple was the symbolic act of a prophet.

his mercy and change their ways will be saved. This calls for repentance; Jesus repeats the Baptist's call for a change of mind (*metanoia*) and a consequent change of direction.

John the Baptist had already warned the Pharisees and Sadducees: *You brood of vipers! Who warned you to flee from the coming wrath? Produce fruit in keeping with repentance. And do not think you can say to yourselves, 'We have Abraham as our father.' I tell you that out of these stones God can raise up children for Abraham. The axe is already at the root of the trees, and every tree that does not produce good fruit will be cut down and thrown into the fire* (Matt. 3:7-10).

The parables of the Good Samaritan, the Pharisee and the Publican, and the Vineyard, and the conversation with Simon the Pharisee illustrate these prophetic themes. Those who are approved by God are those who show mercy and beg for heart cleansing from God. Sadly the Jewish leaders did not give priority to these qualities. Jesus warned them that they were liable to follow their forbears in rejecting the prophets and killing him.

Discerning the Kingdom

Jesus did not berate people for inadequate views of the messianic kingdom, but for failure to respond to what they heard him say and saw him do. He proclaimed the new day of God's rule in the affairs of Israel, which would affect the world. He pointed to his actions as signs of the coming kingdom, and hinted that in his own person lay the key to understanding God's new activity. He prophesied that the kingdom would come in power and judgment after his death.

John the Baptist seems to have accepted the signs that Jesus gave, but others did not. Jesus was disappointed that his contemporaries did not discern that God was doing a new thing through him. Instead they wanted a sign that would prove his messianic identity.

The heart of the matter in Jesus' view was Israel's failure to recognise that in him the kingdom had arrived and to respond to the invitation to enter. The parable of the Great Banquet (Luke 14:15ff.) eloquently expresses Jesus' complaint. Like the host of the feast Jesus has sent out the invitation in God's name, *'Come, for everything is now ready'* (v.17).

The kingdom of God is ready. Come and enter in. But the Jewish leaders do not. They prefer their old ways.

Jesus explained to them that, *The Law and the Prophets were proclaimed until John. Since that time, the good news of the kingdom of God is being preached, and everyone is forcing his way into it* (Luke 16:16). It is not that the old covenant was wrong; it was incomplete. Everyone in Israel admitted that things were not as they should be, the nation longed for the Messiah. But when Christ came they were not ready for the new covenant he brought.

The coming of the kingdom exposed other deficiencies, which were to be enlarged on later by Paul and the author of Hebrews. The annunciation that the kingdom is at hand resulted in people trying to force their way in (Luke 16:16). The tax collectors and sinners were particularly eager to get in. But the Pharisees and scribes and elders stayed outside.

The conversation with Nicodemus (recorded in John 3:1ff.) illuminates the gap between Jesus and Jewish authorities. Nicodemus could see that Jesus' miracles marked him out as a man of God, but he could not understand the outline of the kingdom Jesus projected. For one thing Jesus said that entry into the kingdom would not be by membership of the house of Israel, but by repentance ('water') and by spiritual new birth. Jesus berates this leading theologian for his lack of discernment: *You are Israel's teacher and do not understand these things? I tell you the truth, we speak of what we know, and we testify to what we have seen, but still you people do not accept our testimony* (John 3:10-11).

Jesus' preaching emphasised the truth that the Pharisees could not rely on their heritage to get them into the kingdom. Reliance on their birth as Jews, worship at the Temple, the blessings of Jerusalem and the knowledge of the Law would all fail to give them entrance into the kingdom (Matt. 21:43; 23:37f.; 24:1f.). Their failure to enter the kingdom was compounded by the way they prevented others from entering: *Woe to you experts in the law, because you have taken away the key to knowledge. You yourselves have not entered, and you have hindered those who were entering* (Luke 11:52).

The only way into the kingdom - and it is a narrow door, not only for Gentiles but also for Jews - is through true repentance and faith, which produce the fruit of changed lives. That is precisely what Jesus proclaimed from the moment he began his public preaching in Galilee: *The time has come. The kingdom of God is near. Repent and believe the good news!* (Mark 1:15).

Far from being given the privilege of free entry into the kingdom reserved for them, Jews found themselves facing greater demands than were placed on nearby Gentiles (Luke 10:13-15). For those to whom much has been given, of them much will be required (Luke 12:48). In this Jesus repeated the judgement of the prophets that went before him, who had declared that chosen Israel was to be judged precisely because of her privileges.

Salvation is not something Jews can take for granted, nor will it be granted except on God's terms. The annunciation of a coming saviour (Matt. 1:21) indicates that Israel needs to be saved. Israel wanted salvation from Rome. God wanted to give salvation from Satan, to break his power and set the captives free (Luke 11:20). That this meant every Jew needed to be set free was not at first apparent (John 8:33), because Jesus concentrated on extending God's mission of mercy to sinners, outcasts and even Gentiles. But by the end of the Gospel record it is clear that all need the grace of forgiveness (Luke 24:47).

Pharisees, like Simon, need forgiveness just as much as the prostitute at his door. So Jews are bluntly told by Jesus: *Unless you repent you too will perish* (Luke 13:3, 5). Those who are confident of their righteousness and despise others will not be justified; sinners who repent will be (Luke 18:9-14). So the tables will be turned and the first will be last. Some Jews will find themselves outside the kingdom not just now but on the day of judgement, whereas repentant sinners and believing Gentiles will be in.

Jesus saw Israel under judgment, because she did not recognise the coming of God's rule or the appearance of God's king. His lament over Jerusalem and prediction of its destruction are signs not only of Israel's disobedience, but of the blindness of its leaders.

Understanding God

Jesus' most profound criticism of religious leaders concerns their failure to understand God. This can be illustrated from the parables of the Lost

Sheep and the Lost Son (Luke 15:1-32). Ostensibly these stories were
told to show that God rejoices over sinners who repent. The Pharisees
would not have disagreed with this proposition. They too believed in
the repentance of sinners and in God's ability to forgive. What they
apparently could not comprehend was why Jesus should associate with
sinners **before** they repent. *This man welcomes sinners and eats with them,*
they muttered (Luke 15:2).

The parables reveal some surprising things about God; his ways are
not our ways and his thoughts are not our thoughts. To know him is to
know the God of surprises.

First, God loves sinners even **before** they return to him and repent.
He loves the sinner, just as the shepherd loves his erring sheep, the woman
her lost coin and the father his rebellious son. This is very shocking – and
always has been – to morally law-abiding people, especially to those
who are strict in their religious observances and obedience to divine
commands. Kenneth Bailey has ably demonstrated no Middle Eastern
peasant farmer would act as the father in Jesus' parable did.[99] He would
have thrashed his younger son for the monstrous request that he should
be given his inheritance before his father died and he would never have
given the son any inheritance money to leave home and squander as he
pleased. The father in Jesus' story was utterly different from the proper
traditional model. We have got used to this idea of a God who lets the
prodigal go and runs to meet him on his return. But the Pharisees and
teachers of the law were predictably taken aback.

Second, even more shocking is the picture of God as one who
willingly **suffers** shame and rejection, in order to forgive and save his
children. A casual reading of the parable suggests that the father resided
serenely at home waiting for his sons to respond to his love. Looked
at through the eyes of a Middle Eastern peasant the picture looks very
different. Bailey shows that at every turn in the story the father suffers
either from his sons or from the scorn of his fellow villagers or from
both, but above all from the pain of rejected love.[100] Jesus' view that the
Messiah must also suffer rejection and death was equally shocking. How
could God fail to look after himself and his own? Even John the Baptist

[99]   K.E. Bailey, *Poet & Peasant*, Grand Rapids, 1983, pp.142-206.
[100]   op.cit. pp. 158ff.

wondered how Jesus could be the all conquering Messiah, when he was so slow to take the reins of power and rule.[101] That God would send his son to die as a ransom for many out of love for the world would have seemed outrageous to Jewish leaders.[102]

Third, God's concern is all **inclusive** for all the flock and both sons, not just for the safe and respectable, therefore he gives priority to saving the lost one out of a hundred. From the very beginning of his ministry Jesus surprised the orthodox by his determination to include the excluded. At Nazareth he pointedly quoted Isaiah 61:1, 2, to show that God was on the side of the poor, the prisoners, the blind and the oppressed. He went out of his way to minister to those whom Pharisees and Essenes often excluded from their fellowship meals on the grounds of uncleanness, such as, the blind, the lame, the demon-possessed, the lepers, the deaf and dumb, the deformed, the woman with an issue of blood, prostitutes and tax collectors. He even went further and ministered to Gentiles, predicting that many of them would be included in the kingdom, whilst Jews would be left outside.[103]

Fourth, God loves the elder son, even though the elder son abuses God in his own self-righteousness, and **leaves the way open** for him to come to know God. The elder son's complaint is very revealing: 'All these years I've been slaving for you and never disobeying your orders'. How the father longed that his first born would exchange the slave mentality for the freedom of a son.[104] But the parable does not finish there. The door is not closed on the elder son. The Pharisees and scribes are left to ponder their response. Would they rejoice as God does in having mercy, or would they resent his generosity to the 'unclean' and leave the family.[105] However harsh some of Jesus' words were against the Pharisees, they are the harshness of the prophet not the final sentence of the judge, for here he left the door open, as he did on the cross, praying, *Father, forgive them, for they know not what they do.*

---

[101] Luke 7:18ff.
[102] Mark 10:45, cf. John 3:16.
[103] See Luke 13:28-30 and parallels.
[104] Cf. John 8:34-36.
[105] K.E. Bailey quotes the Syrian commentator I. Sa'id, who points out that the older son's language removes him from the fellowship of the family, op.cit., p.199.

This last point suggests why the religious fail to understand God; their insight into God's ways is obscured by pride and self-righteousness. It is this pride which blinds (Luke 18:9-14). As a result the religious leaders fail to see God in Jesus. Jesus complains frequently in John's Gospel that the Jews do not accept him, because they do not know God (John 5:37; 7:28f.; 8:47). To accept him is to accept God (Matt. 10:40). To know God is to know Jesus (John. 8:42, 47, 55). To see him is to see God (John. 8:19; 12:45; 14:9). But they could not see this far. 'Are we blind?' they ask Jesus. *If you were blind,* he replies, *you would not be guilty; but now that you claim you can see, your guilt remains* (John 9:40, 41).

Paul

Like Jesus, Paul accepted the pillars of Judaism: the law, the temple, the covenant and the revelation of the oneness of God. He spoke of himself as an Israelite, a descendant of Abraham and a member of the tribe of Benjamin (Rom. 11:1). He affirmed that God had not withdrawn the privileges he had given to his people. *Theirs is the adoption as sons; theirs the divine glory, the covenants, the receiving of the law, the temple worship and the promises. Theirs are the patriarchs, and from them is traced the human ancestry of Christ* (Rom. 9:4, 5). Testifying before King Agrippa he argued that he had remained true to his Jewish foundations and was preaching nothing more than the fulfilment of the Messianic hope: *I am saying nothing beyond what the prophets and Moses said would happen – that the Messiah would suffer and, as the first to rise from the dead, would proclaim light to his own people and to the Gentiles* (Acts 26:22f.).

The Failure to recognise Jesus Christ as Lord

However, writing to the Galatians, Paul contrasted his life in Christ with his previous way of life in Judaism (Gal. 1:13). In Romans he argued that all who are descended from Israel are not Israel, in fact only a remnant will be saved (Rom. 9:6f.; 27). The Jews that Paul criticised and the Judaism that he rejected have one thing in common: they have made the same mistake that he made, they deny that Jesus is the Christ. They have stumbled over the stumbling stone of a crucified Messiah and have refused to believe in him (Rom. 9:32f.). The failure to recognise Jesus for who he is and the decision to hold on to the past were wrong, Paul believed, on several counts.

First, Jesus is the Lord, despite the apparent disaster of his crucifixion and the rejection by the chief priests. Paul had learnt this the hard way, struck down on the road to Damascus. Seven times in the Acts 9 account of Paul's conversion, Jesus is called Lord. In the Pauline letters the phrase 'Jesus is Lord' occurs 230 times. Paul's preaching could be summed up as proclaiming 'Jesus Christ as Lord'.

Second, Christ surpasses everything that Paul had previously held dear. *If anyone else thinks he has reasons to put confidence in the flesh, I have more: circumcised on the eighth day, of the people of Israel, of the tribe of Benjamin, a Hebrew of Hebrews; in regard to the law, a Pharisee; as for zeal, persecuting the church; as for legalistic righteousness, faultless. But whatever was to my profit I now consider loss for the sake of Christ. What is more, I consider everything a loss compared to the surpassing greatness of knowing Christ Jesus my Lord, for whose sake I have lost all things. I consider them rubbish, that I may gain Christ ...* (Phil. 3:4-8). Similarly in 2 Corinthians 3:7-11 Paul dismissed the faded glory of the Mosaic covenant, as having no glory in comparison with the glory of the new covenant.

Third, the new covenant provides a universal way of salvation, which is open to all, both Jews and Gentiles. The limitation of the old covenant was that it excluded Gentiles. Instead God has prepared a new way of righteousness for all, which comes by faith in Jesus Christ (Rom. 3:21-30; Eph. 2:11-3:6).

The mistake of relying on works of the law

Paul's attitude to the law has been the subject of considerable debate since the publication in 1977 of E.P. Sanders' major work, *Paul and Palestinian Judaism.*[106] Sanders argues that to classify Judaism as a religion of 'works' and the gospel as the way of 'grace' is to misrepresent both Judaism and Paul. Israel was chosen by the grace of God to be his covenant people. The law was not given by Moses, so that Israelites should attempt to earn salvation by gaining merit through meticulous observation of its

[106] See E.P. Sanders, *Paul and Palestinian Judaism*, London 1977, p. 543. Sanders argues that in Judaism 'salvation is by grace but judgment is according to works'. As far as covenant relation with God is concerned 'getting in' is by grace but 'staying in' is by obedience to the law. Sanders argues that Paul does not contrast Judaism as a religion of 'works' with the gospel as the way of 'grace'. For the contrary view see J.R.W. Stott, *The Message of the Romans*, Leicester, 1994, pp. 25ff.

regulations. Paul understood this. According to Sanders, the one thing that Paul found lacking in the Torah was that it excluded the Gentiles, whereas righteousness by faith in Christ includes Jews and Gentiles equally on the same basis. That Paul was concerned to set forth the gospel as the way for both Jews and Gentiles is clear from Romans and not in dispute. What then of Paul's attack on justification by works of the Law?

Paul's fundamental criticism of justification by law-keeping is that reliance on the works of the law produces false pride and self-righteousness. This manifests itself in different ways. In Romans 2 Paul points out to Jews, proud of their possession of the law, that mere knowledge of the law will not justify them, if they do not keep its commands (Rom. 2:17-23). Similarly boasting of circumcision is valueless, if the Jew breaks the law. Paul listed many things he had been proud of before he met Christ, including his birth as a Hebrew of the Hebrews, of the tribe of Benjamin (Phil. 3:3ff.). This too was worthless and misleading, because all Israel are not Israel, but only a remnant chosen by grace (Rom. 11:6). The only praise worth having is the praise that comes from God (Rom. 2:29).

Pride in achievement is as dangerous as pride in privilege. In Philippians Paul wrote of his own discovery of a righteousness that surpassed anything he had achieved by keeping the law. He contrasted the righteousness that he had received as a gift from God by faith in Christ with *a righteousness of my own that comes from the law* by observing its commands. Paul felt that he could not have been faulted by the standards of legalistic righteousness. But this *confidence in the flesh*, that is in himself, was misplaced and no better than rubbish in comparison with the gift of God's righteousness, where all the praise went to God (Phil. 3:3-9). Faith promotes reliance on God alone. In Romans 10:1-4 Paul laments that his fellow Jews, who reject Christ, ignorant of God's righteousness, 'sought to establish their own righteousness'. They pursued a law of righteousness, but failed to attain it, *because they pursued it not by faith but as if it were by works* (Rom. 9:32). Man is totally dependent on God for justification by faith alone, therefore boasting is excluded (Rom. 3:27).

Furthermore, Paul highlighted the powerlessness of the law in various aspects. His argument in Romans 2 – 3 is not that human beings are incapable of obeying the law, but that no one does in fact keep the law in its entirety. Therefore no one will be declared righteous before God by law keeping (3:20). Paul underlines the Jew's predicament by quoting Moses' words:*Cursed is everyone who does not continue to do everything written in the Book of the Law* (Gal. 3:10 quoting Deut. 27:26). He reminds the Galatians that a return to the law by circumcision would require that they obey the whole law, resulting in certain condemnation when they failed (Gal. 5:3). The law is also powerless to break the control of sin, for all, Jews and Gentiles alike, are under sin's power (Rom. 3:9). It cannot liberate anyone from bondage to sin or set the slaves free (Gal. 3:22; Rom. 8:3). It follows that the law cannot give life (Gal. 3:21). In fact it does the opposite, it causes condemnation and death (Rom. 7:10; 8:1-4). Only a change of heart will bring about a new situation and this the law cannot do. The true Jew is one who is inwardly changed by the circumcision of the heart. No man can do this, it is the work of the Spirit (Rom. 2:29). The written code cannot change people. It is the Spirit not the letter of the law that has the power to create a new person (Rom. 7:6; 2 Cor. 3:3-7). Paul concludes his letter to the Galatians emphasising that the only thing that counts is a new creation (Gal. 6:15).

In addition, Paul implies that his fellow Jews have misunderstood the purpose of the law. He hints at this in 2 Corinthians 3, saying, *Even to this day when Moses is read, a veil covers their hearts* (2 Cor. 3:15). Therefore they do not understand what Moses intended. The purpose of the law is to expose sin and condemn it. It makes us conscious of sin and speechless in the presence of the holy God (Rom. 3:19-20). In Colossians Paul describes the law as a shadow of things to come, pointing forward to the reality which is found in Christ (Col. 2:17). In this sense the law belongs to the era before Christ, since Christ is the end and fulfilment of the law (Rom. 10:4). Paul's argument in Galatians refutes the validity of a distinction between 'getting in' fellowship with God by grace and 'staying in' by obedience to the law. For him both justification and sanctification are by grace through faith and to begin by grace and end by law was a disaster.

The Pillars of Judaism reinterpreted

As Paul reflected on the implications of what Christ had done for Israel as well as for the world, he began to reinterpret the pillars of Judaism.

Election was extended beyond Israel to all nations. Writing to the Ephesian church of Gentiles and Jews, Paul specifically broadened the concept of election and extended it back in time to eternity (Eph.1:4). In doing so Paul followed the lead already given by John the Baptist and Jesus, who denounced the racial presumption of Jewish leaders in thinking that election was based on physical birth (Matt. 3:9; John 8:39ff.).

The Temple in Jerusalem was no longer the focus of Paul's worship. There is another temple, not made with human hands, inhabited by the Spirit of God, where believers worship. In this temple Gentiles are no longer excluded or marginalised. Writing to Gentiles Paul said, *Do you not know that your body is a temple of the Holy Spirit, who is in you, whom you have received from God?* And again, the secret of this temple is *Christ in you, the hope of glory* (1 Cor. 6:19; Col. 1:27).

The Law has been fulfilled in Christ and it is now his word that is law for the believer (Gal. 6:2). The new law is otherwise described as the law of the Spirit of life, where law is a principle and a power not a set of commandments (Rom. 8:2).

There is only one God and Father of all, but the name that is above all names is no longer called Yahweh but Jesus (Phil. 2:9f.).[107] Jesus Christ is the Lord (Yahweh),[108] before whom every knee must bow and every tongue confess.[109] The one God has shared his Lordship with the risen and ascended Christ.[110] Everything is subjected to him, so that he in turn will be subjected to the Father, and the doxology rings out to the grace of the Lord Jesus Christ and the love of God and the fellowship of the Holy Spirit (Phil. 2:9ff.; 1 Cor. 15:25ff.; 2 Cor. 13:14).

---

[107]   See J.D.G. Dunn, *The Partings of the Ways*, London & Philadelphia, 1991, pp.188ff.

[108]   Paul uses *kurios* for Yahweh in OT quotations about nineteen times, and applies several such passages to Jesus. For example in Rom. 10:13 he quotes Joel 2:32 – *Everyone who calls upon the name of the Lord will be saved* – as applying to the Lord Jesus. See Dunn, op.cit., p.189.

[109]   The clear reference to Isa. 45:23, one of the most strongly monotheistic passages in scripture, is striking confirmation of the high position attributed to Christ.

[110]   See Dunn, op.cit., p.191.

Hebrews

The writer of Hebrews mounts a critique not of legalism but of the sacrificial system. His argument is that the sacrificial system given by God under the old covenant relates to the sacrifice of Christ as shadow to real (10:1). The coming of Christ and his death on the cross not only usher in the longed for kingdom, they also have radical implications for Jewish religion. The temple with its array of sacrifices is rendered out of date. The new has come; the old order has passed away.[111]

Hebrews gives great prominence to the contrast between the old and new covenants.[112] The old covenant is faulty, ineffective (8:7ff.) and obsolete (8:13). Interestingly, Hebrews finds that what was wrong with the first covenant was the people, not the revelation. *God found fault with the people* (8:8). Hebrews quotes Jeremiah 31:31-34, to show that the new covenant will change the heart by putting God's law in the minds and hearts of the new Israel (8:7-12). Christ is the mediator of the new covenant. Compared with the old this one is better (7:22), superior (8:6) and eternal (13:20). Significantly for the reasoning of Hebrews, Jesus had talked of establishing the new covenant only at the end of his ministry, when he was about to die. The new covenant was established by the shedding of his own blood, for every covenant needs to be ratified by blood sacrifice (9:16ff.). His sacrifice is very different from all that preceded it, not only because it is the blood of a man not of an animal, but also because he is the perfect Lamb of God, who takes away the sin of the whole world.

Hebrews therefore goes on to compare the results of the two sacrificial systems. The old sacrifices needed to be offered day after day (7:27), but the sacrifice of Christ was offered once for all (9:26). The old sacrifices were not able to purify the conscience of the worshipper (9:9); the blood

---

[111] It is currently regarded as incorrect language to say that the Mosaic covenant was 'superseded'. However, Hebrews suggests the idea of supersession, not however in the sense that the old covenant was rejected and abolished but in the sense that it was fulfilled, so believers in Christ were no longer under the old law.

[112] The Church of England discussion document, *Sharing One Hope?* London, 2001, p.23f., suggests that there are three theories about the relation of Judaism to Christianity held by Christians. First that there is one covenant for both Jews and Christians, second that there are two parallel covenants and third that the two are totally different religions. Hebrews does not conform to any of these alternatives but propounds the fulfilment view of Matt. 5:17, that the Mosaic covenant has been fulfilled, not abolished, and brought to completion in the new.

of Christ cleanses our conscience from guilt (9:14; 10:22). In fact the blood of bulls and goats can never take away sins (10:4). The old sacrifices were powerless to transform those who offered them (7:11, 19), but the sacrifice of Christ makes his worshippers perfect and holy (10:10, 14).

This has implications for the priesthood. The high priest of the old covenant was a sinner, who had to offer sacrifices for his own sin (9:7), in a man-made, earthly tabernacle. Christ on the other hand is without sin, a priest for ever, entering the heavenly tabernacle by his own blood, having obtained eternal redemption for all (9:11, 12). He has sat down at the right hand of God in the seat of divine authority (10:12ff.). The authority of Christ, the ascended high priest, guarantees the finality of the new revelation. It was with this conclusion that the writer began his letter (1:3). The logical consequence is that the new covenant supersedes the old, just as Jesus, the prophet, priest and king, replaces Moses and Aaron, in the order of the priest-king, Melchizedek.

There are also consequences for the status of the temple. The temple and the tabernacle, on which it was modelled, were copies of the heavenly original (9:24; 8:5). Now Christ has opened the way into the heavenly temple itself and made it possible for believers to do what no high priest could do, to enter daily into the most holy place, into God's own presence (10:19ff.). There can therefore be no value in reverting to the man-made tabernacle model and temple worship, which were only a copy of the true and heavenly sanctuary.

Jesus' treatment of the Samaritans

Are the Samaritans to be treated as part of Judaism? The New Testament always distinguishes Jews from Samaritans. On the other hand Samaritans are not classed as Gentiles. J.D. Purvis argues that, "there are good reasons for viewing Samaritanism as a variety of Judaism."[113] He points out that, "both Jews and Samaritans understood themselves (first and foremost) as carriers of Israel's sacred traditions."[114] Samaritans worshipped YHWH and revered Moses as prophet and lawgiver. Regarded as heretics by the

---

[113] J.D. Purvis, *The Samaritans and Judaism* in *Early Judaism and its Modern Interpreters*, ed. R.A. Kraft and G.W.E. Nicklesburg, Philadelphia and Atlanta, 1986, p.91.
[114] Op.cit., p.91.

Jews, they held to the Pentateuch in the Samaritan recension, but not to the rest of the Old Testament. What made them heretics in the eyes of the Jews was their rejection of the temple in Jerusalem and their worship instead on Mt. Gerizim as the holy mountain.

Jesus and Samaritans

Treated as outcasts by the Pharisees, Jesus reached out to the people of Samaria and included them within the scope of God's mercy. The parable of the Good Samaritan makes a hero out of the despised race. On another occasion Jesus commends the only one of 10 lepers to return to give him thanks, who was a Samaritan. Despite their past and their doctrines, the New Testament includes them in the gospel embrace.

The meeting that Jesus had with the woman of Samaria recorded in John 4 is of great significance for the study of the attitude of the New Testament to religions. Note the following:

- Jesus risks his reputation to lead this Samaritan woman and her townsfolk to belief in himself as Messiah[115] and saviour of the world.

- Jesus is dismissive of Samaritan religion: *You Samaritans worship what you do not know* (v.22). Compare this with Paul's remark to the Athenians, *Now what you worship as something unknown I am going to proclaim to you* (Acts 17:23). Compare this also with the modern approach to inter-religious dialogue, in which a blunt statement of this kind would not be permitted.

- In contrast Jesus asserts that *salvation is from the Jews* (v. 22).[116] In the context of John's Gospel this does not mean that Jews are the authors of salvation, but that God's salvation is being delivered to the world through them. Jews have a unique place in the course of divine redemption, but not an exclusive place, hence Jesus' invitation to the woman to look to him as Messiah.

---

[115] Some scholars, such as J.D. Purvis (op.cit., pp.93f.), maintain that there were Samaritans who expected a Messiah figure like Joseph or Joshua. Samaritans, like Jews, had begun to expect an eschatological prophet like Moses, with reference to Deut. 18:18, from the second century BC. See A.D. Crown, *The Samaritans*, Tubingen, 1989, p.275f.

[116] This verse effectively refutes the view that John's Gospel denigrates Jews.

- As in other Gospel narratives Jesus draws a distinction between the worship that was appropriate in the past and the new order, which he had brought. In the past God was worshipped on Mount Gerizim and at Jerusalem, but now the time has come, *when the true worshippers will worship the Father in spirit and truth, for they are the kind of worshippers the Father seeks. God is spirit, and his worshippers must worship in spirit and in truth* (v. 23, 24). Jesus avoided arguing about the Samaritans' distinctive belief in Gerizim and rendered the dispute about Jerusalem and Gerizim irrelevant by saying that it is not 'where' but 'how' people worship that matters. The worshippers God desires know him as Father and are inspired by the Spirit, who purifies their prayers and unites them with the Lord.

- The response not only of the woman but also of many Samaritans from her city, Sychar, contrasts sharply with the reluctance of the Pharisees to see in Jesus the Messiah they were waiting for.

Later when the risen Christ parted from his disciples, he charged them to be his witnesses, first in Jerusalem and in Judaea and then in Samaria. The mission to Samaria was to be an important staging post on the way to the mission to the whole world.

A Model for Dialogue

Jesus' approach to the Samaritans provides a model for Christian-Muslim dialogue. The parallels between the relationships between Jews and Samaritans and those between Christians and Muslims are striking.

Take first the prejudice Jews had against Samaritans, which is repeatedly evident in the Gospels. Compare this with the prejudice that most Christians have against Muslims. Secondly, Jews regarded Samaritans as heretics, because they had their own 'Mecca' on Mt. Gerizim and rejected the holiness of Jerusalem and its temple. Christians originally regarded Islam as a Christian heresy following the lead given by John of Damascus in the eighth century. Thirdly, Samaritans are one step further away from Christians than Jews, as are Muslims. The Samaritan insistence on their own version of the Pentateuch, on their own holy place and on their rejection of the prophetic scriptures made it impossible for Jews to see them as the bearers of God's salvation. Similarly Muslim insistence on their own prophet, their own holy place and their own scriptures make Islam quite different from Judaism and further away from Christ. Fourthly, both groups have much in common. Just as Jews had a great deal in common with Samaritans – one God, one holy book, one holy land, one prophet, Moses, and one sign of belonging, circumcision - and refused to treat them as Gentiles, so Christians and Muslims share much from their common monotheistic inheritance in the scriptures. Fifthly, Samaritans and Jews were divided by atrocities, which both had suffered at the hands of the other. So also Christians and Muslims are divided by history, a history which includes bloodshed and wars.

Jesus' attitude to the age-old hatred of Jews for Samaritans is significant for Christian relations with Islam. He refused to be bound by the communal animosities that dictated the actions of his contemporaries. Doctrinal differences were important, but they had no bearing on the parable of the Good Samaritan except to heighten the standards God requires of his children. On the other hand Jesus did not reject doctrine in the interests of harmony between religions, as so many do today. He was forthright in telling the Samaritan woman that salvation came from the Jews, but only in the context of accepting her completely warts and all and receiving what she had to give him. The fact that she responded by believing in Christ, as did many of her townsfolk, is in sharp contrast to the lack of response to the gospel by Muslims down the centuries. Is the main reason for this rejection the prejudice and hostility that has habitually existed between the two religions?

Chapter Three

Salvation Through Christ and its Implications for Religions

Introduction

THE VIEW CHRISTIANS HAVE TAKEN OF OTHER RELIGIONS has usually been based not on what the New Testament says about religions but on what it says about Christ. The most commonly quoted texts have been John 14:6 and Acts 4:12. Since these say that Christ is the only way to the Father and that there is salvation in no one else, it has been assumed that the New Testament regards other religions as false and of no spiritual value. This has often been interpreted to justify Christians in rejecting religions, such as Islam, Hinduism and Buddhism, as worthless and having nothing to offer. Others have contested such assumptions and questioned the validity of using these texts to dismiss the value of other faiths.

It is important, therefore, for the study of the New Testament attitude to religions to review what it says about salvation through Christ. What precisely is stated and what conclusions should legitimately be drawn from the teaching about Christ as Saviour?

The implications of what is said about Christ for the New Testament view of religions

The New Testament presents Christ as the one who mediates salvation to the world. What follows from this? In what sense is he the only way to the Father? Is he the only saviour, or are there other ways to God? What is implied by the statement that every knee shall bow and every tongue confess that Jesus Christ is Lord? Is Christ Lord of Christians only or Lord of all?

We will focus on what the New Testament has to say about Christ's role in salvation, which has clear implications for the place of other religions. In one sense everything that is said about Christ may have implications for Christian relations with other faiths. Here we confine our attention to those texts, which in themselves have a bearing on the New Testament view of religions. Most Christian missiologists now agree that other faiths contain much that is true and that they should not be completely rejected. Opinion is divided on whether religions are salvific or not, in other words whether they may be used by God as means of salvation for their adherents.

The Way to the Father

The New Testament presents Christ as competent to save the world, because of his close relationship with God. In what sense was Jesus' relationship with God qualitatively different from that of the prophets who came before him? What did Jesus claim and what was claimed for him by the Gospel writers?

Mark 1:11. In Mark, Jesus' ministry begins with the divine signal of a voice from heaven saying: *You are my Son, whom I love (agapetos); with you I am well pleased* (Mark 1:11). As this account of what the voice said seems likely to have come from Jesus himself, just as the record of his temptations must have come from Jesus, Mark 1:11 represents his own acknowledgement of the Father's commissioning.

It is significant that at the very outset of his ministry Jesus is called 'Son' and that he acknowledges his calling. The use of the adjective *agapetos* (beloved) emphasises the uniqueness of his relationship as Son to the Father. It has been said that, "Sonship is the supreme category of interpretation of the person of Jesus in the Gospels."[117] Jesus' awareness of an intimate relationship with God was expressed not only by describing himself as the Son, but even more so by speaking of God as his Father.

---

[117]   H. Marshall, *Jesus the Saviour*, London, 1990, p.143.

The title 'Father' is found 170 times on the lips of Jesus in the gospels, of these sixty-one times occur in the Synoptic Gospels.[118] Jesus addressed God as 'Father' 16 times in the gospels (excluding parallels). He prayed to God as 'Father' in all the prayers attributed to him in the gospels, with one exception (the cry of dereliction, 'My God, my God…', when Jesus used the words taken from Psalm 22).[119] "Whereas there is not a single instance of God being addressed as Abba in the literature of Jewish prayer", says Jeremias, "Jesus always addressed him in this way (with the exception of the cry from the cross, Mark 15:34)."[120] Jesus dared to address God as Abba, a word no Jew had ever used in prayer. He spoke of God as 'my Father', never praying to God as 'our Father'.[121] Jesus' use of Abba expressed a special relationship with God.

What the role of the Son was to be is spelt out in John 1:51, where Jesus says, I tell you the truth, you shall see heaven open, and the angels of God ascending and descending on the Son of Man. As Son of Man he was appointed to mediate between the Father and humanity, to be himself the ladder between earth and heaven.

Matthew 11:25-27 / Luke 10:21-22. This saying in Matthew and Luke has no exact parallel in Mark. It has often been referred to as a bolt from the Johannine blue, though its Semitic language and style are noted by scholars.[122] Matthew 11:25-27 and Luke 10:21-22 reflect Jesus' special relationship to his Father noted above and must be seen against the background of the Son of Man sayings in the Synoptics, as a whole.[123]

In Matthew 11:27 Jesus says: *All things have been committed to me by my Father. No-one knows the Son except the Father, and no-one knows the Father except the Son and those to whom the Son chooses to reveal him.* The only

---

[118] Jeremias gives the following breakdown of these occurrences: Mark 4, Luke 15, Matthew 42 and John 109 times. In the Synoptics excluding parallels there are 51 times when God is called 'Father' in words attributed to Jesus. See J.Jeremias, *The Prayers of Jesus*, London, 1967, p.29.

[119] Jeremias, op.cit., p.55.

[120] Jeremias, op.cit., p.57.

[121] Cf. John 20:17. See J. Jeremias, *Abba*, Tubingen, 1966, especially pp.33ff. Also H. Marshall, op.cit., pp.135ff.

[122] See J. Jeremias, *The Prayers of Jesus*, p.45ff.

[123] The Son of Man sayings in Mark are characterised by three themes: the Son's authority (Mark 2:10,28), the Son's sacrifice (Mark 8:31; 9:12, 31), and the Son's exaltation (Mark 13:26; 14:62; cf. Matt. 25:31ff.).

difference in Luke's version is that 'knows the Son' / 'knows the Father' is expanded to 'knows who the Son is' / 'knows who the Father is'.

From this saying, with its four line stanza, we learn four things.

First, 'all things' have been revealed by God to Jesus. The word 'committed' (*paredothe*) is used of the handing down of knowledge from teacher to pupil.[124]

Second, nobody knows the Father as Jesus knows him.[125] This knowledge is not theoretical or the abstract knowledge of theology concerned with the learning of propositions and statements. It is rather the relational, personal, direct knowledge of the Father, which Jesus enjoyed, born of his constant experience of fellowship with his Father.

Third, nobody knows the Son except the Father. The real identity of Jesus can only be known by his Father, for their relationship has no parallel in human wisdom or spirituality. The world does not know him, but the Father does.

Fourth, Jesus is the sole mediator of the revelation of the Father to the rest of the world.[126] What prophets and wise men of the past longed to know, he knows. Jesus is not only the one who has received the revelation, he is also the one who reveals it to those whom he chooses.

What is new in this saying is that it spells out the implications of Jesus' claim to a unique relationship with the Father. Here, as elsewhere, Jesus speaks of 'my Father', not of 'our Father', perhaps because this is in the context of his prayer in the preceding verses. This is not a surprise, because in the rest of the Gospel narratives he clearly distances his relationship with the Father from the experience of God shared by his disciples and others. From the moment of his baptism and hearing the voice from heaven Jesus has difficulty in explaining his identity to

---

[124]　Cf. Mark 7:13; Luke 1:2.

[125]　Jeremias argues that Jesus used an Aramaic saying in the form, 'just as only a father really knows his son, so only a son really knows his father.' But whatever the reference might have been in colloquial Aramaic, the text as we have it makes clear that Jesus used it to assert his special relationship with his heavenly Father. For since God has transmitted to Jesus the revelation of himself, so the Son alone can pass on to others the real knowledge of the Father. J. Jeremias, *The Prayers of Jesus*, p.50f.

[126]　Some have suggested that Jesus did not envisage a mission to the Gentiles. See the next section for discussion of this issue.

the world, but never to the Father. The Father alone knows the truth about him from eternity. It follows that the revelation of God as Father in all its fullness can only be given by the Son, for he alone can initiate human beings into the intimacy of this relationship. There can be no other mediator of the Father - Son relationship, and no one else can call upon the Holy Spirit to make this revelation possible.[127]

John 1:1-18. The Prologue of John's Gospel (1:1-18) is one of the key texts for an understanding of the relationship of Christ to the Father, and his role in creation and salvation. This has implications for the Christian view of religions, even though they are not mentioned. In the context of the plurality of world religions, the opening of John's Gospel could not be more striking.

In the beginning was the Word, and the Word was with God, and the Word was God (1:1). Primacy is given to the Word (*logos*), the Word is associated with God from eternity and the Word is defined as God. The meaning of these statements is amplified later by the whole of John's Gospel, but even from this opening the keynotes begin to resound. God communicates eternally through his Word. His Word is an essential part of his being. He is the God who speaks and is never silent, not the unknown and unknowable Being posited by philosophers. The way to know God is to receive his Word.

To any of John's readers, who were familiar with the Old Testament, the words 'In the beginning' would have recalled the opening of Genesis. Whereas Genesis declares, 'In the beginning God...', the Prologue says, 'In the beginning the Word...'. Genesis says God created all things, the Gospel says all things were created through the Word. Genesis says God created light and life, the Gospel says the Word is the source of life and light, indeed he is the life and light of mankind. Lesslie Newbigin aptly comments that the Word is "not merely declaratory but creative and life-giving."[128]

The term *Logos* (Word) rings bells both with the Old Testament and with Greek philosophy, also with Philo, the Hellenised Jew of Alexandria,

---

[127] Cf. Luke 10:21 and John 14:16ff.
[128] L. Newbigin, *The Light Has Come: an Exposition of the Fourth Gospel*, Edinburgh, 1982, p.3.

who wrote under the influence of both. *Logos* is frequently used in the Septuagint[129] in passages concerning God's creative word and prophetic word. In line with this usage the role of the Logos both in creation and revelation is central to John's Prologue. The Logos can also be compared with the personification of Wisdom in Proverbs.[130]

Stoics emphasised the importance of the Logos, or indwelling reason, which is to the world what the soul is to the human body. In the resulting pantheistic world-view the soul of man and the soul of the universe find their affinity with each other, when man lives according to reason.

Philo combines both Greek ideas and the personification of Sophia in Jewish Wisdom literature. In Philo the Logos is the agent of creation and the link between God and the world. The Logos in human beings is the same as the Logos in heaven (the 'real' man), therefore humans can gain knowledge of God through the indwelling Logos.

The rest of the Prologue and the rest of the Gospel make clear that, despite similarities, John does not identify the Logos[131] with Philo's concepts or with Greek speculation. The Logos is identified with Christ as the self-expression of God and is no mere personification of an abstract quality, nor a rational element in the mystery of an unknowable, impersonal Being. The Logos, Christ, is the personal revelation of the God who wills to make himself known to the world (1:18). God speaks and his Word is eternally present with him and inseparable from him. He reveals himself to the world, in contrast to those philosophies and religions that declare God to be unknowable, unthinkable and beyond all personal qualities. The Logos has become flesh and has lived among us, in order to express the glory of God through grace and truth (1:14). It is true that no one has ever seen God, but the only begotten Son has made him known. The only begotten, or one and only, who is at the Father's

---

[129] The Greek translation of the Old Testament ascribed to the third century B.C.

[130] See especially Prov. 8:22-31; cf. Sirach 24.

[131] John's daring use of the Greek philosophical term *Logos* was to be highly significant for the future relationship of Christianity to Greek culture and religion. The Hellenisation of the Gospel begins with the New Testament's use of Greek, especially of philosophical terms like *logos*. John's meaning was Hebraic, but the use of *logos* language opened the way later for the Early Fathers to claim that the best in Greek philosophy was inspired by God and could be assimilated by the church and made part of the Christian's heritage.

side, is the Logos, the Word made flesh, Jesus Christ. Jesus is the clue to the understanding of all things and of God himself (1:18).

What then of verse 9? Many have taken this to mean that everyone coming into the world receives illumination through reason and conscience, according to Platonic and Stoic ideas associated with the Logos.[132] If this were so, it might suggest that by using inner illumination religions could form an alternative pathway to God.[133] This interpretation assumes that the correct translation of the text should be, *The true light illuminates all men who are coming into the world.*

There are two objections to this view. Firstly, the subject of the words, 'coming into the world' is 'the true light' not 'all men'. This appears to be the case, because the coming of light is the theme. Also in the next verse (v.10) light is said to be in the world, it is logical therefore to expect that it should previously have been described in verse 9 as coming into the world.

Secondly, to translate the word 'lightens' (*photizei*) as 'illuminates' is misleading, as if everyone is inwardly enlightened.[134] In the next verse John notes that despite the presence of the Logos in the world and the creation of the world by the Logos, the world did not know him. Later in the Gospel John emphasizes the point that there is no universal knowledge of God (see esp. 3:19-21). Barrrett concludes, "It is not true that all men have a natural affinity with the light."[135] So *photizein* ('to lighten') should be translated by its basic meaning, which is 'to shed light upon', 'to bring to light', 'to make visible'. A study of all the texts in the Fourth Gospel where the word light occurs indicates that light is associated with judgement (see esp. 3:19). What is more, John specifically mentions that men stumble apart from the light, because they do not have it in themselves (11:9f.). Verse 9 cannot therefore be taken to mean

---

[132]   Clement of Alexandria and Marcion, though eager exponents of Logos Christology, did not quote John 1:9 in support of their views.

[133]   L. Newbigin, op.cit., p.6: "It has often been assumed that this inner illumination is to be identified with the various religions of mankind. Nothing in the text suggests this."

[134]   Jeremias called this a "Platonic understanding", which is "in contradiction to v.5 as well as to vv. 7f." J. Jeremias, *The Central Message of the New Testament*, London, 1965, p.81f.

[135]   C.K. Barrett, *The Gospel according to St. John*, London, 1955, p.161. See also J. Jeremias, op.cit., p.82.

the opposite and should properly be translated: *The light, which shines upon every man, was coming into the world.*

This does not mean that humans come into the world without any spiritual potential. Far from it. Men and women are made in the image of God (Gen. 1:27). Consequently the New Testament assumes that people know about God and have the capacity to worship him, even if their knowledge is distorted by sin (cf. Rom.1:19ff.; 2:14f.). The Spirit of God is omnipresent in creation and no one is beyond his influence. There is no need to read unbiblical ideas into John 1:9, given the divine origin of mankind and the role of the Spirit in the world. On the other hand human beings are not endowed by nature with a spiritual enlightenment that enables them to know God without the help of his revelation, especially in Christ. The question remains: how has the light of Christ shone on those who lived before his incarnation and subsequently on those who have never heard of him?

In the Prologue the relationship of Christ to God is portrayed not as the way but as the Word. God is so inextricably linked with his Word, that what God is the Word is, and what the Word does God does. So the Word is the source of light and life and acts as the creator. Above all the Word, incarnate in Jesus Christ, reveals God with unparalleled completeness. Whereas in the past the people of Israel had heard the word of God spoken by prophets, now in Christ they saw the likeness of God and the glory of God.

John affirms that there is only one light and one source of light. The light came into the world to overcome the darkness and to shine upon all. Christ, the light of the world, shines on all people, not only on Jews (and Christians).[136] What was previously hidden is now made visible. There is therefore only one way to know God and that is to come to the light and listen to the Word.

John 14:6. This text is often quoted and expounded in isolated splendour, as if it stood on its own. In the light of the evidence of Christ's teaching, as a whole, it is clear that John 14:6 gives vivid expression to claims

---

[136] John's message to his Jewish contemporaries was this: the Messiah has come for all humanity not just for Israel. The emphasis on 'all' is repeated 4 times. Through Jesus Christ all things were made (v.3). He came that all might believe (v.7). His light shines on all men. To all those who receive him he multiplies his gifts of grace (v.16).

which can be found on Christ's lips elsewhere in the Gospels.[137] At the same time this stands as a summary of the claims of Jesus to be the one and only way to the Father.

Most striking and inescapable is the focus on the person of Jesus. Thomas asks to be told the way. Jesus points to himself - not 'I have the way' but 'I am the Way' is his reply. No other founder of a world religion has pointed to himself and said, 'I am the Way'. Great religious pioneers like Buddha, Muhammad and Guru Nanak have always pointed away from themselves and said, 'This is the path, follow it.' But for Christ his person is the path, and the path is not a philosophy nor a theology nor a creed. That can only be because the person is the Messiah, the Son of the Blessed. In language that the Qumran sect could have appreciated, he declared with Messianic insistence, that he is the key to the kingdom. To be connected to him is to know the Truth, to be united to him is to have the Life, to follow him is to be on the Way.

The text only makes sense in the context of the biblical revelation of God as creator and men and women as fallen, divided from God by rebellion and therefore in need of a way back to him. If humans are not fallen and have no duty to live in fellowship with a personal creator, then they might be free to find their own way in this life, and any way would do provided it achieved its goal. Here, in the immediate context of the betrayal and crucifixion, 'I am the Way' refers to the sacrificial purpose of Christ's giving of himself to save humanity. The way to the Father is not an abstract statement of truth that can be separated from the person of Jesus. It is through him and his death and resurrection that the way to the Father is opened up. It is because of the identity of the Son that his death has eternal consequences. It is through his relationship with the Father that his death and resurrection can unite us to God.

Similarly, Jesus is both the Truth and the Life. He reveals the truth, which he is, just as he not only speaks the word of God but is the Word. He gives the Life, which he is, so whoever lives and believes in him will never die (John 11:25). To partake of the living bread, which he gives, that is his body, is to receive eternal life (John 6:51). Jesus is the Truth and

[137]   For the picture of the Way, cf. 'I am the Door' (John 10:9). For the idea of the Truth, cf. John 6:32 and John 15:1. For the claim to be the Life, cf. John 6:35; 11:25. For the denial of any other way to the Father, cf. Matt. 11:25ff.; Luke 10.21f.

the Life, not only because he has been sent by the Father, but because the Father is in him and he is in the Father (v.10), and his words and acts are the words and acts of God (v.10).[138] To see Jesus is to see God (v.9).[139]

As a result no one comes to know the Father except through the Son, that is to say no one enters into an intimate relationship with the Father except through the Son. Though negatively stated the purpose is positive, since the sole reason for Christ's mission to the world is to make the way possible. There is an echo here from the beginning of the Gospel, where the Son of Man is revealed to be the point where earth and heaven meet, he is the place of revelation, he is the gateway to heaven, he is the way (John 1:51). Now that Jesus' mission is almost complete he intends to close all other options and shut his disciples up to the one road, which will be there for them when they have recovered from the annihilation of all their human hopes and dreams at the execution of their master.

Some commentators have sought to interpret this passage in such a way as to leave room for other paths to God.[140] They want to acknowledge the truth of Christ's words and yet at the same time to say that there are other ways and other religions that have spoken of God as Father. However it is one thing to ascribe the word 'Father' to God, it is another to be initiated into the intimate relationship Jesus enjoyed with the Father. Similarly, for Jesus to talk about the Way does not affirm religions that also speak of a Way. Some think John 14:6 should be interpreted in the light of a Logos Christology. Since Christ is the light of all people, he must also be working in the good and generous faith of other men and women who follow other 'ways' and 'paths.'[141] As we have seen above, John's view of the Logos does not indicate that human nature possesses inner illumination, but points to Christ as the source of light itself, the light which has shone on humanity from the beginning. However John does affirm that the Word incarnate in Jesus Christ has always been at work in the world from creation and implies that he will always be at work causing his light to shine on everyone.

---

[138] Cf. John 12:44-50
[139] E. Hoskyns, *The Fourth Gospel*, London, 1947, p.455.
[140] K. Cracknell, *Towards a New Relationship*, London, 1986, p.86.
[141] *Ibid.* p.106

Others suggest that the Way is to be understood as the indwelling Logos, a spiritual essence, to be distinguished from Jesus of Nazareth. To argue that the Logos is different from the man Jesus Christ is to repeat the attempt to divide the Jesus of history from the Christ of faith. John's Gospel does not make this error. It goes to great lengths to identify Jesus, the Son of Man, with that which pre-existed before him (*before Abraham was I am*) and to that which is eternal (*I am the Light of the world* and *I am the Bread of Life*). So here, it is the man Jesus, who is the Way, the Truth and the Life.

However, before we jump to the conclusion that this text proves that all other religions are false trails or dead ends, leading nowhere, we should note some other considerations. First, there are no negative conclusions drawn in this passage about Judaism or any other religion. Second, though the words, *no-one comes to the Father but by me* make a negative statement, the purpose is positive, since Christ came to open the way to the Father for all mankind. Third, Jesus said these words to his inner group of apostles; they were not a public proclamation to people of all faiths. So to use John 14:6 as a basis for attacking other religions is questionable. Fourth, what Jesus claims to be is the way to the Father.[142] As the one closest to the Father it is his unique privilege to initiate his disciples into the intimate relation with his Father, which he has always enjoyed. This does not prove that other religions have nothing to offer their followers, though they cannot give what Christ promises to those who follow in his way. To know God as Father we are dependent on the word made flesh. To enter the Holy of Holies, access can be found only through the sacrifice of Jesus.

John 14:6 must be seen in the context of all the New Testament teaching on the relationship of God to humanity and should not be lifted out as a dictum on its own. How this text fits together with the implicit teaching of Scripture about people of other faiths is a question for later discussion in this study.

Postscript: John 20:30-31. John 20:30-31 summarizes the purpose of the author in writing the Gospel. The aim is that the reader may have

[142] For Paul's view of the importance of knowing the Father, see Gal. 4:6f. (cf. Rom. 8:15), where he describes the coming of Christ and the gift of the Spirit to the believer, as that which transforms both Jews and Gentiles from slavery to sonship.

life, which in this Gospel is shorthand for eternal life, the divine life that comes from knowing God and his messenger, Jesus Christ (17:3).

Notice the wholly positive tone of this statement. There is no condemnation of religions, no threats of judgement to come, but there are implications attached to believing in Jesus. He is the true Messiah, the Son of God, as defined in the Prologue. If eternal life comes through him, it implies that the believer did not have life before. However John does not say that there is no other way to obtain eternal life, just that God's way of giving life is through his messenger, his divine Son.

If Jesus is the Messiah, the divinely appointed means of knowing God, why should anyone look elsewhere? For no-one has ever seen God and no-one else has revealed him apart from the only begotten of the Father. This was true for Jews like John, and, if for Jews, then with even stronger reason for the Gentiles also, that is for people of all races.

The Saviour of the World

John's Gospel

The title 'Saviour of the World' occurs only twice in the New Testament.[143] Surprisingly it is Samaritans who describe Jesus in this way (John 4:42). The theme of Jesus' universal role in salvation is repeated in a variety of ways throughout the Gospel, though the title occurs only once in John's Gospel. Whereas the Synoptics describe the death of Jesus and the events leading up to it at great length, it is John who sets this story in the context of the world, not just of Israel.

At the beginning of the Gospel, John the Baptist mysteriously points his disciples to the Lamb of God, who takes away the sin of the world (1:29). Later Jesus' dialogue with Nicodemus turns into an exposition of Christ's mission to the world. The Son of Man will be lifted up on the cross not just for Israel but for the world (3:14-17).

---

[143] John 4:42; 1 John 4:14. See also 1 Tim. 4:10 for the phrase 'Saviour of all men'. In Titus the titles 'God our Saviour' and 'Jesus our Saviour' are combined three times, indicating the divine extent of Jesus' saving role (Tit. 1:3,4; 2:10,13; 3:4,6).

The 'I am' sayings in John express Christ's world embracing ministry. He is not limited to Israel. His love reaches out to the nations and invites all to follow him out of darkness, for *I am the light of the world* (8:12). The wording of the other sayings is also significant. In each case there is a width and universality in the language: whoever comes, whoever enters, whoever hears, whoever believes - will receive.

I am the bread of life. He who comes to me will never go hungry, and he who believes in me will never be thirsty (6:35).

I am the gate; whoever enters through me will be saved. He will come in and go out, and find pasture (10:9).

I am the good shepherd; I know my sheep and my sheep know me -- just as the Father knows me and I know the Father -- and I lay down my life for the sheep. I have other sheep that are not of this sheep pen. I must bring them also. They too will listen to my voice, and there shall be one flock and one shepherd (10:14-16).

I am the resurrection and the life. He who believes in me will live, even though he dies; and whoever lives and believes in me will never die (11:25f.).

Also relevant are the words of Jesus, predicting his crucifixion and its intended impact: *I, when I am lifted up from the earth, will draw all men to myself* (12:32).

The general thrust of these sayings indicates the all-inclusive embrace of Christ's saving work rather than an exclusive rejection of the world beyond Judaism.

Acts

Acts 4:12. *Salvation is found in no-one else, for there is no other name under heaven given to men by which we must be saved.*

A great deal of ink has been spilt on this verse. How should it be understood?

The context is not only the healing of the beggar crippled from birth (Acts 3), but also the preaching of the apostles, Peter & John, 'proclaiming in Jesus the resurrection of the dead'. The authorities were disturbed that thousands had believed the apostles' claim that the crucified and resurrected Jesus was the Messiah (3:18-20, 4:4, 11).

This verse raises several questions. First what is meant by salvation (*soteria*) and to be saved (*sothenai*)? The verb *sozo* and the noun *soteria* can refer to healing or physical deliverance as in 4:9. But equally the words may also refer to spiritual salvation and mean salvation from eternal death and judgment and all that might lead to such death e.g. sin, as in Acts 2:21, 40, 47 & 5:31. In 4:12 the sense of healing predominates in the first usage and spiritual salvation in the second. But it makes no sense to translate, "Healing is found in no-one else and there is no other name under heaven given to men by which we must be healed." Even Cracknell, who emphasises the healing aspect, admits that "the usual translation is the most likely, and healing is in any case an aspect of salvation."[144] Prophets healed people. What is distinctive about Jesus is that he is the Messiah, who has come to deliver his people from sin and death.

What does *no other name under heaven given to men* refer to? It surely relates to the religious leaders' challenge: *By what power or what name did you do this?*(4:7).

Peter replies: *It is by the name of Jesus Christ of Nazareth, whom you crucified but whom God raised from the dead, that this man stands before you healed* (4:10). He is the Messiah *you builders rejected* (4:11). Besides this, there is no other name given to men by God by which we must be saved (4:12). Peter relies on the authority of Jesus as Messiah. He gave the power to heal the cripple, just as he healed many in his life-time, and the apostles rely on him for salvation.

There is also a clear allusion to the meaning of the name of Jesus, 'the Lord saves'. The name had been given by the angel (Gabriel) to Mary: *you are to give him the name Jesus* (Luke 1:31). The angel of the Lord also gave the name to Joseph: *you are to give him the name Jesus, because he will save his people from their sins* (Matt. 1:21). Peter is evidently thinking of more than the healing of a cripple. That healing was a picture of the deliverance God had given to all people through Jesus Messiah. The double negative 'in no-one else' and 'no other name' emphasizes the exclusive assertion to a Jewish audience of the Messiah's role in salvation.

How applicable is Peter's statement to Gentiles (and so to modern religions)? Commentators are agreed that Acts 4:12 amounts to a

[144]   K. Cracknell, op.cit., 1986, p.108.

declaration of the universal extent of Jesus' saving power. For example, J.V. Taylor writes, commenting on this verse: Jesus "was the totally unique saviour, because he was totally universal."[145] However we must remember that Peter is speaking to Jewish leaders. Cracknell is right to note that Peter is "appealing to the Jewish leaders that such a healing is reason for them to accept their Messiah."[146]

What the verse does not say is also important. Despite the negatives in which it is couched the verse does not say that apart from believing in Christ all people are doomed to perdition, nor that all Gentile religions are devoid of truth. What it points to is the particular role of Jesus to be the bearer of universal salvation. He alone is the saviour of the world, because he alone among prophets and religious leaders has died for the sins of the world and risen again to deliver humanity from the power of death, and will come again to restore creation to its intended glory (3:18-21).

Acts 10:36-43. The importance of the encounter between Peter and Cornelius and God's revelation to both (Acts 10) has already been noted. At the heart of this story is the message Peter gave to the large gathering of friends and relatives in the centurion's home at Caesarea. Peter is gentle and positive in his speech to Cornelius (10:36-43). There are no denunciations of Gentile religion, nor is there anything comparable to Acts 4:12 for a Gentile audience. However Peter does include the following points: Jesus Christ is Lord of all (10:36). God has appointed Jesus to be the judge of all, both the living and the departed (10:42). Through the name of Jesus forgiveness of sins is given to all, who believe in him (10:43).

Peter confesses to being astounded that God shows no favouritism, but accepts men from every nation who fear him and do what is right (10:34,35). Though this is the same Peter who had told the leaders of Israel that there is salvation in no one else, he is amazed by God's all-embracing purpose in including all nations as well as Jews in his offer of salvation. Peter now began to realise that Jesus is saviour of all, because he is Lord of all. Gentiles could no longer be excluded from the family

---

[145] International Review of Mission, 1979, *The Theological Basis of Interfaith Dialogue*, p.378.

[146] op.cit., p.108.

of God. So the words *everyone who believes* (v.43) means every Gentile
as well as every Jew. God wants to include all races in the new Israel
(10:43-48; cf. 15:7-11).

Acts 17:30-31. The high priest and his theologians in Acts 4 might well
have objected to Peter's assertion that there is salvation only in the
name of Jesus by saying: 'What about Abraham and the patriarchs?
Do you think they were not saved because they had never heard of
Jesus?' Gentiles too might have asked whether the Gospel meant that
their forefathers had died under judgment. Paul replies to this possible
objection in his speech at the Areopagus (17:22ff.):

> In the past God overlooked such ignorance, but now he commands
> all people everywhere to repent. For he has set a day when he will judge
> the world with justice by the man he has appointed. He has given proof
> of this to all men by raising him from the dead.

The idea that God overlooked the ignorance of the Gentiles was
put forward by Paul on other occasions (see Acts 14:16; Rom. 3:25). The
coming of Christ brings in a new era when God's gospel is on offer to all.
Now there is no excuse, Christ's offer is for all and obliges all to respond
and repent. God will judge all at the last day on the basis of the Christ
event. The saviour of the world will also be its judge. It is important
not to miss the word 'justice' in v.31. Christ will not judge arbitrarily or
unfairly, but justly. He will take everything into account.

Romans

The Letter to the Romans is the place to look for a systematic treatment
of the gospel in relation to the world's religions. Paul is concerned to
show that the gospel is for all, including Gentiles (1:5). *It is the power of
God for the salvation of everyone who believes, first for the Jew, then for the
Gentile* (1:16; 2:10). *For God does not show favouritism* (2:11). Jews need the
gospel as much as Gentiles, for *Jews and Gentiles alike are all under sin* (3:9).

It is in this context that Paul reveals God's solution for the human
predicament. A way of being made righteous before God has been made
known apart from the Law of Moses (3:21). This way is through faith in
Christ, who has sacrificed himself for the sins of all through his atoning death
on the cross (3:24f.). The result is that all, Jew and Gentile, are on the same

level and are given the same way of salvation by faith in Jesus (3:26). For God is not the God of Jews only, but the God of Gentiles too, consequently there is only one way to the one God and that is by faith (3:29f.).

In this manner God demonstrates his justice, because he provides a means of salvation for sinful human beings, who have all fallen short of the purity of God. He is also just in treating everyone alike and in overlooking the sins committed by Gentiles in the past out of ignorance of his law (3:25f.).

The universality of God's saving work through Christ is stated positively. But the implication of Paul's argument is that, because faith in Jesus Christ is God's way for all, there are no other God-given ways. Specifically to try to get to God by keeping the law, whether it is the law of Moses or the moral law of conscience, is doomed to failure, because *no-one will be declared righteous in his sight by observing the law* (3:20). The only way forward is by faith and dependence on God. This route goes back to Abraham, the father of all who believe, both Gentile and Jew (4:11f.). Paul proceeds to expound the primacy of Abraham and to show that faith has always been the path to God (4:1-25). We will return to this important topic in a later section. For the moment we note that Paul's argument is that for all who believe, faith in Christ is now the means by which they are forgiven and given a right relationship with God (3:21-26).

Pastoral Epistles

Not quoted as frequently as John 14:6 and Acts 4:12, 1 Timothy 2:4ff. is striking in its context, where Timothy is told to pray for all people, including their rulers, because God wants *all men to be saved and to come to a knowledge of the truth* (2:4). The text continues:

For there is one God and one mediator between God and men, the man Christ Jesus, who gave himself as a ransom for all men -- the testimony given in its proper time (2:5,6).

This affirms with equal emphasis not only the oneness of God, but also the oneness of the pathway from man to God. The Greek highlights the oneness of both: *One is God and one is the Mediator (eis gar theos, eis kai mesites).* The words recall the Shema: *Hear O Israel: the Lord our God, the Lord is one (Dt. 6:4)* and also Isa. 45:5: *I am the Lord, and there is no other, apart from me there is no God.* In contrast the Gentile world thought of many mediators, angels and gods, and therefore of many approaches to the supreme Being. But since God is one, not many, there can be only one mediator, not many.

The meaning of the word 'mediator' (*mesites*) needs unpacking. The word signifies an intermediary and was used both for an arbiter in legal disputes and for a negotiator of business deals. But Christ is more than a mere legal arbiter. He is the Go-between God or the ladder between earth and heaven (John 1:51).

The ground for this indispensable role is Christ's voluntary sacrifice of himself as an atonement for all. Verse 6 echoes Jesus' words in Mark 10:45: *the Son of Man came …to give his life as a ransom for many.* There are two important additions to Mark 10:45 in the wording of 2:6. The addition of the preposition *anti* (in place of) reinforces *lutron* (ransom), as does the preposition *huper* (on behalf of). The effect of these two additions is to emphasize that Christ has given himself as a ransom **in place of** and **on behalf of** all people. A ransom was the price paid for the release of slaves or captives. The implication is that people need a ransom, because they are enslaved to evil and unable to free themselves. This ransom has been paid by Christ's death, the one for the many.

The humanity of Jesus is highlighted: the mediator is the man, Christ Jesus, because he represents man to God. Though he is the pre-existent Son of God, Jesus identified with man, in order to lift us to God. He crossed the dividing line between God and sinful humanity, to bring mankind across that divide and unite us with God.

1 Tim. 4:10 & Tit. 2:11 also bear witness to the universality of Christ. Christ is called the saviour of all men (1 Tim. 4:10) and has appeared to all men to bring them salvation (Tit. 2:11).

Hebrews

Hebrews was apparently written primarily to Jewish Christians, though some contest this. The writer urges the believers to stand firm in their loyalty to Christ and not to fall away or go back to their old life. In eloquent language he grounds his appeal on the superiority of Christ's person and his sacrificial work.

The letter begins in magnificent style contrasting Christ with all that came before him:

In the past God spoke to our forefathers through the prophets at many times and in various ways, but in these last days he has spoken to us by his Son, whom he appointed heir of all things, and through whom he made the universe. The Son is the radiance of God's glory and the exact representation of his being, sustaining all things by his powerful word. After he had provided purification for sins, he sat down at the right hand of the Majesty in heaven (1:1-3).

Christ is superior to angels (ch.1), to Moses (ch.3) and to Aaron (ch.7), but that does not mean that the past is annulled or discredited. The prophets spoke God's word and prepared the way for Jesus.

Past revelation is fulfilled in Christ; it is superseded but not rejected.

Hebrews does not address the world of Gentile religions. What it does do is to expound salvation through Christ as the new covenant. The old Mosaic covenant was just a shadow of the reality revealed and established by Christ.

Therefore, brothers, since we have confidence to enter the Most Holy Place by the blood of Jesus, by a new and living way opened for us through the curtain, that is, his body, and since we have a great priest over the house of God, let us draw near to God with a sincere heart in full assurance of faith, having our hearts sprinkled to cleanse us from a guilty conscience and having our bodies washed with pure water. Let us hold unswervingly to the hope we profess, for he who promised is faithful (10:19-22).

It follows that there is no alternative salvation and Judaism offers no other way into the Holy of Holies, least of all to those who had been believers and then denied their Lord (10:26-29).

The Lord of All

In the great Christological passages of Ephesians 1:3-2:23, Philippians 2:5-11, and Colossians 1:15-23, Christ's pre-existence, divinity and lordship are exalted in paeans of praise. Christ came not just for some Jews and God-fearing Greeks, an elite band of faithful followers, but for all. The universal extent of his embrace leaves no part of humanity untouched. He has created all things and all people (Col.1:15f.). All creation moves toward that day when every knee shall bow and every tongue confess that Jesus the Messiah is Lord (Phil.2:11). Therefore the gospel has been proclaimed to every creature under heaven (Col.1:23). Christ is supreme in everything and for everyone (Col.1:18).

In addition to overlapping themes the passages cited from Philippians, Ephesians and Colossians highlight different themes. Three themes of significance for this study are the following: the name above all names (Phil. 1), the ruler of all things (Eph. 1), and the pre-eminence of Christ (Col. 1).

The name above all names (Phil. 2:6-11)

Paul declares that God bestowed on Jesus the name that is above all names (v.9). What was that name? This could not have been 'Jesus', because he already had that name. Therefore the name must have been 'Lord' *(Kurios)*. This becomes clear from a comparison of Phil. 2:9-11 and the Septuagint version of Isa. 45:18-25, especially the wording of v.23, which is used by Paul.

In the Septuagint version God says: *that to me every knee shall bow and every tongue shall swear to God*. Paul writes: *that at the name of Jesus every knee will bow (in heaven and on earth and under the earth), and every tongue will confess that the Lord (Kurios) is Jesus Christ* ... What is attributed to God in Isaiah is attributed to Jesus Christ in Philippians. Furthermore in the Septuagint of Isaiah 45 God is called *Kurios* ('Lord', or in Hebrew, *Yahweh*), whereas Paul boldly claims that Jesus Christ is Lord *(Kurios)*. It is this name, Lord, which is the name above all names, and it is this name which is given to Jesus Christ.

Gordon Fee comments that the reference to Isaiah 45:23 "seems to certify that what Paul had in mind is none other than the name, Yahweh itself, but in its Greek form of 'the Lord', which has now been 'given' to Jesus."[147] Howard Marshall concludes that "Jesus shared the status of God and was entitled to the same name of 'Lord' that was borne in the Scriptures to God himself."[148] No wonder then that

---

[147] Gordon Fee, *Paul's Letter to the Philippians*, Grand Rapids, 1995, p.223.

[148] I.H. Marshall, *The Epistle to the Philippians*, London, 1992, p.59. He notes that in Rom. 14:11 Paul applies God's claim in Isa. 45:23 to Jesus.

all will give Jesus the homage that belongs to God, for he is *in very nature God* (v.6).

But as Lord, Jesus is not an overbearing ruler. He has not seized this position or risen to it by his own efforts. He has been given it by God, as a vindication of his self-humbling and his descent to the depths of the cross. His way to Lordship has been the opposite of the sinful human pattern. He has come there through humiliation and self-emptying. Similarly he will not subjugate his opponents by brute force, but will be vindicated in the end by the demonstration of his God-given position, for it is God who will cause all to bow before him and confess his Lordship.

All things summed up in Christ (Ephesians 1)

It is generally accepted that Paul wrote the letter of Ephesians to Christians in Western Asia, whether the letter was directed in the first place to Ephesus or not. In understanding the significance of Paul's praise of Christ in chapter 1, it is important to note the religious background, dominated by the cult of Artemis. The goddess, Artemis, was described as saviour, cosmic Queen and Lord. She was thought to be capable of raising the dead and to have the keys to unlock the gates of Hades.[149] It was all too easy for Gentile converts to think of Christ as being one like Artemis, one among the gods, even if superior in some respects.

Paul's response begins with that extraordinary introductory sentence, verses 3-14, one of the longest Greek sentences in literature. Paul piles on the clauses to present Christ as the unique agent of the Father. In this opening sentence there are no less than thirteen references to Christ, which suggests that Paul was determined to counter any suggestion that Jesus could be put on a par with any other gods or spiritual powers.

At the heart of Paul's doxology is verse 10, which may be translated: *When the times have reached their fulfilment, God will bring to a head everything in heaven and on earth under Christ.* The key word here is the term *anakephalaiosis* ('bring to a head'), which has a wide range of meanings. These include 'recapitulation', 'summing up', and 'gathering together'. Of these 'summing up' and 'gathering together' appear to fit the passage

---

[149] T. Moritz, *'Summing up All Things'* in *One God, One Lord in a World of Religious Pluralism*, ed. A.D. Clarke & B.W. Winter, Cambridge, 1991, pp.88-90.

best.[150] This summing up will take place in the future, when God fulfils all his purposes for creation. What remains to be gathered together are the 'all things' in the created universe.

Some theologians both ancient and modern have seized on the phrase 'all things', to argue that all people, whether followers of Christ or not, will be saved. But there is no hint of such an idea in this verse or in the rest of Ephesians. As in many instances the development of Ephesians and Colossians runs parallel with each other, so it is here. Verse 10 is paralleled by Colossians 1:16-18, where three times Paul writes of 'all things', as the whole created order, both in heaven and on earth. Whereas in Ephesians all things will be brought together in Christ, in Colossians Paul says that 'all things hold together in Christ' (v.17). It is logical to understand Paul to use the words 'all things' in Ephesians to mean all parts of the universe, as he did in Colossians. Christ has created the whole universe, sustains it and will bring it to unity under him as its head. The emphasis in Ephesians is on the fulfilment of God's purposes at the end of time by the unification of everything under Christ. Not only will Christ be the head of all things, but he will also be the one who brings the conflicting elements in the universe to order and unites them under him.[151]

In verses 20-23, Christ is seen as having been exalted to the supreme place of power at God's right hand after his resurrection. This is further expatiated on in verses 21 and following, where Paul's language recalls Psalm 110:1. There, *The Lord says to my Lord: 'Sit at my right hand, till I make your enemies your footstool.'* Reference to the 'footstool' is reflected in the words of v.22: *God placed all things under his feet.* In Psalm 110 the footstool refers to God's enemies, so here Christ is said to be placed far above all, both enemies and friends. Christ has the supremacy over *all rule and authority, power and dominion,* which might challenge his position. These spiritual forces are similar to those mentioned in Col. 1:16. He has also been given a position of honour far above any title that has been or

[150] So here: 'the summing up of the totality takes place in its subjection to the Head' (*TDNT*, p.682).

[151] NEB translates verse 10: *that the universe might be brought into a unity in Christ.* Cf. J.B. Lightfoot, who wrote of "the entire harmony of the universe, which shall no longer contain alien and discordant elements, but of which all the parts shall find their centre and bond of union in Christ" (*Notes on Epistles of St Paul, from unpublished commentaries*, Macmillan, 1895, p.322).

can be given. There is also a reference in v.22 to Psalm 8:6-8, and to the dominion God gave to man at creation, which was forfeited by the fall. Christ as the perfect man has been given the dominion, which it was intended that Adam should exercise.

The obvious implication of Paul's description of Christ and what it means to be 'in Christ' is that Christ stands far above Artemis and every other god or power, who may be feared or worshipped in the world. He cannot be compared with them. He is God's agent for all ages, past, present and future. Before creation God planned to redeem the world through him. *His incomparably great power for us who believe* has been demonstrated in the present age. In the age to come everything will be summed up in him, every opposition will be put beneath his feet and the church will be honoured as his own body.

The Supremacy of Christ (Colossians 1:15-23)

This is the most powerful and comprehensive of all Paul's eulogies on the Lordship of Christ. Paul compiles an impressive list of Christ's attributes and achievements. He is the image of the invisible God, the firstborn of all creation. All things were created by him and for him. He is before all things, the one who holds all things together, the head of the church, the beginning and the firstborn from the dead – i.e. the first of the new creation. All God's fullness dwells in him and God's purpose is to reconcile all things to himself through Christ.

Here we have in addition to an emphasis on Christ's pre-existence and power as the agent of all creation, a statement of his present and future power.[152] Christ is not seen as someone, who will be Lord at the end of time, but the one who is already in the position of absolute power at God's right hand. God has already given him authority and fullness, so that he might have the supremacy in everything. In the end he will be seen to be the Lord and saviour he has been all along.

The reasons for Christ's pre-eminence are threefold. Firstly, as the beginning (*arche*, meaning 'first principle', 'source', 'creative

---

[152] N.T. Wright notes: "Verse 16 thus moves the thought of the poem from the past (Christ as agent of creation), to the present (Christ as the one to whom the world owes allegiance) and to the future (Christ whose sovereignty will become universal)." See N.T. Wright, *Colossians and Philemon*, Leicester & Grand Rapids, 1986, p.73.

initiative'), he is bound to take precedence over and be Lord of all the powers (*archai*) in heaven and on earth. These powers include all forces, rulers and authorities, whether spiritual or human, benevolent or malign (v. 16, 17).

Secondly, Christ is certain to be pre-eminent, *because God was pleased to have all his fullness dwell in him* (v.19).

The third reason for Christ's supremacy is that he has set in train the process of the reconciliation of all things to God through his death and resurrection.[153] The sacrificial shedding of his blood has cosmic consequences, so despite the rampant evil in the world, peace will be achieved through Christ. God and man will be reconciled. The entire universe will be brought to a new unity and harmony. He is the Lord of the new creation, as well as being Lord of the old (v.20).[154]

Therefore, Christ is not yet one more god or one more founder of a world religion. He cannot be, because he has reigned with God from the beginning and through him God reveals himself to be the creator, redeemer and ruler of all. The purpose of Christ is the purpose of God, the sacrifice of Christ is the sacrifice of God, the new creation in Christ is the new creation of God.

The New Testament believes that only the Lord of all has the answer to the disunity and disharmony in the universe, which has been fomented by evil powers. Christ alone has the God-given authority by nature and achievement to reign supreme over all for the good of all. The declaration that Christ is Lord of all is made in a positive mode, there is no explicit denunciation of other religions. But the implication is clear that Christ is the final authority. Other ways, other saviours and other lords, must be second best, if they are valid at all.

---

[153] Cf. Rom. 14:9 and C.H. Dodd's comment: "the attainment of universal lordship was, according to Rom. 14:9, the very purpose of Christ's death and resurrection" (C.H. Dodd, *The Apostolic Preaching and its Development*, London, 1936, p.15).

[154] "What is being claimed is quite simply and profoundly that the divine purpose in the act of reconciliation and peacemaking was to restore the harmony of the original creation ..." (J.D.G. Dunn, *The Epistles to the Colossians and to Philemon*, Grand Rapids & Carlisle, 1996, p.104).

Some conclusions

What implications can be drawn from the New Testament's teaching about Christ, as surveyed above, for its attitude to religions?

Firstly, the belief that Christ is the saviour of all implies that God desires to save all, as 1 Timothy 2:4 affirms. The New Testament is inclusive in its attitude to Gentile peoples, including them in Christ's offer of salvation. The whole thrust of the apostolic witness is to reach out to people of every nation, whatever their religion, and to welcome them into the kingdom.

Secondly, the emphasis on Christ's God-given role as the Way to the Father and the Lord of all allows no room for rivals. Since Christ is the pre-existent Word, his sacrifice on the cross has cosmic significance. No religion can claim the same divine authority to reveal the Father and to provide a way of salvation that brings human beings out of slavery to sin and death. Religions do not have the power to save the world.

Thirdly, Gentiles outside God's covenant with Israel do not live in total ignorance of God. The light of Christ shines on all. All are made in the image of God, however distorted by sin this likeness may be. People of all races should know about God and are capable of worship. The Spirit of God is omnipresent and ceaselessly at work. God is just and has overlooked the ignorance of the nations, who did not know him and were unaware of the gospel.

Fourthly, the New Testament does not draw the negative conclusion that all religions are entirely false. They are simply outdated now that Christ has come. Even the old covenant is reduced to a shadow. Hebrews puts it forcefully: *By calling this covenant 'new', God has made the first one obsolete, and what is obsolete and ageing will soon disappear* (Heb. 8:13). There is no point in clinging to the way of Mosaic sacrifices when the high priest of the heavenly temple has come to offer himself as the eternal sacrifice, to which the Levitical system looked forward. But everything in the past is not rejected as wrong. Similarly Gentile believers do not have to reject what is true in their old beliefs.

Fifthly, people of all religions are expected to respond to God's new offer and follow Christ. Does that mean they must leave their old religion and join a new one? They will certainly have to abandon devotion to other gods and lords. God demands absolute loyalty. But how far this means leaving their religious community remains an open question. Conversion does not require joining the trappings of Christianity. It requires joining the new humanity where all races are reconciled and it involves entering the kingdom of God. But Jewish believers remain Jews, Asian believers remain Asian, and African believers remain African, even if they are now all one in Christ Jesus.

Sixthly, there is a place for plurality. In the gospel economy the conflict between the one and the many is rooted in the contrast between God and men. God is one and his way is one. God is the opposite of duality. Hinduism is right to proclaim 'Advaita', 'no second', for with God there is no other. But in the world there is infinite diversity. So also in the human quest for God, there are as many routes to the way that leads to God as there are people. Religions may be part of the diverse aspirations and desires that lead people to search for God, but if they are to lead to the Father people must come to his way, incarnate in Christ.

Christ's mission to the world and its implications for the New Testament view of people of other religions

The necessity of mission

The apostles and early church might have restricted the preaching of the gospel of the kingdom to Jews and proselytes. This is what happened to begin with at Pentecost in Jerusalem and in the first seven chapters of Acts. It was not as if the world did not figure in their thinking. They had experienced the amazing work of the Holy Spirit speaking through them in the languages of all the pilgrims, who had come to Jerusalem from many parts of the world for the feast of Pentecost. But the apostles' vision was limited initially to the world of Judaism, consisting of Jews and proselytes. If there had been no change in their approach Christianity would have remained a Jewish sect and it would have shared the Jewish aversion to Gentiles without provoking foreigners by preaching to them. What changed the apostles' thinking and convinced them that the church's mission should be extended to all peoples?

Luke's account of the church's expansion in Acts shows that the apostles were slow to grasp the plan that Jesus gave them before his ascension (1:8). Luke traced the progress of the church, as predicted by Jesus, from Jerusalem to Judea and Samaria and on into the Graeco-Roman world. At each stage there was resistance, but there were also powerful reasons compelling the church to move forward into mission.

God's revelation

The first breakthrough came at Samaria. The apostles, alarmed at the number of Samaritans baptised by Philip, sent Peter and John to investigate. Their doubts were removed when they saw the Samaritan believers receive the Holy Spirit, as they laid hands on them. A more momentous breakthrough came when God enlarged Peter's outlook on a Joppa roof and Peter saw the Holy Spirit poured out on Cornelius and his household. The apostles concluded that God wanted to include Gentiles in the church. Of equal importance was the commissioning of Paul to be the apostle to the Gentiles. Subsequently, the free admission of uncircumcised Gentiles into the church was confirmed by the Jerusalem Council, as being in conformity with Scripture and the guidance of the Holy Spirit. In all these developments the leading of the Holy Spirit was decisive.[155]

Christ's commission

All four Gospels and Acts record that after the resurrection Christ commissioned his disciples to engage in mission to the world. Some have suggested that prior to the resurrection Jesus did not envisage a mission to all nations, in view of his remarks to the Syro-Phoenician woman (Matt. 15:24) and his instructions to the twelve (Matt. 10:5f.). But this would be to ignore or discount evidence that suggests that world mission was part of the Messiah's agenda from the beginning. Christ would have been fully aware of those Old Testament prophecies, which envisaged a time when God's mission to the nations would be fulfilled through Israel.[156] These go back to the beginning of creation and specifically to the promise given to Abraham: *and all peoples on earth will be blessed through you* (Gen. 12:3). In Isaiah, one of the Servant Songs

[155] See the following references: Acts 8:4-25; 9:15; 10:1-11:18; 15:1-19.
[156] See D.J. Bosch, *Transforming Mission*, New York, 1991, pp. 16-20.

expresses plainly the outgoing mission of God to the world: *I will also make you a light for the Gentiles, that you may bring my salvation to the ends of the earth* (Isa. 49:6). Paul quotes this text very early in his missionary career at Pisidian Antioch, to justify the mission to Gentiles (Acts 13:47).[157]

The Gospels bear witness to Jesus' welcome for non-Jews and his concern for the world. From the beginning of his life, when the Magi were the first to worship Jesus, there were indications that his coming would be significant for the world. Jesus told his disciples that he was tempted in the wilderness to achieve God's objective of winning the world by bowing down to the devil. That clearly indicates that Jesus was concerned to reach the world, hence the cleverness of Satan's offer to achieve this by a quick and easy means. After his Nazareth manifesto (Luke 4:24-28) he brought down the wrath of his home town, not for claiming that the Spirit was upon him, but for daring to suggest that God (through his prophets) is concerned for Gentiles. In the Sermon on the Mount the disciples are told that they are to be the light of the world. Jesus was positive in appreciating the Gentiles he met. He never gave such high praise to a Jew, as he gave to the Capernaum centurion and to the Syro-Phoenician woman for their great faith. Commenting on the centurion's example, he predicted that the kingdom of God would be opened to people from the four corners of the earth, whilst many Jews would be excluded (Matt. 8:5-12; 15:21-28; Luke 13:28-30). In the parable of the Great Banquet the servant is sent out of the city to the highways to bring in people from beyond the community, symbolising the inclusion of the nations (Luke 14:15-24).[158] In John's Gospel the 'I am' sayings are a vivid expression of Christ's universal ministry. Most obviously relevant are the words, *I am the light of the world* (John 8:12). Before he died Jesus told the crowds, which appear to have included Greeks, *I, when I am lifted up from the earth, will draw all men to myself* (John 12:32).

After the resurrection the Gospels and Acts are unanimous that Jesus gave new instructions to his disciples to take the good news to the world. This was not an afterthought or something tacked on the end by the writers, but the climax of all that went before. As Bosch has shown in

---

[157] See also Isa. 42:6; Amos 9:12 (quoted by James in Acts 15:16f.).

[158] "There is general agreement among contemporary scholars that the latter invitation symbolically represents an outreach to the Gentiles, and that Luke understands it in this fashion" (T.W. Manson, *Sayings*, p.130). Ken Bailey, *Through Peasant Eyes*, Grand Rapids, 1980, p.101.

his analysis of the relation between the Great Commission and the rest of Matthew, "the entire gospel points to these final verses."[159] As the church expanded far beyond the boundaries of Palestine, north and south, east and west, Christians reflected on Christ's words and saw in them the inspiration for a society that welcomed all peoples into the family of God.

Christ's unparalleled achievements

Mission presupposed that something new had happened, that made it possible to invite people of all religions into the kingdom of God. The apostles and evangelists pointed to Christ as the new way. But it was one thing to say that Christ is the Way and another to show to Jews and Greeks what was new about the way of Christ. What had he done that had never been done before?

The apostles' preaching majored on three unusual things that Christ had achieved: his sacrifice on the cross, his resurrection from the dead and the gift of the Holy Spirit.

What was it that made the crucifixion of Jesus an event of universal significance? The short answer is the identity of the person who died on the cross and connected with that the manner and purpose of his death. The execution of the Messiah, the word of the Father, the light of the world and the Son of God had cosmic repercussions. But his death was not unexpected. Jesus warned his disciples repeatedly that he would be put to death. He accepted crucifixion voluntarily and described his death as a ransom for sin and a sacrifice to inaugurate a new covenant between God and man. Jesus did not die as a martyr for a cause, but as the atonement for the sins of the world. His death is unique in the annals of human history and is celebrated with joy as a victory, not with sorrow as a tragedy.

The resurrection of Jesus was the central fact of the apostles' preaching. It vindicated Christ's death, endorsed his claim to be Lord and made him a living reality through his Spirit. It is true that

---

[159] D.J. Bosch, op.cit., p.57. Bosch adds: "Matthew's entire Gospel can only be read and understood from the perspective of the final pericope. The same is true of Luke's Gospel" (op.cit., p.91). See also his quotes on the same page from well known scholars, such as G. Bornkamm on the importance of Matt. 28:18-20 for the whole gospel. Bornkamm calls them "a summary of the entire gospel of Matthew" and U. Luck says they are "the climax of the gospel."

people have revived after clinical death and returned to their bodies. Also, Jesus himself brought Lazarus, Jairus' daughter and the widow of Nain's son back to life. But the resurrection was different. Jesus reappeared in a spiritual body, not to return to life on earth, but on his way back to God. The ascension to God's right hand is part of the resurrection victory.

The third achievement of Christ was fulfilled after his ascension. He had promised his bereaved disciples that he would not leave them alone, but would send his Spirit to be with them. The coming of the Spirit at Pentecost transformed a dejected and frightened group of men into a bold and fervent movement. But it did more. It provided Christ's followers with a spiritual dynamic, communicating God's presence and inner transformation, which has never left them.

The sacrificial death of Christ, the resurrection and the coming of the Spirit at Pentecost have never been replicated in any religion. No other founder of a world religion has voluntarily sacrificed his life for the sins of the whole world. No one else has undergone a resurrection from death as Jesus did. No other religion, including Judaism, has been launched on the outpouring of the Holy Spirit, as happened at Pentecost, with the subsequent offer of the Spirit to all believers.

Christ's universal role

As the first Christians reflected on the extraordinary life, death and resurrection of Jesus and the legacy he had left them, they understood more of the implications of the titles he had been given. The titles given to Christ and the claims made by and for him were not merely laudatory. They reflected the fact that God had done something new through Jesus, which must be communicated to all earth's citizens. At his birth he had been given the name Jesus (Saviour), later he accepted the title 'Lord' and spoke of himself as the Way. We have already seen above how these titles were developed to describe Jesus as the way to the Father, the Saviour of the world and the Lord of all. A Messiah with such titles could not be limited to the confines of Judaism. In fact the titles indicate the compulsion the apostles felt to proclaim Christ as far as they could travel. Paul expressed this feeling of compulsion in many of his letters. Take for example, Romans 15:17-20:

Therefore I glory in Christ Jesus in my service to God. I will not venture to speak of anything except what Christ has accomplished through me in leading the Gentiles to obey God by what I have said and done -- by the power of signs and miracles, through the power of the Spirit. So from Jerusalem all the way round to Illyricum, I have fully proclaimed the gospel of Christ. It has always been my ambition to preach the gospel where Christ was not known, so that I would not be building on someone else's foundation.

The goal of mission

When the church began its mission to the Gentile world, expanding from a purely Jewish base, it may not have had a clear idea where it was going. But there were guidelines already in place in the teaching and commission of Jesus. These were important and are important now in defining what the church should be aiming at in mission to the world. These in turn have implications for the New Testament view of religions.

Proclamation. Luke-Acts defines the goal of mission as the progressive proclamation of Christ's message from Jerusalem through Judea and Samaria to 'all nations' and to 'the ends of the earth' (Acts 1:8; Luke 24:47). Mark records Jesus as saying that the gospel must be preached to all nations (Mark 13:10). Paul's aim was 'to preach the gospel where Christ was not known' and he claimed to have fully proclaimed the gospel of Christ from Jerusalem all the way around to Illyricum (Rom. 15:19f.).

Discipling. Jesus told his apostles to *go and make disciples of all nations* (*panta ta ethne*, Matt. 28:19). Proclamation was to be followed by a call for response, just as Jesus had preached the kingdom and called disciples to follow him (Acts 20:21). Paul's prayer was *that all nations might believe and obey God* (Rom.16:27). Those who responded were to be incorporated in the church, the body of Christ.

In-gathering. At the end of time there will be an in-gathering of people from all nations into the kingdom of God. Jesus forecast this in the Gospels, speaking of the time when people would come from east and west and take their places at the feast with the patriarchs in heaven (Matt. 8:11). This theme is taken up in some parts of the book of Revelation, most notably in the prediction of the *great multitude that no-one can count, from every nation, tribe, people and language* who will stand before Christ in heaven (Rev. 7:9); also in the vision of the heavenly Jerusalem, where *the glory and honour of the nations will be brought into it* (Rev. 21:26).

These goals are notable for what they do not contain as well as for what they look forward to. They do not set the target as the conversion of all or many or most of the nations, nor do they aim for statistical success, in terms of the number of baptisms or new churches planted. Proclamation, discipling and the growth of the church are to be pursued, but not at all costs, and certainly not by coercion.

The implications of mission

How did the practice of mission and evangelism affect the attitude of the New Testament writers to people of other religions? How did it affect the relations between Christians and Jews who refused to follow Jesus as Messiah? Once the church agreed to preach to everyone and make disciples of every nation, what did that suggest about the other religions around them in the Roman empire? Did it mean that they were defective or that Christians had something others did not have? What sort of impact did the adoption of mission to the world have on the apostles and first Christians?

Respect for all races and religions. The change from a mission to Judaism to mission to all nations had a surprising effect on Peter. He gained a new regard for non-Jews. No longer did he refuse to visit them or have any social intercourse with them. Instead he admitted that God has no favourites and treats Gentiles just the same as he treats his people. This had not been his view as a Jew, for whom the term Gentiles was little better than 'dogs'. As Tacitus noted Jews 'regard the rest of mankind with all the hatred of enemies' (*Histories. 5.5*). Paul ceased to look down on them as 'foreigners', but saw them as the recipients of God's new covenant, a covenant equally for both Gentiles and Jews.

Humanity reunited. Paul considered that Christ came to make of the two divisions of humanity, Jew & Gentile, one new race. He grasped the astonishing truth, that in Christ not only are all human beings equal, because they are created by God in his image, but they are also equal under the new covenant. The old division into Jews and people of other races has been abolished.

Privileges reversed. The New Testament is very positive about Greeks and Romans and people of other races, because it realises that God has great plans for the nations. They are to be included in his plans. The kingdom of God is for all the peoples, east and west, north and south. The time has come when the doors of the kingdom are open to them as well. The mystery has been revealed – the time has come to invite the Gentiles in. They did not get the first or even the second invitation in the parable of the wedding feast, but now that Jews have turned theirs down, God has given invites to all the nations. So they are the privileged ones now, just as Israel was privileged under the old covenant. They are privileged, but not their religions. Those religions have some truth in them, but they have had their day and all are now called on to respond to the call of the man from the dead, the resurrected Lord.

But the New Testament does not attack any contemporary religion. It does not spend its time running down the cults of Artemis and Cybele, or the doctrines of Stoics and Epicureans, or decrying those who worship Hermes and Zeus. It simply broadcasts God's invitation to all humanity to respond to the message of salvation through his agent Jesus Christ, with the warning that God's invitation cannot be lightly rejected and the time is short in which to respond.

Cultural diversity accepted. The radical decisions of the Jerusalem Council meant that non-Jews did not have to adopt Jewish culture in order to join the church. They did not have to become like Jews. They did not have to change their culture to join the kingdom or fit into the church. Compare this with the modern objection to Christian mission, that it forces Asian and African converts to become westernised. According to this view, to become a Christian is to become westernised and to abandon your own culture. That was not the case in the first century. The danger then was that Greeks and Romans might think they had to become like Jews, in order to follow Christ. Paul fought hard to prevent that happening and so opposed all attempts to circumcise converts according to Jewish rites. Converts did not have to abandon their culture and cease to be Greeks or Ephesians or Romans.

A different division. The old division between Israel and the rest was dissolved. A different division took its place, a division into two worlds, the world of darkness, which is made up of people regardless of their race, religion or socio-economic status and the world of light, which is also made up of people regardless of their race, religion or socio-economic status.[160] Everyone is by nature under the prince of darkness. It is Christ who offers to transfer those who believe in him into the world of light. This offer is given to the Jew and also to the Gentile, there is no difference. To begin with this did not cause the church to look down on those who were still in darkness, but did motivate them to preach the good news that Christ offered to all, both Jew and Gentile.

The implications for the salvation of people
who do not hear the Gospel

What is the fate of people belonging to other religions who do not hear about Christ? A great deal has been written on this question and still more is being written. Some will agree with Lesslie Newbigin who reminded his readers that when Jesus was asked a similar question he told the crowd they should strive to enter the narrow gate, which leads to life and avoid speculation. Others would say that what the world urgently needs is the preaching of the gospel, not reasons for thinking people may be alright without it, for there are very few God-fearing souls in any community. Both points are valid, but we still need to ask what light the New Testament sheds on this difficult question, because the answer will affect our attitudes and actions.

The New Testament does not give us a direct answer to this question. It does not say either that no one will be saved apart from believing in Christ, or that some people will be saved. But there are passages, which have a bearing on the subject.

---

[160]   Teresa Okure from Port Harcourt, Nigeria, has the following note in her missiological study of John: "To the modern mentality missionary endeavour is almost synonymous with efforts to meet the needs of 'the Third World', a kind of substitute for their lack of technological development. The general impression given then is that those in the 'developed countries', have no need of missionary activity, or of evangelization. To this way of thinking the author of 1 John would probably say you are wrong and deceive yourselves (1:6,8). For his schema recognizes two, not three, basic worlds, the world of light to which all believers belong regardless of nationality and social status, and the world of darkness to which unbelievers belong, regardless of nationality and social status (3:19-21)." Teresa Okure, *The Johannine Approach to Mission*, Tubingen, 1988, p.296 n.11.

Matthew 11:20-24

This is the most striking of those texts that refer to the principle of diminished responsibility and its bearing on the final judgement. In the end when God calls everyone to account before him will he give any concessions to those who have not had a chance of hearing of the gospel of repentance and faith? Jesus indicates that he will. In these verses in Matthew Jesus first of all lays down the principle that those who have heard his message and been presented with evidence of his truth and power will be judged more severely than those who have not heard. This should immediately warn us against thinking that God's judgement will fall most severely on outsiders who have had none of the privileges open to Christians and that he will reject them all on the grounds that they have not heard the gospel. Secondly, Jesus bluntly says that the citizens of Tyre and Sidon would have repented long ago if they had seen his miracles. Does that suggest that they will be given an opportunity to repent in the next life or that they will be exonerated, because it is clear to God that they would have repented if they had had the opportunity? What Jesus does say is that it will be 'more bearable' for Tyre and Sidon on the judgement day than for the Jews who saw his miracles. Thirdly, Jesus goes one step further in saying that it will be even more bearable for Sodom, that symbol of wickedness, on the judgement day than for his contemporaries in Capernaum. Again he gives a reason for this prediction. Sodom would not have been destroyed if its population had seen Christ's miracles, presumably because like Tyre and Sidon they would have repented and thus averted disaster.

This passage does not say the people of Tyre and Sidon and Sodom will be saved on the judgement day, but it does give grounds for hope that God will treat them mercifully.

Matthew 25:31-46

Many have argued that the parable of the sheep and the goats shows that God will judge non-Christians by their deeds. In particular God will accept or condemn people according to whether or not they have acted in a Christ-like manner to the poor, the hungry, the naked, the sick, the foreigner and the imprisoned. At first sight this is what Jesus appears to have been saying. But if this were so, it would be a fairly arbitrary list and it would also be strange to find a parable that teaches salvation by works rather than by faith as in the rest of the New Testament. There is a further problem. Those who use this parable to suggest that people of other religions can be saved by the way they treat the poor and disadvantaged often overlook the fact that, if these actions were to be the criteria for salvation from judgement, then they would apply to both Christians and non-Christians alike, and so Christians would be saved by their works.

In order to decide what the parable means and how it should be applied, the exegesis of v. 40 is crucial. Both 'sheep' and 'goats' are astonished, because neither group recognised Jesus, nor were they conscious of either serving him or neglecting him. He appeared to them *incognito* in the form of *one of the least of these brothers of mine* (v.40). How are we to understand who *these brothers of mine* stand for?

In his treatment of this parable TW Manson comments[161] that what is being commended is not upright living or kind-heartedness as opposed to their opposites, but whether people have sided with God or not, in the person of Jesus. The emphasis is on the words 'I' and 'me' not on the actions of the sheep. Feeding the hungry, clothing the naked and so on were vital, because they were done for Jesus Christ. The king clarifies this in v.40 by saying that what was done for his brethren was done for him. In Matthew's Gospel there is no doubt about the meaning of the phrase *my brethren*. Jesus speaks of his disciples as *my brethren* on two occasions (12:48, 49; 28:10). Also the principle that help given to a disciple is help given to his master, Jesus, is laid down in 10:40-42. The identification of 'my brethren' with 'my disciples' also makes good sense of the actions commended. When Jesus' followers are engaged in mission and exposed to the opposition of a hostile world, they are in need of hospitality and support, especially when imprisoned.

We conclude that this parable does not teach that people, who belong to other religions will be judged by their actions in support of the poor and oppressed, but that people will be judged by whether or not they have sided with the kingdom of God. The test of that will be how they have treated Christ's disciples. This, of course, does raise the possibility that a Muslim, a Hindu, or a Buddhist may be welcomed into heaven,

[161] T.W. Manson, *The Sayings of Jesus*, London, 1949, pp.249-252.

because they sided with Christ's disciples in the hour of their need, even though they did not realise the significance of what they were doing

Acts 10:34, 35

As a result of his meeting with Cornelius, Peter learnt that God shows no favouritism in his dealings with human beings, whether they are Jews or people of other faiths. Far from writing people off, because they have not heard of Jesus and his gospel, God *accepts men from every nation who fear him and do what is right* (10:35).

How are we to interpret these conditions for acceptance by God? Some think this means that God saves people of other religions who believe and are morally upright and there is no need to preach the gospel to them, because they are already approved, accepted and saved. Others hold the opposite viewpoint that only those who are converted, baptised and filled with the Spirit as Cornelius was can be saved. They hold that those whom God accepts are given the opportunity to hear the gospel, repent and believe in Jesus Christ, as Cornelius was, whereas those who do not hear and believe in Christ are not saved. Others believe that God-fearers like Cornelius, who have not heard the gospel, are nevertheless saved on the grounds that they feared God and did what is right, according to the light they received. Clark Pinnock[162] takes John Stott[163] to task for limiting the scope of the phrase 'acceptable to God' to mean those who are not justified by faith but are acceptable in a weaker sense. Instead Pinnock quotes Matthew Henry with approval: "God never did, nor ever will, reject or refuse an honest gentile, who, though he has not the privileges or advantages that the Jews have, yet, like Cornelius, fears God, and worships him, and works righteousness; that is, is just and charitable towards all men, who lives up to the light he has, both in a sincere devotion and in regular conversation."[164]

As already indicated in our discussion of Cornelius in the first chapter, verse 35 should be understood within the context of the whole of Acts 10:1 – 11:18 and not lifted out and treated as a statement on its

---

[162] Clark H Pinnock, *A Wideness in God's Mercy*, Grand Rapids, 1992, p.165.
[163] J.R.W. Stott, *The Message of Acts*, Leicester, 1990, p.198f.
[164] Matthew Henry, *Commentary on the Whole Bible*, Vol.VI, p.133, quoted by Pinnock, op.cit., p.165.

own. Two things are abundantly clear from the Cornelius story. First, that God did commend Cornelius for his prayers and almsgiving before he met Peter, but that he still needed to repent, believe in Christ and be filled with the Spirit, in order to enjoy the fruits of salvation. The story emphatically refutes the idea that non-Christians do not need the gospel, but can be saved by their own religious devotion. Second, Peter received a double rebuke for (a) thinking that all Gentiles were unworthy of God's attention and (b) that God did not want Gentiles to hear the gospel and join the church.

The meaning of this text depends on how the word 'acceptable' (*dektos*) is interpreted. Is it equivalent to 'saved' or something else? In view of the context and the fact that Cornelius is told by the angel that Peter *will bring you a message through which you and all your household will be saved* (11:14), it is clear that Cornelius was not saved before Peter came to him. He experienced salvation later when he believed and was filled with the Spirit. This suggests that *dektos* means he was approved and accepted with a view to salvation. Cornelius was fortunate to hear about Christ and believe. What about those like him who have not heard and cannot hear about Christ? Does this mean they will be saved or not? Can a person be accepted and not saved? Theoretically, yes. Cornelius was 'acceptable' to God and an angel was sent to him. If he had died before he met Peter, he would not have been 'saved'. But would he have gone to hell? Here we need to distinguish between the experience of being born again ('saved') and being received into heaven (also 'saved'). Compare this with the New Testament's three tenses for salvation, past, present and future: we have been saved, are being saved and will be saved. Here there are also the three stages of being accepted, saved and received into heaven. A non-Christian who is accepted by God on account of his faith and godly behaviour has reached the first stage. If he/she has no opportunity of hearing the gospel in this life, we would nevertheless expect God in his mercy to receive such a God-fearer into heaven, on the grounds of God's impartiality and this person's faith. This helps to distinguish between two questions. Has a God-fearing non-Christian who is acceptable to God but is deprived of the knowledge of the gospel been 'saved' now in this life? Answer, no. Will the same person enter heaven? Answer, yes.

John Stott is right in saying that *dektos* ('acceptable') does not mean 'justification'. Cornelius was not saved in the full sense of the word before he met Peter. However to say that God considers a person to be acceptable (*dektos*) to him is a powerful commendation. God does not say such things lightly. God heard and answered the prayers and longings of Cornelius. Will he not similarly answer the prayers of people of other religions who cry out to him with faith and obedience? God responds to true faith in himself. This ties in with what Paul says about saving faith in Romans. This will be referred to later in the discussion of Romans chapter 4. 'Saving faith' normally leads to salvation through Christ in this life, but if not, will it not lead to salvation in the next life?

Acts 10:35 implies that some people of other religions actually draw God's attention to themselves by their faith and righteous action. True they have not attained salvation nor have they merited justification, but God has heard their prayers. Such people need the gospel preached to them, so that their heart's desire can be satisfied by the joy of the Spirit, the fellowship of the Father and the forgiveness of the Son. It is not true that they are so satisfied by their own devotions that they do not need Christ. Nor is their worship so inadequate that they are doomed to hell, if they do not hear and believe in Christ. The truth is somewhere between these two notions. God is impartial and sees beyond the confines of the people of God, whether Jew or Christian, to those choice souls like Cornelius, who are God-fearing and upright. Such people are acceptable to him and he will act to save them whether in this life or the next.

Some, who are concerned to assert that the gospel of Christ is the only way of salvation given by God, argue that God-fearing non-Christians, who have never heard of Christ, cannot be saved because no one is perfect. This would be to ignore their faith and apply different standards in judging them than we allow for ourselves. Just as a Christian believer is not saved by works but by grace operating through faith, so a God-fearing person ignorant of Christ is saved not by the perfection of their observance of the dictates of conscience, but by faith in God and reliance on his grace. Similarly a God-fearing person, who has never heard of Christ and fails to keep the moral law in every part, is no more disqualified from salvation by their failures than is a born again Christian who falls into sin. For no one is saved by works but by the grace of God received through faith. In the words of J I Packer: "We may safely say (i) if any good pagan reached the point of throwing himself on his Maker's mercy for pardon, it was grace that brought him there; (ii) God will surely save anyone he brings thus far; (iii) anyone thus saved would learn in the next world that he was saved through Christ."[165]

Cornelius is the example, par excellence, of those devout followers of other religions, who are accepted by God. But he is not the only one. Right from the beginning of Acts 10 it is not Cornelius alone but Cornelius and his whole family who are commended for being *devout and God-fearing* (v.2). Later a large gathering of Cornelius' family, servants and friends heard Peter's message and were filled with the Spirit. Luke also records that Paul consistently sought out the God-fearing Gentiles wherever he went and they together with Jewish converts formed the core of his churches. Whether there are few or many such people in the world, we are not told. Experience suggests there are few, but more than some may expect.

What makes a person acceptable to God? Two things are mentioned here: that they 'fear him' (*phoboumenos auton*) and 'do what is right' (*ergazomenos dikaiosune*). Concerning the first we have already seen that Acts designates Gentiles who worshipped the one Creator God of Israel as God-fearers or God-worshippers. They not only feared God, but also worshipped him and directed their prayers to him; above all they put their faith in him. It is this faith in God, which commends them to him. But it is not a bare faith unaccompanied by evidence of a godly life. The test of the genuineness of their faith is that it produced deeds of righteousness (*dikaiosune*).

We conclude that Acts 10:34, 35 is of immense importance in defining the biblical attitude to people of other faiths.[166] There is nothing here to support the pessimism, which says that there is no hope for people of other faiths who have never heard of Christ. Nor is there support for the optimism that says people are saved by their own religions and do not need the gospel. What is clearly taught are the following three truths.

---

[165] J.I. Packer, *God's Words*, Downers Grove, 1981, p.210.

[166] It is "perhaps the most powerful pointer to the inclusiveness of God's saving activity" and contains "important clues for a Christian understanding of the status before God of those who are not Christians in our day" (*Towards a Theology for Inter-Faith Dialogue*, Anglican Consultative Council, 1986, p.24f.).

First God treats all his creatures on the same terms. He does not have one set of criteria for Christians and another for non-Christians. He does not judge non-Christians by their deeds but Christians by their faith. He is looking for faith and righteousness from all his creatures.[167]

Second God does not judge people by their national identity or religious label. A Muslim from Mecca or a Hindu from Benares is not automatically rejected by God, because he is not a Christian believer, as some appear to think. God judges people from every nation and religion according to the way they respond to him in the light of the knowledge they have. People from every part of the world are capable of putting their faith in God and doing what pleases him, whether they know Christ or not.

Third, those who are God-fearing and do what is right are accepted by God. There can be no quibble about that. To them God will send his messengers with the way of salvation, so that they may enter into fellowship with their Lord. Where this is not possible, as for many centuries it has not been possible, e.g. in Saudi Arabia, God will surely accept their faith as he did Abraham's 'as righteousness'. To them Jesus gave this promise of fellowship with faithful Abraham: *I say to you that many will come from the east and the west, and will take their places at the feast with Abraham ... in the kingdom of heaven* (Matt. 8:11).

Romans 2:1-16

Romans 2:6-16 is often cited as a passage, which affirms that non-Christians are able to attain salvation without believing in Christ. The main texts are verses 7, 10 and 15. These appear to suggest that Paul believed non-Jews could attain eternal life if they lived according to the dictates of conscience and pleased God by their works. The passage must be viewed in the context of Paul's argument from 1:18 – 3:26, where he aims to show that since neither Jew nor Gentile can be declared righteous, God has provided a new way by which believers are saved through grace by the sacrifice of Christ. Since all fall short of God's requirements, it would be strange if Paul intended to suggest in 2:2-16 that people of

---

[167] J.A. Alexander sums it up well: "The essential meaning is that whatever is acceptable to God in one race is acceptable in any other." J.A. Alexander, *A Commentary on the Acts of the Apostles,* quoted by J.R.W. Stott, op.cit., p.198.

other religions could gain salvation through their good deeds. What then was he trying to say in these verses?

In 1:18-32 Paul describes those who have deliberately turned their backs on all that they knew of God and devoted themselves to gross evil. In 2:1-16 he turns his attention to those who think that they are morally superior and judge others (v.1, 3), yet do the things they condemn. From 2:17 – 3:8 he specifically addresses Jews, who believe that they are superior to the rest of humanity and are favoured by God, because they have the law and the covenants. He shows them that the very law they trust in condemns them.

What then is the meaning of 2:7, 10 and 15? Paul's purpose is to establish God's impartiality – not the process of salvation – that is why he includes the statement: *for God does not show favouritism* (v.11). In his thesis, *Paul as Apostle to the Gentiles*, Daniel Chae says, "Paul's argument for God's impartiality in 1:16 – 2:11 serves as a stepping stone to his affirmation of the legitimacy of Gentile salvation."[168] Paul wanted to show that God was absolutely fair in treating both Jews and Gentiles in the same way. Though the Gentiles did not have the law, they had the moral law written on their hearts and were capable of doing good.

In his commentary on Romans Cranfield[169] lists ten possible interpretations of v. 6 – 11, especially with reference to those who do good. These are compressed by Chae into four main views of Paul's 'judgement according to works', as (i) self-contradictory, (ii) merely hypothetical, (iii) meaning the 'work of faith', (iv) God will judge all by their works. Cranfield favours the latter and believes that Paul had Gentile Christians in mind. The fact that non-Jews sometimes do what the law requires does not mean they are saved by some good deeds, because their consciences will both accuse and defend them. To be justified they will have to rely, like Jews, on Christ. Here Paul's point concerns the justice of God's judgement not the way of salvation.[170] Paul does not say that those Gentiles who live according to their consciences will be saved.

---

[168]   Daniel J.S. Chae, *Paul as Apostle to the Gentiles*, Carlisle, 1997, p.105.
[169]   C.E.B. Cranfield, *A Critical and Exegetical Commentary on the Epistle to the Romans*, Vol.I, Edinburgh, 1975, pp.151-153.
[170]   J.R.W. Stott, *The Message of Romans*, Leicester, 1994, p.87.

The reverse is the case, for just as the law is a schoolmaster to lead Jews to Christ, so conscience drives non-Jews to Christ by convicting them of their guilt.[171]

To sum up: Romans 2:6-16 does not provide any grounds for believing that people of other faiths can be saved by their good deeds apart from faith in Christ. It does however show that they are able to do good by living according to the light they have from God through conscience.

Romans 4

There is only one way of salvation for human beings and that is the way of faith. This way is open to people of all faiths, all times and all nations. The way of faith in God has been available to mankind from the beginning of time and will remain open till the end of the world.[172]

In Romans 4 Paul sets out to establish the principle of salvation by faith from the example of Abraham. He has already firmly stated in 3:28-30 that just as there is only one God, so there is only one way for Jews and Gentiles to be justified and that is by faith. Here 'Jews' and 'Gentiles' stand for the whole of humanity, both those who know the God of Israel and those who do not, both those who belong to the people of God and those who do not.[173] Does this undercut the revelation of justification by Christ? Paul asked a similar question: does faith undercut God's revelation to Moses of the law? (3:31). Certainly not, he said, and turned to the example of Abraham to prove the primacy of faith.

---

[171]　Rom. 2:15 can be used to show people of other faiths why Christians rely on Christ for forgiveness, because our consciences accuse us of our many failures to live a perfect life and drive us to Christ.

[172]　Although Clark Pinnock's thesis in *A Wideness in God's Mercy* can be criticised on various counts, he is surely right in affirming the faith principle. "In my judgement, the faith principle is the basis of universal accessibility. According to the Bible, people are saved by faith, not by the content of their theology. Since God has not left anyone without witness, people are judged on the basis of the light they have received and how they have responded to that light. Faith in God is what saves, not possessing certain minimum information" (op.cit., p.57f.).

[173]　Paul refers to three distinctions that separate Jews from Gentiles: keeping the Law (v.28), belonging to the Jewish race (v.29), and circumcision (v.30). But none of these give the Jew any ground for boasting, because God is only looking for faith, and justification is by faith alone.

Paul begins his exposition of Abrahamic faith by quoting Genesis 15:6: *Abraham believed God, and it was credited to him as righteousness.* He points out that on account of faith God forgives the sinful and acquits them as if they were righteous. Paul deliberately says of God that he *justifies the wicked* (4:5). Abraham did not deserve to be forgiven. In God's sight he was guilty of wickedness, as was David, whom Paul cites next (v.6, 7). This is important in our thinking about God-fearing non-Christians. They are not justified because they are better than other people, but because of their faith. It also follows that if they exhibit true faith in God, this faith is not nullified by their transgressions, but credited to them for forgiveness.

Someone may then object by saying: 'Justification is only for those who have become Christians'. Paul refutes a similar objection in v. 9-11 raised by Jews, who said that God only justifies the circumcised. 'Wrong', said Paul, 'Abraham was justified before he was circumcised'. Therefore Abraham *is the father of all who believe but have not been circumcised, in order that righteousness may be credited to them* (v.11). Abraham is the father of *all who believe* in God while they are still unidentified as belonging to the people of God, i.e. are in an uncircumcised state. Since Abraham lived long before Jesus and had never heard of the gospel of forgiveness by Christ's death on the cross, this is a powerful sign of hope for all, who have never heard of Christ. Abraham is the father of the unknown company of those who have put their faith in God all down the centuries despite never hearing about Christ. The fact that he is also the father of Christians who live by faith does not mean that only Christians have saving faith in God and no one else (v.12).

Abraham was not only made righteous through faith, but also received a promise that he would inherit the world (v.13, 14). The pattern of Abrahamic faith therefore affects the world and is valid for all far beyond the Abrahamic religions of Judaism, Christianity and Islam. Faith lays hold of the promise of God's blessing for the world, so then those who have a faith like Abraham's are not only children of faith, but also children of promise and heirs of God. Paul specifically identifies the type of faith that is honoured by God, as Abraham's faith (v.16). Abraham's acts of faith preceded his submission to circumcision and dated from the time when he belonged to a polytheistic culture in the ancient civilization of Ur (in modern Iraq). Abraham is therefore the forerunner not only of non-Jewish Christians, but of all who obey and believe in the creator God, whatever their religious label.

This is all possible by grace (v.16), the unlimited, universal generosity of God. Faith is not another work meriting God's attention, but the simple outstretched hand of a helpless child relying totally upon its father's care. All who live by faith are children of Abraham and are heirs with him of God's promised blessings. Paul quotes Genesis 17:5 to remind his readers that God had called Abraham *a father of many nations* (v.17). He did so to encourage Gentile believers to realise that they need not submit to Mosaic law, as the Judaisers desired, but could trace their spiritual roots back beyond Moses to Abraham. The same would be true for all those unknown believers who have lived without knowledge of Christ, for their faith is endorsed by God in his dealings with the father of all the faithful.

Paul goes on to expound the true quality of Abraham's faith (v.18-22). The aged and childless patriarch had been promised the marvel of being the father of many nations. How could that be? Abraham did not ask; he faced the facts and did not waver, because he believed God would do the impossible and keep his promise. That is the faith God is looking for and has been looking for among all those who have never heard the name of Christ.

Paul concludes by linking the faith of Abraham to the faith of all who believe in Jesus, as described in 3:22-26, and so ends the digression concerning Abraham (v.23-25). Note: *The words "it was credited to him" were written not for him alone, but also for us* (v.23,24). And we may add, 'not only for us but also for all who believe in God as Abraham did'. His example cannot be limited to those who believe in Jesus, for the essential quality of his trust was that it rested in God. Since biblical writers assume that human beings know about God and should trust God, it cannot be argued that non-Christians cannot have faith in God. Nor is their limited knowledge of God a fatal drawback, since Abraham's knowledge of God was fragmentary compared with the revelation we have in Christ. On the other hand it is true that the revelation of God in Christ was designed to make faith attainable by the masses in a way that was not possible before. Paul delighted in the universality of the gospel, which made salvation available to people of all nations on equal terms with the Jews.

Despite the powerful evidence of Romans 4 on the principle of salvation by faith in God alone, there are those evangelicals who claim that salvation is only possible for people who believe in Christ and therefore those who have not heard of him cannot be saved.[174] This view is sometimes called restrictivism. However to argue that faith in God is not adequate for salvation is to be guilty of splitting the Trinity, as if faith in Christ is effective but faith in God is not! Those who wish to restrict the possibility of salvation to those who hear the gospel, also argue that saving faith in the Old Testament was limited to Abraham and his descendants. They say that only Jews could be saved, because of their covenant relationship with God, which provided them with the revelation they needed to believe.[175] This argument is also unbiblical, because it ignores the covenants that preceded the Mosaic covenant and refuses to accept the biblical teaching on general revelation. The covenants God made with Adam and Noah embraced humanity and concerned the salvation of the human race. The covenant with Abraham was specifically given for the blessing of the nations (Gen. 12:3). As for general revelation, we have seen that Paul's argument in Romans 1-3 is entirely dependent on the adequacy of man's knowledge of God and his moral laws.[176] Faith in God was possible, even though salvation by works was not.

Salvation is not limited in the Old Testament to Abraham and his Jewish descendants. Some of the non-Jews who are mentioned as being accepted by God include Abel, Enoch, Noah, Melchizedek, Job and Naaman. No one doubts that the men of God who lived before Abraham were saved and Hebrews 11:4-7 tells us how they were saved – they were saved by faith. We have noted already that Melchizedek is given special prominence in Hebrews. Some have argued that we know little about this king of Jerusalem and therefore cannot deduce any theological principles from what is said about him. That is not what the writer of

---

[174] E.g. D.A. Carson, *The Gagging of God*, Leicester, 1996, pp.297f. A. Fernando, *Sharing the Truth in Love*, Grand Rapids, 2001, p.216f.

[175] D.A. Carson, op.cit., p.298.

[176] Cf. Vatican II: "Those also can attain everlasting salvation who through no fault of their own do not know the gospel of Christ or his church, yet sincerely seek God and moved by his grace, strive by their deeds to do his will as it is known to them through the dictates of conscience"(*Dogmatic Constitution on the Church*, chap. 16).

Hebrews thought! He deduced some very radical conclusions from the three verses given to him in Genesis 14:18-20 (Hebrews 7:1-22). Similarly it is said of Job that we know very little about him, but we certainly know a great deal more about him from the 42 chapters of Job than we do about many Old Testament prophets. In particular we know how his faith was refined and focused through suffering to rest in God alone.

Reliance on the atoning sacrifice of Christ for the sins of the world is vital in explaining how people, who lived before Christ, could be forgiven by God. Scripture indicates that the sacrifice of the cross was planned before the foundation of the world (Rev.13:8). Just as Christ's sacrifice is effective for all who have lived since he died, so the cross is the ground on which God forgave all who lived before him. Since Christ's sacrifice was planned from eternity, it is effective both BC and AD, and is therefore effective for all who believe in God. It is not only effective for all time but universally for all people in all places. The cross is God's means of salvation for all who have a faith like Abraham's, even if like him they have never heard the gospel of Jesus.

Galatians 3

In Galatians 3 Paul refers to Abraham and again quotes Genesis 15:6 (3:6). Once again he shows the Gentile Christians that they do not have to listen to the Judaisers and submit to the yoke of the law, because they are children of Abraham and inheritors of the gospel God gave him for the nations. They are justified by faith just as Abraham was, not by law, which is impotent to save.

Once again Paul expounds the principle of Abrahamic faith as the key to salvation. He affirms that *those who have faith are blessed along with Abraham, the man of faith* (3:9). Some assume that this faith must be faith in Christ. But Paul does not say so. Paul was writing to Gentile Christians and it was true that they had been enabled to believe by Christ. Nevertheless Paul's argument relates to Abraham, whose example predates Jesus and anticipates his work. The fundamental principle that Paul aims to establish is that salvation is by faith in God, who provided for the salvation of the nations through Abraham.

Paul also says that justification by faith is not something entirely unheard of before Christ, for it was anticipated in the promise to Abraham.

That is why he can say, the gospel was announced in advance to Abraham (v.8). What was that gospel? It was the gospel of the inclusion of the people of other faiths and nations who had been excluded from Israel, i.e. those who had not heard the gospel. It was and is God's purpose to make known the good news of salvation for the entire world. This is not universalism, for the Scripture foresaw that God would justify the nations **by faith.** Without faith it is impossible to please God (Heb.11:6). On the other hand salvation by faith is not restricted to those who have faith in Jesus. The preaching of Christ clearly portrayed as crucified for the sins of the world (v.1) is the means God has provided for the liberation of all who believe (v.14, 22). But for those who have never heard the good news, Abraham is still the symbol of hope, for he had never heard of the cross, yet was adjudged to have the faith that saves.[177]

The only hope for people who have never heard of Christ is not devotion to their faith or religious observances, and not fasting and uprightness of life, but faith in God alone on the pattern of Abraham. What God is looking for is not the extent of their knowledge but evidence of their faith.

---

[177] It will be asked, 'Who are these people who have never heard the gospel, yet have faith in God alone?' An answer to that question deserves a book in itself, but one example can be given here. Guru Nanak, the founder of what has become Sikhism, was convinced that no one can be saved apart from the grace of God. He rejected all other ways. He was a monotheist, who believed in one God only, and knew that human beings are doomed without the grace of God. He cast himself entirely on the mercy and grace of God for salvation.

Chapter Four

Relations Between Christians and People Of Other Religions

WHAT PRACTICAL ADVICE WAS GIVEN TO CHRIST'S FOLLOWERS living in the pluralist world of the first century with Greek and Roman and Jewish neighbours? What was to be their attitude to people of many different religious cults? How were they to behave towards people who might be hostile toward them? Most of the evidence comes from the New Testament letters. But first we begin with the teaching and example of Jesus in the Gospels.

What advice did Jesus give his disciples?

On a superficial reading of the Gospels it appears that Jesus did not tell his disciple how to relate to non-Jews. But in the Sermon on the Mount he had three key things to say, which reveal his attitude to all people whatever their religious affiliation. He taught his disciples to follow these principles and he reinforced his teaching by his own example. These three keys to harmonious inter-faith relations are:

- Love your neighbour, especially your enemies, and pray for those who persecute you.

- Do not judge or you too will be judged, for in the same way you judge others, you will be judged.

- Do to others what you would have them do to you.

Jesus practised what he preached. That is one reason why he is respected by the followers of many religions. I recently read about an Arab, who is proud to trace his ancestry to the prophet Mohammed. He studied many religions and finally began to read the New Testament. What impressed him about Jesus was that here was a religious leader who lived exactly as he taught others to live.

Here is the challenge for Christ's followers: can we practise what he preached?

Love your enemies : Matthew 5:43-48

Who were the enemies Jesus was referring to? The immediate audience that was listening to Jesus consisted of disciples, the crowd was in the background, and the teaching of the Pharisees was in part what he sought to refute. Although the Pharisees often opposed Jesus, it seems unlikely that he had them in mind. The mention of tax collectors and pagans (v.46f.) suggests a more obvious enemy. The Romans and those who collaborated with them were the people his Jewish audience would most likely have thought of as enemies. The Roman military and the administration of the procurator, Pilate, were the ones who persecuted them.

Once again Jesus challenged the assumptions and prejudices of his hearers. He called on them to love their oppressors as they loved their own people, their brothers by race and religion. As in the parable of the Good Samaritan, so here Jesus broadened the concept of neighbour to include all non-Jews. In this case the conclusion was even more shocking than in the parable, because here Jesus called on Jews to love the hated Romans who did them harm. Jesus saw the look of incredulity on his disciples' faces as he said these words, so he gave them a reason. The reason Jesus gave for this offensive teaching was not that the word 'neighbour' includes everyone, but that God loves everyone and so his people must do the same. Love is also defined not as a sentiment but as an action. God does good to all, so must we. God gives to all, so must we (v.45). God's love is perfect in the sense that it embraces all without distinction (v.48).[178] Or as the parallel verse in Luke puts it: *Be merciful,*

---

[178] The word 'perfect' (Gk. *teleios*) means 'complete'.

just as your Father is merciful (Luke 6:36). God even does good to the 'unrighteous', such as the tax collectors and pagans.

The application to our multi-faith society could not be clearer. Not only are we to love people of all religions and none, we are also to love those we consider collaborators with evil and to love them even when they persecute us or God's people. In these days when Christians are attacked and killed in many countries, it is all too easy to adopt a collective hostility to the adherents of other creeds. The first step in countering such instinctive prejudice is to pray for those we perceive as enemies, asking God to bless them as generously as he has blessed us. The second step is to express love in action by doing whatever we can for those who are not Christians. If our love is of God it will be practical, generous and long-suffering.

We know Jesus had enemies and he had some harsh things to say to them. But he never rejected them and showed what love means by dying for them and forgiving them. What does it mean for us to love people of other faiths who persecute us? Can we forgive them? Can we keep talking to them? Can we do them some good?

Judge not : Matthew 7:1-4

Just as tough for some of us are Jesus' warning words: *'Do not judge, or you too will be judged'*.

In our critical age these warning words of Jesus are likely to be ignored. We are so determined to exercise our critical faculties that any suggestion we should curb them is likely to be seen as a threat to our freedom. So what did Jesus mean? He taught us to be discerning; for example, a few verses later he told his disciples to watch out for false prophets (7:15-20). Most commentators, therefore, understand 'judge' in this context to mean 'censorious condemnation of another'.[179]

We have no right, says Jesus, to pass sentence on people, as if we had the authority to judge them. That is God's prerogative, which he will exercise on Judgement Day. If we abrogate to ourselves God's role, we will be judged. In fact the way we judge others will be used as the

[179] See R.A. Guelich, *The Sermon on the Mount: A Foundation for Understanding*, Waco, 1982, p.350.

measure by which God will judge us (v.2). Clearly many of us who think we are Christ's disciples do not believe this, otherwise we would be more restrained in our speech and more generous in our thinking. Could it be that God will condemn us as severely as we condemn others?

Some of us are very critical of people of other faiths and condemn them for their beliefs and practices.

Bonhoeffer[180] argued that when we condemn others not only do we behave as if we are the judge not God, but also our condemnation of others has no positive effect. It does not spring from a desire to reconcile others to God, but actually sends them further away from God. In the process we ourselves are separated from the other person and from God. So however right we may be in criticising the errors in the beliefs and practices of others, we are wrong to aggravate the disunity between us.

Jesus calls on us to examine ourselves. Do we have an attitude of superiority from which we look down on others and reject them? One sign of such superiority is to be judgmental and dismissive of people who belong to other faiths. This can easily occur if we assume we are superior to others, because we belong to the one and only Saviour of the world. The fact that Christ is superior does not make us superior. Besides though he was God, Christ humbled himself and took upon him the form of a servant. The humility of Christ is not a threat to other faiths. That is one reason why so many religions respect Jesus despite his exclusive claims. Unfortunately his followers often give the impression that they look down on others even in the act of sharing the good news from God.

In verses 3-5 Jesus puts his finger on the fault of the Pharisees. They saw the faults of others, not their own. The point of the contrast between a speck and a plank is not that we criticise people for the very same sins we commit. It is worse than that. We see the peccadilloes in others and miss the huge sins in our own lives. Of course the peccadilloes might seem large to us but they are small in comparison to our own sins. It is easy to see things that we think are wrong in people of a different creed and culture, and to wish to correct them. Jesus suggests that quickness to criticise and correct springs from self-righteousness. We do this because we are confident of our rightness with God, instead of humbly walking

[180] D. Bonhoeffer, *Ethics*, Minneapolis, 2005, pp.313ff.

with God and being open to his correction. He expects us to look in the mirror of his word and see how large our own faults are, so that we admit them and remove them. We are expected to remove a monster, because it is so large we cannot miss it. Only then can we see clearly to help remove a minute speck from a brother's eye.

Does this mean that we should not use our critical faculties? Are we to avoid all critical study of other religions and their scriptures? Surely not. As we have seen the New Testament rejects false religious beliefs and practices such as idolatry. In 7:1,2 Jesus warned us not to condemn people and reject them, but he did not reject the right use of the mind to discern what is untrue and to expose ways that do not lead to God. Criticism is valid not only of things but of people, so Jesus told us to watch out for false prophets and to discern them by what they do. The injunction 'condemn not' does not mean that we should be so uncritical that we accept people for what they claim to be without checking their credibility, or that we accept their teaching without scrutiny. The repeated words of Jesus, 'You have heard it said … but I tell you' in Matthew 5:21-44 show that he consistently examined what others taught and contrasted the true with the misleading. In 7:3-5 he does not say that it is wrong to remove even the tiniest hindrance to spiritual vision, only that it is hypocritical to ignore our own blindness by focusing on the minor blemishes of another.

Jesus was critical of his own people. In keeping with the prophetic tradition of Israel he spoke bluntly to warn his people so that they might be saved, rather than uttering the bland words they wanted to hear. In relation to non-Jews like the Capernaum centurion he was gentle, and on trial for his life he even impressed Pilate. In all cases Jesus was careful not to pass dismissive judgement on Jews or Gentiles, even if he had to correct their errors. He was always conscious that he came to save not to reject and condemn.

For us there is particular value in relating to those whose ideas and practices are different from our own. As we relate to people of other faiths, the closer we get to each other the more we are challenged. Sometimes unconsciously they hold up a mirror to us, in which we can see where we need to change. Or through them we may discern our blind spots. When our eyes are opened we may see what God is doing in our brother and what he wants to do to reconcile this child of his to himself. Instead of hostile condemnation we can be agents of healing and reconciliation, when our eyes ore opened.

The Golden Rule : Matthew 7:12

In everything, do to others what you would have them do to you.

It is easy to say treat others as you would like to be treated by them – even those who do not believe in God think this is a fine saying. To practise this teaching is very hard. To love others as we love ourselves and behave toward them in this way requires at least four steps.

First it implies that we must treat even those we do not understand or appreciate with respect. It is easy to respect those we admire, but what about people of a different culture who do things that seem to us strange and offensive. They may also find our ways obnoxious. Before we write each other off, we should try to understand why they behave as they do

Next we should treat people of other faiths as one of us, one of God's creatures, one with us in the human family on earth. At the heart of racism is the divide between 'them' and 'us'. 'They' do not belong to 'us' and 'they' are inferior to 'us'. Such an attitude should be impossible for a disciple of Christ, for we know we are all created by God, all are equal and all belong to one race, the human race.

Next we are to realise that God loves others as much as he loves us, for he has made them in his image and died for them. Seeing people from God's viewpoint is an essential step toward getting out of the self-centred mode in which we were born. As long as we remain in ego mode we cannot treat others as we should. Viewing people as God views them helps us to see their worth.

The next step is to see things as others see them. Put yourself in their shoes and try to see everything from their viewpoint. Jesus took on flesh to see things from our side. How much easier it should be for us to imagine how our fellow human beings feel. Even so it takes a positive act of the will and the imagination to see things from another's situation.

When we have begun to see people of other faiths with respect, with equality, with God's love and from their viewpoint we are able to begin to do what Jesus had in mind. This approach will help us to avoid rejecting others out of prejudice and belittling their faith. Positively, we will be able to love others. For example, instead of fearing our Muslim neighbours, we should accept them as one of us, get to know them, help them out when they are in need, support them in trouble, welcome them to eat with us, pray for them and share with them the spiritual blessings God has given us.

To see how Jesus practised the Golden Rule we can examine the ways he treated the people he met, as recorded in the Gospels. Everyone was different and therefore he dealt with everyone differently according to their needs. Take for example the story of his encounter with the Samaritan woman. Despite her unconventional behaviour Jesus gave her respect, treated her with equality as a fellow human being, saw her deepest needs and led her patiently toward a new beginning. Notice also that she was a foreigner and a member of a different religion. She belonged to what Jesus regarded as a heretical sect. None of this put Jesus off or affected the respect and care he showed her.

In the verses that precede 7:12, Jesus spoke of God as the Father who loves to give. Just as we like to receive gifts, so God intends that we should give good gifts to others, for that is his nature. What good gifts would we want to be given, if we had grown up in another religious community? What would it mean for us to do to the followers of Mohammed, Sai Baba, Guru Nanak, Buddha or any other religious leader around us, what we would like them to do to us? When we seek their best interests, not our rights, then we will be on the way to fulfilling the Golden Rule.[181]

What advice is given in the New Testament to members of the *ekklesia* concerning their relations with people of other religions?

The lofty claims made for Christ by his apostles must have sounded laughable to their contemporaries. Whether in Ephesus, Athens, Corinth or Rome, Christians were a tiny minority in a sea of other faiths. Often regarded as members of an outlandish Jewish sect, the small groups of Jewish and Gentile believers must have struggled to assert their new

---

[181] R.A. Guelich, op.cit., pp.379ff.

identity as followers of the Way. How then were they taught to relate to their neighbours, whether worshippers of one God or many?

The answer to this question is to be found in the letters of the New Testament.[182] Although these are mostly concerned with the spiritual growth of the disciples and with their internal relationships in the church, there is evidence of the advice they were given for their interaction with society around them. This teaching can be divided into four parts, according to whether the advice concerns relations with all non-believers, with Gentiles, with Jews or with governments.

Relations with outsiders

The relation of believers to non-believers is grounded in the nature of God, as revealed by Christ. Christ has demonstrated the essence and extent of God's love. Just as his love was not confined to the circle of the chosen few, but extends to all his creatures, so believers were to reflect his unlimited love. This conviction is plainly expressed in the first letter of John: *God is love. Whoever lives in love lives in God, and God lives in him* (4:16). The same point is also stated negatively: *Whoever does not love does not know God, because God is love* (4:8). Although John was primarily writing about love for the brethren, he knew that God loves all. Therefore believers were to reflect God's love both for their brother Christian and for their brother man. The extension of love for the brethren to love for everyone is explicitly made in 1 Thessalonians 3:12: *May the Lord make your love increase and overflow for each other and for everyone else.*

Writing to the small band of Christians in Rome, Paul applied the command to love your neighbour as yourself to their situation in a pagan society. He called on them to love all their fellow-men (Rom. 13:8-10). This was a confident move, showing no signs of paranoia or of a minority complex. Following as it does on a paragraph urging respect for and submission to the Roman government, it shows that Paul wanted Christians to react positively to people around them. Though most of their neighbours would have been worshippers of many gods and devotees of the emperor, they were to treat them with the same love they

---

[182]   Our concern in this section is to see what advice was given to the rank and file members of the early church by their leaders.

owed to each other. Paul's language is striking. He has told his readers to pay their debts, and owe no-one anything. But there is one thing they should always owe, the debt of love for their fellow human beings. They are reminded of the Decalogue and told they will fulfil it, if they love their neighbour, because *love does no harm to its neighbour* (13:10).

Writing more to Jewish believers than to Gentiles, James also quoted the neighbour love command (James 2:8). He called it *the royal law*. His application was different. He used the command to attack favouritism. His target was the people who ignore the poor but flatter the rich. However the stress on inclusivity is similar. God's love reaches out to all, so the believers must do the same.

Love is practical, as 1 John 3:18 teaches. Some aspects of love in action for those outside the church are mentioned in the Epistles. Here are a selection. Love is based on respect. Respect for everyone whatever their religion is fundamental to a harmonious society. Peter called on God's elect throughout the provinces that covered a large part of modern Turkey to *show proper respect to everyone* (1 Peter 2:17). James reminded his readers of the call to be merciful, a prominent theme of Jesus' teaching in the Gospels (2:13). The writer to the Hebrews seems to have had more in mind than the need to provide hospitality for visiting preachers, when he wrote, *do not forget to do good and to share with others* (13:16). Paul told the believers in the multi-ethnic port of Corinth, *Do not cause anyone to stumble, whether Jews, Greeks or the church of God*. He was referring to disputes over eating food offered to idols, but the principle was of wider application. Paul certainly took it to be so and urged the believers to *try to please everybody in every way* and aim for *the good of many* (1 Cor. 10:31-11:1).

After love, the second most prominent theme in the advice given to believers concerning their relations with everyone around them is peace. *Make every effort to live in peace with all men* (Heb. 12:14). The spread of the gospel depended on peaceful conditions.[183] Early Christianity did not advance by military conquest, in keeping with the example and teaching of its founder. Despite opposition from Jews and Romans, the believers

---

[183] See 1 Tim. 2:2,4, where Paul recognises the link between peaceful conditions and the spread of the gospel.

were taught not to respond with aggression of any kind.[184] Paul, who knew more than anyone else about the violent backlash of those who were provoked by the preaching of the crucified Messiah, also knew the importance of passive resistance. He urged the Christians at Rome to *live at peace with everyone*. But significantly, he prefaced this instruction with the words: *if it is possible, as far as depends on you* …(Rom. 12:18). He knew both that the behaviour of others could not be guaranteed and that Christ himself had predicted that his mission and message would bring division not peace.[185]

Whatever others might do, it was important not to return evil for evil, wrong for wrong, hatred for hate, but rather to be kind to everyone (Rom. 12:7; 1 Thess. 5:15; Tit. 3:3; 1 Pet. 3:9). All this is summed up in one sentence in the letter to Titus, where Christians are told: *Remind the people to be subject to rulers and authorities, to be obedient, to be ready to do whatever is good, to slander no-one, to be peaceable and considerate, and to show true humility towards all men* (3:1, 2). The Cretans were notoriously quarrelsome. The Greek historian, Polybius, accused them of habitually engaging in "insurrections, murders and internecine wars."[186] They were bluntly told that a Christian's aim is to be 'peaceable' (lit. 'not a fighter'). To this end they were to refrain from slandering anyone and to behave with humility (lit. 'meekness') to all.

A third concern of the writers of the Epistles was that Christians should win the respect of outsiders, however hostile they might be. This is an important theme of Peter's first letter. Writing to Christians suffering severely under persecution, Peter advised them to be sure that they did not in any way deserve punishment because of wrongdoing, but rather earned the respect of others by the way they bore unjust attacks. *Live such good lives among the pagans, that, though they accuse you of doing wrong, they may see your good deeds and glorify God on the day he visits us* (2:12). Paul commended the Thessalonians for their reputation as model believers throughout Macedonia and Achaia. But this did not prevent him also advising them that they must work hard to *win the respect of outsiders* (1 Thess. 4:12). They were to do this by getting their hands dirty to earn

---

[184]   For the response to persecution see the next section.
[185]   Luke 12:51.
[186]   W. Barclay, *The Letters to Timothy, Titus and Philemon,* Edinburgh, 1956, p.296.

their own living, so as not to be dependent on others. It was especially important for Christian leaders *to have a good reputation with outsiders*, so that they would not disgrace the church (1 Tim. 3:7).

There was one more important obligation on believers and that was to pray for everyone. Paul wrote: *I urge, then, first of all, that requests, prayers, intercession and thanksgiving be made for everyone – for kings and all those in authority* (1 Tim. 2:1ff.). This is an impressive passage, for it requires that the church pray for all including the emperor, kings and governors, who were often enemies of the church. It also requires prayer for all people, whatever their status, race, religion or gender. Also noteworthy is the wealth of words used to describe this prayer. The four different terms used for prayer suggest a comprehensive submission to God of the needs of everyone in society. The object of the prayer is not only the wellbeing of people and the peace of the world, but also that all should be saved and come to a knowledge of the truth.

Relations with people of other religions

Although the New Testament does not set out to define the way Christians were to live with their unbelieving neighbours, everyday issues affecting food, work, family and friends are dealt with.

Food. Many religions have strict food laws and these drastically affect the way their adherents treat outsiders who do not belong to their community. In the first century Jews had such strict food laws that they could not eat with Gentiles. Most current world religions attach importance to directions about the eating of food. For example, high caste Hindus have traditionally refused to eat what is cooked by a low caste person. Muslims shun those who eat pork and insist on buying, cooking and eating halal meat, just as Jews insist on eating food that is kosher. Paul, in sharp contrast to his upbringing, declared that food has nothing to do with spirituality. *Food does not bring us near to God; we are no worse if we do not eat, and no better if we do* (1 Cor. 8:8). What we eat does not affect our standing with God. What matters to God is righteousness, peace and joy inspired by his Spirit, not food and drink (Rom. 14:17). Therefore we should judge no one on the basis of their eating habits, whether vegetarian or non-vegetarian. As a result of Paul's radical stand, Christians were free to socialise with their neighbours of other faiths (1 Cor. 10:27). They could visit their homes or invite them for a meal with their family.[187] This made them very different from Jews, who tended to cut themselves off from social intercourse, because of their food restrictions. Christians were not confined to living in a ghetto of their own making, and were free to mingle with the polytheistic communities around them.

Work. Paul's approach to the work situation of slaves and masters was equally radical. This is relevant to the relations of believers and Gentiles, since converted slaves and masters were far more likely to be Greek or Roman than Jewish. Take first the advice that Paul, and also Peter, gave to slaves who had joined the church. It seems fair to assume they would have been working for owners, who were not Christians. Were they to refuse to work for pagan masters, because they believed in many gods and worshipped idols? We may be so used to the language of the New Testament that Paul's comments seem innocuous. But if we were to imagine ourselves living 2000 years ago in the place of those slaves and to hear Paul say, *Obey your pagan master, as if he were Christ*, would we not be shocked? Paul said to Christian slaves at Ephesus: *Obey your earthly masters with respect and fear, and with sincerity of heart ... serve (them) wholeheartedly, as if you were serving the Lord, not men* (6:5,7). Whatever his religion, race, character or behaviour, the master was to be respected and obeyed, because of his God-given role in society. Christians could work for unbelievers, just as much as for fellow believers. This was both demanding and liberating: demanding, because the standards for work and loyalty were set so high and liberating, because the Christian slave was no longer working for a tyrant but for Christ. Therefore the rewards on offer were far higher than the master's terms. The slave could aspire to the same rewards as a free man, *because you know that the Lord will reward everyone for whatever good he does, whether he is slave or free* (6:8).[188] Peter takes up the agony of the mistreated slave and lifts his status by comparing him to Christ, who was enslaved and executed for no fault of his own. Christ did not retaliate, nor should Christian slaves retaliate

---

[187]   See Ben Witherington, *Conflict and Community in Corinth: A Socio-Rhetorical Commentary on 1 and 2 Corinthians*, Grand Rapids and Carlisle, 1995, p.227. Witherington comments: "Paul distinguishes between eating at home and eating in temples and strictly forbids the latter."

[188]   In Colossians 3:24, Paul identified the reward as *an inheritance from the Lord*.

against unbelieving overlords, however cruel, for God will vindicate them as he has vindicated his Son. Clearly the religious affiliation and practice of an employer should have no effect on the Christian's respect, loyalty and work.[189]

The teaching for slave owners follows similar lines. How were Christian masters to treat their slaves, most of whom would have been polytheists? Whether their slaves were believers or not, should make no difference to the owner's behaviour. *Masters, treat your slaves in the same way*, wrote Paul. They are not to threaten them, but to provide for them and give them what is fair and just (Eph. 6:9; Col. 4:1). The reason given for this even-handed approach removes any grounds for the assertion of superiority or even a patronising attitude. Employers were to remember *that he who is both their Master and yours is in heaven, and there is no favouritism with him* (Eph. 6:9). Before God slaves and masters were both on the same level, even though on earth they had different positions and status. God will not side with the believing master against the slave, whatever his religion. If the slave became a believer, as Onesimus did, then the owner's responsibility was even greater, and he was expected to treat him as a dear brother in the Lord (Philemon 16).

Family. In many communities a change in religion by husband or wife has been the signal for rejection, persecution, expulsion, divorce and disinheritance. Not so in the early church. Paul, as in other matters, took a different line from the Jewish practice he had been brought up to observe. For converts at Corinth he ruled that new Christians should stay with their unbelieving partners, unless the partner wished to leave. In 1 Corinthians 7:12-16 Paul gave his ruling on this contentious matter. He mentioned two important principles. First, that the unbelieving husband or wife and the children of their marriage have been sanctified by their relationship with the converted partner. The thought seems to be that the believer's relation with God extends to their partner and children, because the one who has been sanctified is set apart for God. Although believers are not encouraged to marry unbelievers, in the case of a couple

---

[189] See also Tit. 2:9, 10, where it is assumed that the masters are not believers. Therefore it is important that Christian slaves give up their old habits of stealing and talking back, thereby demonstrating the attractive power of a gospel that changes the untrustworthy into reliable servants.

where one partner has been converted after marriage, the conversion of the one leads to blessing for the other partner and their children.

The second principle is that, *God has called us to peace* (v. 15). Harmony in the home is of the greatest importance. Wherever possible this should be achieved by keeping believer and unbeliever together. But if the friction and tension between husband and wife becomes too great and the unbeliever wishes to leave, he or she should be free to do so and the believer should not be blamed for letting their partner go. Here again Paul's advice had the effect of fostering good relations with pagan communities and mitigating the dislocation caused by conversion.

Friends. More controversial are the references in the Epistles, which suggest that Christians should avoid friendship with the world. The sharpest warning against contact with unbelievers is given in 2 Corinthians 6:14 – 7:1, where Paul says, *Do not be yoked together with unbelievers.* This has often been used in church history by exclusive groups to justify their withdrawal from contact with those they disapproved of. How should this passage and the warnings against friendship with the world be understood?

Before dealing with 2 Corinthians 6:14ff., it will be helpful to look at other warnings against the ways of the world. A typical example is James 4:4: *You adulterous people, don't you know that friendship with the world is hatred towards God? Anyone who chooses to be a friend of the world becomes an enemy of God.* The context shows that, what James was attacking was not contact with non-Jews, but loving what the world loves. In particular he denounced his readers' motives, such as envy and greed. They wanted something to spend on their own worldly pleasures (v.4). James issued a call for purity of heart, submission to God and resistance to the real enemy, the devil (vv. 7-10). Similarly, the well known passage in 1 John 2:15ff. targets love of the world, and the lusts and boasting it inspires. Peter encouraged the brethren not to avoid people in the world, but to abstain from sinful desires and the things pagans chose to do. They were to treat the world as a foreign country (1 Pet. 2:11; 4:3). In his letters to Ephesus and Colossae, Paul instructed the church not to live as the Gentiles do and as they had once lived (Eph. 4:17; Col. 3:7). *Have nothing to do with the fruitless deeds of darkness, but rather expose them* (Eph. 5:11). Paul specifically made the point, when writing to Corinth, that he was not asking believers to avoid all contact with Gentiles. *In that case you would have to leave this world* (1 Cor. 5:10). The warnings in the New Testament are directed not against meeting with unbelievers, but against living as the world lives.

What then of 2 Corinthians 6:14 – 7:1?[190] Paul concluded this section by an appeal for purity of body and spirit, not by a call to have nothing to do with people who did not belong to the church (7:1). In the earlier verses he clearly identifies idolatry as the evil, which the new converts must totally abandon. Since they had been idolaters, so it was vital that they should break completely with this aspect of their past. The reason given is that they now belong to the temple of God, indeed, as a company of Christian believers,[191] they are *the temple of the living God.* There can be no compromise on this point. Hence Paul's strong contrasts in vv. 14,15 between righteousness and wickedness, light and darkness, Christ and Belial.[192] Viewed in context, the injunction not to be yoked with unbelievers, prohibits permanent relationships being formed between Christians and those who worship other gods. Separation from the world involves separation from ungodly people as well as from worldly ways. Respect for neighbours is one thing, union with opponents is another. Whatever love for neighbours demands, it does not require living like the world or alliance with the world.

The nature of the church as a multi-ethnic community comprised of people from many nations as well as Jews made it radically different from the synagogue. Nowhere was the contrast sharper than in its attitude to Gentiles. Israel's hostility to the nations was only partially mitigated by the phenomenon of the Jewish diaspora. In the church on the other hand, converts from all races were accepted on equal terms. The nations were no longer excluded, but embraced as beloved by God. Therefore the distinction between Jews and Gentiles ceased to have its old

[190]   It is standard practice for commentators to note that these verses break the train of thought between 6:14 and 7:2, and appear unusual for the puritanism they express.

[191]   See 1 Cor. 3:17.

[192]   C.K. Barrett comments that, "the question (v.15) is intended rather to make the point that one cannot be a believer and an unbeliever at the same time than that Christians and non-Christians may have no contact with each other" (*The Second Epistle to the Corinthians*, London, 1973, p.199).

significance. Gentiles could no longer be thought of as enemies, second class or outsiders *per se*, and outsiders could no longer be equated with Gentiles. For Paul the fundamental distinction between people was no longer racial, but between the new humanity in Christ and those who still belonged to the old order of Adam.[193]

Relations with Jews

All the writers of the New Testament Epistles were Jews. They believed in Jesus as the Christ, Israel's Messiah. This has not deterred some modern writers, both Christian and Jewish, from accusing them of being anti-semitic. Whether it is possible for a Jew to be anti-semitic or not, this accusation sharpens the debate about Jewish-Christian relations in the early church. What do the Epistles have to say about the teaching given to believers concerning their Jewish neighbours?

Luke's account in Acts shows that Paul was attacked by Jews on numerous occasions and in at least ten different cities. Jews instigated mob violence, plotted to kill him and at Lystra stoned him and left him for dead. In 2 Corinthians Paul revealed that he had been given the Jewish punishment of thirty-nine lashes on five separate occasions (2 Cor. 11:14f.). Despite these attacks, Paul never encouraged the church to ignore Jews, attack Jews or be hostile to them. Paul criticised those who were Jews outwardly but not inwardly and was grieved by Israel's rejection of Jesus. He warned his followers of the errors of the Judaisers – Jewish Christians – who wanted Gentile converts to be circumcised and to conform to Mosaic laws. But he remained positive about his own people to the end. In the last glimpse we have of him in Acts, when he arrived in Rome, he went first to the synagogue, winning some and turning to preach to Romans only when his own people had turned against him (Acts 28:17-28).

Paul's views on his fellow countrymen are fully articulated in Romans 9 – 11. What is important here is his advice to Roman Christians on their relations with Jews, who opposed Christ. He vehemently rejected the Jewish accusation that he no longer cared for his fellow Israelites (9:1-5). He passionately longed for their salvation and argued that their

---

[193] See Ephesians 2:11-22; 1 Corinthians 15:22, 45-49.

God-given privileges cannot be taken away from them. At the same time he repeated what he had said earlier in the letter (3:9-30), that there is no difference before God between Jew and Gentile. God is Lord of all and blesses all, who call on him for salvation (10:12, 13). In chapter 11 he specifically addressed Gentile believers and warned them about their attitude to Jews, of whom there were many in Rome. They are not to boast of their superiority over those Jews, who are still outside the kingdom, for that same boasting had been the cause of Israel's undoing (v.18-21). Unbelieving Jews remain natural branches of the olive tree[194] and can be grafted in again if they do not persist in unbelief (v.23f.). It is God's intention that all Israel will be saved (v.25f.). If there was any element of anti-semitism in the church at Rome, Paul wanted to root it out before it could grow any further. *As far as the gospel is concerned, they are enemies on your account; but as far as election is concerned, they are loved on account of the patriarchs, for God's gifts and his call are irrevocable* (Rom. 11:28).

In Paul's first letter to Corinth there are two references to Jews. In 9:20 Paul explained that though he had ceased to adhere to the Jewish customs and law, which he had once observed, he still identified with Jews, in order to share the gospel of Christ with them. This principle of identification as a means of mission, he must have learnt from the incarnation. It is significant for New Testament teaching, because Paul offers himself as an example for Christians to follow, as well as to appreciate. If the believer is strong enough, he or she can place themselves under the restrictions of Jewish law, in order to come alongside their Jewish neighbours and convey Christ's message to them. In 10:32, the unusual grouping together of Jews, Greeks and Christians is connected with the instruction: *Do not cause anyone to stumble*. How might Jews be caused to stumble? In the context of food offered to idols, the most obvious way to cause a Jew to stumble would be to compromise over idolatry. Paul would undoubtedly have wanted his practice of eating with Gentiles to be free from anything that would have given justifiable cause for concern. After all, the Council of Jerusalem had stipulated

[194] "It is only branches which have been cut off, not the whole tree which has been cut down; God has not started afresh from the beginning. The blessings they (Gentiles) share with Jewish Christians must be seen therefore as stemming from the source of Israel...." (James D.G. Dunn, *World Biblical Commentary Vol. 38 Romans 9-16*, Dallas, 1988, p.673).

that the very minimum requirement for Gentile converts was *to abstain from food polluted by idols* (Acts 15:20). On the rejection of idolatry both Jew and Christian should be at one. The principle of avoiding giving offence that might cause someone to stumble is also of wider application. Despite Jewish opposition, Paul directed his churches to be sensitive to Jewish opinion.

The Jewish writer of the book of Revelation had some sharp things to say about Jewish communities in Smyrna and Philadelphia.[195] They are denounced as counterfeit Jews, therefore synagogues of Satan (2:9; 3:9). The real Jews are those who belong to the new Jerusalem and follow the Lamb. Commentators presume that the large and well established Jewish colonies in the cities of Smyrna and Philadelphia must have used their power and influence to persecute the small groups of Christian believers. They probably objected most to the Jewish believers in the churches of the province. Rev. 2:9 does not imply a condemnation of all Jews or the whole Jewish nation, but only that the synagogue in Smyrna had been particularly hostile to Christians and involved in their persecution. It is also worth noting that in the previous letter the church of Ephesus was warned of a similar fate and told that it could lose its place in God's kingdom. Believers are not asked to retaliate against Jews. They are assured that Christ will vindicate them and deal with their oppressors, revealing who are the real people of God.

It should be remembered that this is not the sum total of advice given to believers concerning their attitude and behaviour toward Jews. All that was covered in the first section on the Christian's love for his neighbours, applied to the Jews. Believers were particularly expected to pray for the people of Israel, with whom they had so much in common.

Relations with Political Authorities

So far we have considered the teaching given to Christians on their personal dealings with individuals. The New Testament also defines the relationship of the church with political authorities. The main passages are Romans 13:1-7 and 1 Peter 2:13-17, with important references in Titus

---

[195] See W.M. Ramsay's notes on the Jewish Communities in the Province of Asia in his classic, *The Letters to the Seven Churches of Asia*, London, 1904, pp.142-157.

3:1 and 1 Timothy 2:1-4. The authorities referred to are primarily those of the Roman imperial power and its subsidiaries.

Both Paul and Peter are at one in commanding submission to the emperor and those under him. This they did despite the fact that Paul wrote to Christians in Rome, who lived under the shadow of the imperial presence. Peter may have written his letter from Rome, a few years later, sending it to churches in Asia Minor, who were under the jurisdiction of the Roman governor. Their positive attitude to Rome is remarkable considering that Nero may have already begun to reign, when Peter wrote his first letter. It would be several centuries before the faithful were ruled by a Christian king.

Christians are to support the government under which they live and submit to its laws, because the authorities have been established by God (Rom. 13:1).[196] Rulers and their officials have a moral responsibility, as upholders of law and order, to do good and to punish wrongdoing. No doubt Paul had experienced the beneficial side of Roman justice, which had protected him on more than one occasion from violent mobs. But his argument is theological. He accepted the Old Testament teaching, that Yahweh rules over the kingdoms of this world and it is by his decree that kings rule and princes govern. On the practical level it was essential that the Christian community in Rome should establish a reputation for loyalty and trustworthiness, which would benefit Christians in the rest of the empire. The new congregations were losing their Jewish ethnic identity and therefore the privileges, which the Roman state gave to Judaism. The responsibilities of the Christian citizen to the imperial authority had to be clarified.[197] Paul could not afford churches to turn into centres of subversion, so anyone who was thinking of rebellion was roundly condemned (13:2). Peter is quick to tell those who have enjoyed the intoxicating taste of Christian liberty, not to use their freedom as a cover-up for evil (2:16).

---

[196] Commenting on Romans 13:1 and Cullmann's view that the authorities (*exousiai*) are angelic powers, Dunn observes, "There is nothing therefore in the usage to support the suggestion that *exousiai* here mean also angelic powers behind and acting through political authorities" (JDG Dunn, op.cit., p.760).

[197] "A community which no longer identified itself in ethnic terms could therefore no longer claim the political privileges accorded to ethnic minorities" (JDG Dunn, op.cit., p.769).

This teaching has practical implications as well. Taxes must be paid (Rom. 13:6). 'Give to Caesar, what belongs to Caesar.' The rulers, as God's servants, work full-time for the wellbeing of the populace, so they deserve to be paid and have the right to levy dues. Both Paul and Peter call on Christians to 'respect' (lit. 'fear') and 'honour' the authorities, whether the emperor, his governor or those under them. They are to be honoured as 'God's servants'. Paul repeats the title three times and uses two different words: *diakonos,* the word used for Christian ministries and *leitourgos,* which can mean 'public servant' as well as 'priest'.

As already noted above, Paul believed that the churches had a duty to pray for all people, especially for kings and those in authority (1 Tim. 2:1-5). Paul gave two reasons why Christians should pray for their rulers, even though they worshipped other gods and promoted emperor worship. First, that Christians might enjoy the benefits of peace and protection from violence. Second, that God desires all people to be saved from the emperor down to the lowest slave.

Sadly the relations between Christians and the imperial power changed dramatically not long after Paul and Peter wrote their letters. The Neronian persecution and the years 63-68 AD proved traumatic for the whole church. During those years both apostles are said to have been executed in Rome. Persecution intensified under Domitian. By the time the book of Revelation was written, probably in the AD 90's, the imperial authority was viewed as the agent of the devil (Rev. 13). All inhabitants of the earth worshipped the beast. Verses 15-16 suggest a reference to the enforcement of the cult of emperor worship, since all who refused to worship the image were to be killed (as were thousands of Christian martyrs). Believers were taught to look to God alone to rescue them and reward them in heaven. Even in those dire conditions their only resort was to passive resistance.

Were Christians encouraged to aim for the conversion of their neighbours of other religions?

The scandal of conversion is the major cause of controversy between Christians and the adherents of other faiths in many parts of the world today. Conversion to Christ seems to take people away from their religious communities and transfer them into a new and sometimes foreign community. It causes division in families. To convert from one faith to another implies that there was something missing, something wrong, something inadequate about the religion into which the convert was born. There is a leaving, as well as a cleaving to the new faith. This creates a sense of loss in the family of the convert. Baptism is seen as a cut off point after which the convert ceases to belong to his or her old community. If there is a wave of conversions, communities fight back to preserve their numbers; conversion may then become a political issue. Has this always been the case? How were the first century Christians taught to share their faith? Did they aim for the conversion of their neighbours?

A survey of the Pauline letters shows that Paul was most concerned for the spiritual growth and faithfulness of the church members to whom he wrote. He spoke of himself as the herald and evangelist and preacher and did not ask them to be evangelists. However Christians were encouraged to share their faith and the Epistles mention five different ways in which this was to be done.

By example

Since the New Testament writers laid such store by the example of Jesus, and Paul did not hesitate to ask his churches to follow his example, it would be no surprise to find that the apostles were concerned that their followers should lead by example. The most striking instance of Paul commending a church's example occurs in his first letter to the Thessalonians. Paul was eloquent in his praise of the Thessalonians (1 Thess. 1:6-10). He commended them not only for imitating him but also for being a model (*tupos*) to all the believers in Greece. The Greek word used, *tupos*, originally meant the mark left by a blow, or the print of a nail, as in John 20:25. It then came to mean a copy or an image, and so to be an example or pattern as here. Paul called no other church a pattern for believers. The Thessalonians were called a model for believers in Macedonia and Achaia, the two provinces of Greece (v.8). So effective was their witness, says Paul, that the word of the Lord rang out from them, or 're-echoed' (*execheo*), 'everywhere'. It reverberated like thunder and resounded like the call of a trumpet.

The example of the Thessalonians is commended not only for its effect on believers but for its witness to Greeks. In particular, Paul notes that, *They tell how you turned to God from idols to serve the living and true God, and to wait for his Son from heaven, whom he raised from the dead – Jesus, who rescues us from the coming wrath* (v.10). Luke recorded in Acts 17:4, that when Paul preached in Thessalonica, some Jews were persuaded, but they were outnumbered by many God-fearing Greeks. What impressed Paul was the response of Greek believers in getting rid of their idols. This was the clearest mark of their conversion. They became a model for others to follow.

Elsewhere in the Epistles there are a few references to the importance of witness by example. Peter instructed wives, whose husbands had not yet believed in the gospel, to win them over by their behaviour. Instead of preaching at them, they were to rely on the work of God in their lives. Their purity and reverence and inner beauty would be more effective than words. In similar fashion Titus was told to teach slaves to impress their masters in everything, so that they would be attracted by the message of God's salvation (Tit. 2:10). Paul told the Philippians, *conduct yourselves in a manner worthy of the gospel* (1:27).

By defending the faith

The tiny churches founded by the apostles in the Roman Empire were put under intense pressure by Jewish and polytheist opposition. New converts were not expected to be spokesmen for the gospel. Public speaking was left to the apostles.[198] Believers were told to have the courage to defend their faith when challenged and to give an answer (*apologia*) to their opponents (1 Peter 3:15). The word *apologia* may mean a defence in court (2 Tim. 4:16), but the defence could also be given in informal situations. This would appear to be the meaning in this context, where Christians were to give an answer to anyone at all times for the questions they might ask. Converts might face accusations on any occasion from family, friends, neighbours or hostile crowds. They were to be ready with an answer for their belief in Christ. The emphasis is not only on defending the faith, but also on using the occasion *to give the reason (logion) for the hope that you have*. The Christian is not to be aggressive, but to respond with a reasoned explanation of the way of

[198] See e.g., 1 Tim. 2:7; 2 Tim. 1:11; Rom. 15:15-20; 2 Cor. 4:1-12, 6:1-10; Eph. 6:19-20; Col.4:3,4.

salvation, which inspires him or her. They are to do this with *gentleness and respect*[199] for God and men (v.16). Did Peter remember the occasion when he was accused by two girls and a man of being a follower of Jesus, and failed so miserably in reply?

Paul advised the Colossians to be alert and wise in their conversations with outsiders (Col. 4:5, 6). Like Peter he told them to be always ready to answer anyone who questioned them. It is significant that Paul asked his readers to pray for him, that he would have courage and clarity in proclaiming the message of Christ, but he did not ask his readers to imitate him and engage in public preaching. But they do have a part to play in answering the questions of unbelievers. When their pagan neighbours interrogated them about their new-found faith, they were to make the most of the opportunity to explain what they believed. Paul stressed (as did Peter) the importance of being gracious in the way they talked about their faith. Their conversation should also be *seasoned with salt*. Since salt was valued most as a preservative, it suggests that Paul wanted them to have something wholesome and effective to say, not platitudes and evasions.

There were times when Christians had to defend not only themselves, but also the truth of the gospel (Phil. 1:7, 16, 27). Paul urged the Philippians not to be frightened by the attacks and insinuations of their opponents. They were to stand firm, *contending as one man for the faith of the gospel* (v.27).

By proclaiming the gospel

Occasionally Paul conceded that ordinary Christians might also take part in the proclamation of the gospel. This was the case when he was imprisoned at Rome (Phil. 1:12-30). He admitted that most of the brethren in Rome had been encouraged by his example to preach the word of God fearlessly (v.14). Some preached as rivals of Paul and others preached out of love for him. Either way he was glad that Christ was preached in the city and to the palace guard.

The whole church was called to mission. Despite the special role of apostles as witnesses to the resurrection and as spokesmen for the

---

[199] 'Respect' inadequately translates *phobos* ('fear'), which is more likely to indicate fear for God than fear of man.

faith, there was to be no priestly class in the new Israel. Peter gave a magnificent declaration of the new identity of the scattered groups of believers, to whom he wrote in Asia Minor. He called them *a chosen race, a royal priesthood, a holy nation, God's own people* (1 Pet. 2:9, 10). As the people God had chosen, with a priestly calling, they had the joyful task of declaring to the world what God had done for them, both corporately and individually. Peter's words recall the words of the Psalmist: *Declare his glory among the nations, his marvellous deeds among all peoples* (Ps. 96:3). But the declaration had a new meaning, because the church was open to all peoples, not to one race only. In its ranks Gentiles and Jews had been brought together to form a new humanity. The church was a living demonstration of an open society, which anyone could join, whatever the tribe or religion they had been born into. What were they to declare? Peter singles out three things that God had done for believers, especially for Gentiles. He had brought them out of darkness into light, out of exclusion into inclusion in his people and out of judgement into mercy. They could sing this declaration in worship, but they could also share it in words with the people around them. The declaration was a personal statement and a priestly offering. It was an act of personal testimony to what they had seen and heard and experienced, not the recalling of what God had done in past history. It was their priestly role to represent God to their communities.

By confessing the Lordship of Christ

The book of Revelation implies a different form of witness: the martyr's confession of the Lordship of Christ. The martyrs are said to have been killed, *because of the word of God and the testimony (marturia) they had maintained* (6:9). They are praised for overcoming Satan, *by the blood of the Lamb and by the word of their testimony* (12:11).[200] The implication is that the martyrs refused to bow to the emperor and obey the decree to worship Caesar. For them Christ alone is Lord. There can be no other Lord. Their testimony (*marturia*) was their confession of Jesus as Lord and their faithfulness unto death. In the end this proved the most powerful method of promoting and preaching the way of Christ.

---

[200] In both Rev. 6:9 and 12:11, the Greek word for testimony is *marturia*.

By prayer

Christians are taught to pray for everyone, whatever their race or religion, because God wants all people to be saved and to come to a knowledge of the truth (1 Tim. 2:1-8). The instruction given to Timothy is clear in requiring Christians to pray for everyone. It is not so clear what they are to pray for. The first reason given for praying for everyone, including kings and those in authority, is that people may live in peace. Verses 4-5 seem to indicate a second reason that peace is necessary, so that all may come to know the truth about Christ and the ransom he has paid to be the all-sufficient mediator between God and men.

Summary

Christians were nowhere told to aim for the conversion of their neighbours. What they were told to do was to attract people to Christ by their example, to defend their faith when challenged, to preach the message of Christ boldly and to pray for everyone that God would save them. Those who were bold enough to confess their faith in Christ as Lord and remained faithful to death were assured of a martyr's crown, but not urged to do so that many would be converted by their example.

If the believers were given an aim for sharing their faith it was to make Christ known and to glorify their Lord by their example. Although they would undoubtedly have been glad when outsiders confessed Christ as Lord and joined the church, conversion was not the issue it has now become. No-one was asked to persuade followers of other gods to leave their religious community. Although believers gave up the worship of idols, that was not without parallel, as some Greeks disapproved of idolatry and those attracted by Judaism became monotheists. Believers were not told to aim for the baptism of non-believers. In any case baptism was not a controversial public issue. There is no evidence to suggest that pagans regarded baptism as cutting off converts from their ancestral communities, as is the case today.

There could also have been no question of forcible conversions. Christians were a small and powerless movement. Force and intimidation were frequently used against them. They had no physical power or weapons with which to defend themselves. They relied on God and the spiritual power of their Saviour and Lord. They had no material inducements to offer people, so there was no possibility of anyone becoming a follower of Christ because of offers of money, food or employment.

The aim of church members was to be faithful witnesses. God did the rest, and added to their number those who were to be saved by his grace.

How were Christians taught to respond to persecution by people of other religions?

Acts shows that initially persecution came from the Jewish authorities. When the church began to spread beyond Antioch into Asia Minor and Greece, opposition came not only from some Jews, but also from the local populace and from Roman authorities. The advice given to Christians, instructing them how they should react to persecution, is most impressive. If Christians had always followed this advice and were to follow it now, the world would be a different place and the church's reputation would not have been marred. The church might not have been more popular, but it would have been more credible.

The fact of persecution was taken for granted. There is hardly a letter in the New Testament, which does not refer to opposition and suffering in some form. From the very beginning the church grew through opposition and converts were told to expect suffering and to remain faithful whatever the hardships (Acts 14:22). To suffer is part of the Christian's calling, and the reason for that is not hard to find, for Christ suffered, so why should his followers be exempt. Instead it was seen as a privilege to endure with Christ, to follow his example and to share his sufferings (1 Pet. 2:21; 2 Tim. 3:12; Phil. 1:29f.; Col. 1:24).

Persecution took different forms. Acts describes mob violence, plots, beatings, court proceedings, imprisonment, stoning and attempted murder. Paul added his own list of hardships in 2 Corinthians chapters 4 & 6. But it was not just the apostles and evangelists who were attacked, ordinary Christians also faced hostility. From scattered references we can piece together the following examples of what Christians were subjected to. Verbal abuse was clearly the most common feature, subjecting believers to public insults, threats, slander, cursing and the like (Heb. 10:33; 1 Pet. 3:9, 16; 4:14). Physical assault was common. But worse could follow, such as litigation, being driven out of house and home, confiscation of property, loss of employment, arrest, imprisonment and, in the worst scenario, death (Acts 8:1-3; 22:4, 5; Heb. 10:34; Rev. 2:10; 12:11; 13:15-17).

Opposition was inevitable. How were the new converts to respond? The teaching of the New Testament provides an astounding treasury of non-violent response, from which believers could draw in their hours of humiliation. There is not a word of retaliation, not a hint of armed resistance, not even a mention of self-defence. At the same time this teaching cannot be equated with either stoicism or passive resistance. It went far beyond both in its positive embracing of suffering, inspired by the joy of heaven. What the apostles wrote is convincing and compelling, for they lived what they taught. The teaching can be divided into negative and positive injunctions.

No retaliation

On the negative side, believers are told not to do certain things, when persecution comes to them. Most importantly they are not to hit back. This point was expressed in various ways. They are told not to repay evil with evil, not to trade insults, not to threaten their opponents, not to retaliate and not to seek for revenge.[201] Romans 12:17-21 provides a useful summary: *Do not repay anyone evil for evil …Do not take revenge …Do not be overcome by evil*. The example to follow is Jesus Christ, who refused to retaliate and never stooped to use force, though evil rained down upon him (1 Pet. 2:21-24). Despite being warned of the suffering they could expect, believers were encouraged not to be frightened. Their opponents are the ones who should be afraid of God's judgement, whereas they have nothing ultimately to fear, since they will receive the crown of life (Phil. 1:28; 1 Pet. 3:14; Rev. 2:10). Consequently they are not to be ashamed, if they suffer for Christ. Rather than being overwhelmed by shame the disciples should be full of joy, that they have the privilege of bearing Christ's name (1 Pet. 4:16). The blessing that Jesus pronounced on the

[201] These points are made by Paul and Peter in Rom. 12:14-21 and 1 Peter 2:23, 3:9.

persecuted was never far from their minds. All this presupposes that they are not to be surprised by suffering. Every Christian is to expect it. Peter put the obvious into words: *Dear friends, do not be surprised at the painful trial you are suffering, as though something strange were happening to you* (1 Pet. 4:12).

Bless your oppressor

If the negative instruction, telling them what they should not do, is uncompromising in its clarity, the positive advice on what should be done is impressive for the notes of joy and love that sound above the trials the early church endured. Paul and Peter are not satisfied by saying, 'Do not retaliate,' they go on to say you must bless your persecutors. *Bless those who persecute you, bless and do not curse* (Rom. 12:14).To bless your enemy is more than offering a prayer or pronouncing a benediction, it requires being kind to him and generous in his hour of need. This includes feeding your enemy when he is starving and giving him drink when he is dehydrated with thirst (v.20). It is easy to say 'love your enemy', but Paul's graphic phrases show what that entails. To put it differently, to overcome evil you have to use right means and do good to your opponents (v.21).

Rejoice

The characteristic feature of Christian resistance is not defiance but joy. Paul sang hymns in a Greek jail. He rejoiced whilst chained to a Roman guard. So it is not out of character for him to tell the Philippians to rejoice at all times (Phil. 4:4). James and Peter were more forthright. They told their readers to be full of joy when persecution comes. James appears extravagant in saying: *Consider it pure joy, my brothers, whenever you face trials of many kinds* (1:2; cf. 1 Pet. 4:13). But there are reasons for a joyful response to persecution. Believers can rejoice, because they are counted worthy of suffering, they share Christ's sufferings, they bear his name and they will be overjoyed when his glory is revealed. Joy is not a smiling mask covering intense inner pain. It is the reality of knowing God's approval and the result of the Spirit's presence within.

Stand firm

The core response had to be endurance. Unless the believers stood firm in the faith, the church would have been swept away. Like disciplined soldiers they were to stand their ground, however fiercely they were attacked. This called for patient enduring of a constant stream of abuse or succession of hardships, as Paul knew from personal experience (2 Cor. 6:4ff.). The spirit of perseverance was the product of hardship and in time it produced Christians of maturity (Jam. 1:3f.). Those who persevere to the end will receive the crown of glory and the reward of eternal life. This is the crux of the message of Christ to the seven churches in Revelation. Every one of the seven letters ends with a promise to those who overcome. The overcomers are the saints, who resist every temptation to give in to the attacks of the enemy and remain faithful unto death.[202]

Know your enemy

'Know your enemy' is not only a basic requirement for military strategy but also for spiritual warfare. When the church is attacked it needs to know that the prime mover behind persecution is the devil. Paul put his finger on an important principle when he wrote: *For our struggle is not against flesh and blood, but ... against the spiritual forces of evil in the heavenly realms* (Eph. 6:12). This knowledge keeps the saints focused on their real enemy and helps them to hate evil not their attackers. Knowing that they are opposed by the spiritual forces of evil in the heavenly realms should make the church rely upon God and not on its own resources. This was certainly Paul's intention, for he went on to tell his readers to put on the full armour of God, which would enable them to withstand the devil's assaults. The six parts of the armour are designed for defence. They are not intended to be used against people, and despite the martial metaphor, the Christian is not encouraged to engage in any kind of military action against the enemy.

Support the persecuted

Practical steps should be taken as well as the spiritual ones already mentioned. These included support for those who were being persecuted

[202] See the letters to the seven churches in Rev. 2:7, 11, 17, 26; 3:5, 12, 21.

and the visitation of prisoners. In a rare glimpse of the actual conditions faced by Christians, the author of Hebrews revealed that the converts he was writing to had gone through a baptism of fiery opposition at the time of their conversion (Heb. 10:32ff.). If, as seems likely, the main recipients of the letter were Jewish Christians, these verses give a brief indication of the ferocity of opposition from Jews, who felt their compatriots had become traitors by joining the followers of Jesus Messiah. Some commentators suggest that orthodox Jews would have been outraged by the baptism of converts. But there is no reference in Hebrews 10 to baptism. Acts shows that those Jews, who rejected Paul's presentation of Jesus as the Messiah, incited violence without waiting for anyone to be baptised. In Hebrews the believers were commended for standing side by side with Christians, who were being publicly insulted and attacked. They did so because they had been through the same ordeal and did not hesitate to share the public humiliation of their brethren. They were also commended because they had *sympathised with those in prison* (v. 34). In Hebrews 13:3 they are told to: *Remember those in prison as if you were their fellow-prisoners*. Presumably they not only remembered the prisoners, but also visited or helped them in whatever way they could by gifts of food or clothing. Such public identification with those who had been given a prison sentence by the Roman authorities was never without risk. Imprisonment may not have had any connection with Jewish opposition. Hebrews does not give any clue as to when this Roman action against Christians may have taken place, whether under Claudius or Nero or later.[203]

Imitate Christ

The example of Christ is always held up to Christians as the model to follow. The faithful are to suffer like Christ, to suffer for Christ and to suffer for the gospel. Christ endured humiliation voluntarily. He did not have to expose himself to human malevolence. He suffered vicariously, not for himself, but for others (1 Pet. 2:21ff. & 3:18ff.). So Paul believed

---

[203] The Jews were expelled by the emperor, Claudius, from Rome in AD 49. Christian Jews were probably included. See Acts 18:1f. F.F. Bruce thinks the persecution referred to in Heb. 10:33f. was due to the decree of Claudius (Bruce, *The Epistle to the Hebrews*, Grand Rapids, 1964). The Neronian persecution is usually thought to have begun after AD 64.

that in his tribulations he was sharing in the afflictions of Christ for the sake of the church (Col. 1:24, cf. 1 Pet. 4:13). Here on earth even Christ, the sinless Son of God, was unjustly sentenced and had to rely upon the one who judges justly to vindicate him (1 Pet. 2:23). So too, persecuted believers must entrust themselves to the God of justice, who will vindicate them in glory. Above all it was necessary to be faithful to the very end, as Jesus had been, even if that was a martyr's death.

Trust in God's ultimate victory

Revelation undergirds all this by revealing the divine perspective on the appalling agony of the church under the Domitian persecution.[204] The purpose of the apocalypse is to show that God has an answer for the slaughter of the helpless martyrs. A door is opened in heaven to show God reigning in awesome power and to reveal the future. The power of the devil and his agents on earth will be destroyed. The saints will reign and every human being will bow before Christ, when he returns in glory. Then the nations will find their rightful place in the new Jerusalem. Their kings will submit to God and their wealth will be brought into the holy city. The prophetic vision of Christ's return is to be received and believed. The church must rely on Christ, God's Alpha and Omega, the First and the Last, the Beginning and the End, the bright and Morning Star (Rev. 22:13,16). There is no other rock and no other hiding place.

[204] Domitian was emperor from AD 81-96. If Revelation was written late in the first century, its lightly veiled allusions to the killing of many Christians by Rome would fit with the draconian punishments inflicted by Domitian on all who refused to worship Caesar as Lord.

Part II: The Emerging Picture

What conclusions can be drawn from the survey of the New Testament evidence regarding religions in the first century A.D.? The purpose of the second part of this book is to outline some answers from the New Testament to the questions with which we began in the Preface.

How does God regard the devotees of world religions? Are religions valued or condemned? Is there only one way to God? Is Christian mission to the world only another form of imperialism?

How the New Testament evidence is to be applied to world religions in the 21st century is another subject. The aim here is to find biblical principles that will guide Christians in their relations with people of other faiths.

Chapter Five

God's View of
People of Other Faiths

How does God regard people of other faiths? Does he treat them like second-class citizens? Is God able to communicate with the devotees of world religions? Do they have the spiritual capacity to approach God and exercise true faith in him?

No Favourites

GOD HAS NO FAVOURITES. HE TREATS EVERYONE EQUALLY, whatever their racial or religious label. Acts 10:34, 35 spells this out unambiguously: *Then Peter began to speak: I now realise how true it is that God does not show favouritism but accepts men from every nation who fear him and do what is right.*

If there was one revelation that shattered the attitude of Peter and his fellow apostles to the Gentile world, it was this. No longer could they shelter behind the tenaciously held belief that God was partial to Jews and that all people of other races and religions would have to become Jews in order to gain God's favour. This may seem obvious to us, but in all the centuries that have followed there have been (and still are) Christians, who believe that God is partial to them and gives them preferential treatment.

Acts 10:34, 35 stands out as a key text defining the Christian attitude to other religions. The scope of the statement is universal. God treats people of all nations equally, including Israel. The whole encounter between Peter and Cornelius elaborates on the meaning of God's impartiality toward the nations. He hears the prayers of those who call upon him. He accepts those who fear him and do what is right. He communicates directly with God-fearers in any religion through visions or any other means he chooses. He does not regard any non-Christian as unclean and teaches his servants not to call anyone impure or unclean.

Therefore God wants to bless those of any nation who worship him in faith and obedience, just as he blessed Cornelius. He desires that God-fearers should know the good news of Christ. He gives the Holy Spirit to all who believe in Christ regardless of race and religious background, just as he gave the Spirit to his Jewish disciples. So then all depend equally on God's grace for salvation and enter the kingdom of God on the same basis (Acts 15:8-11).

To this Paul also adds his testimony in Romans 2:11: *God does not show favouritism.* The confines of Paul's Jewish outlook on the Gentiles had also been shattered by a revelation from God. His experience on the Damascus road is the only incident to be given more space in Acts than Peter's meeting with Cornelius. Together, these two encounters with the God of the nations transformed the first disciples from being a Jewish sect into an outgoing world-affirming faith. But we still need to digest the implications of both and apply them to the Christian attitude to people of other religious communities.

In Romans Paul emphasises the equal standing of Jews and Gentiles. To those who do evil there will be trouble, *first for the Jew, then for the Gentile.* To those who by persistence in doing good seek glory, honour and immortality, God will give eternal life (Romans 2:6-10). Paul goes on to spell out the justice of God's even-handed approach: *Is God the God of Jews only? Is he not the God of Gentiles too? Yes, of Gentiles too, since there is only one God, who will justify the circumcised by faith and the uncircumcised through that same faith* (Rom. 3:29, 30).

Paul never ceased to marvel at God's all embracing love for the nations, but he was not the only one. So the New Testament is bursting to tell the good news to everyone – the secret that God is for the whole world as well as for Jews. Because the apostles received and obeyed the revelation of the God who loves all and has no favourites, people from every country on earth have entered the kingdom of God. God continues his impartial treatment of people of all races and religions, whether they are Christians or not. This includes judgement as well as blessing, for partiality does not mean that God is morally neutral and impervious to our actions, whether we do good or evil.

God does not label people according to their religion. He treats everyone as his creatures.

God-given Potential

From the biblical perspective every human being is a unique person created, loved and valued by God, whatever their religion, race, gender, education or wealth. In Christ the privileges given to Israel are extended to all nations. This was powerfully expressed by Paul, for example in his letter to the believers in Ephesus, in what we would now call western Turkey: *Through the gospel the Gentiles are heirs together with Israel, members together of one body and sharers together in the promise in Christ Jesus* (Eph. 3:6).

In the missionary churches of Asia Minor and Greece, Jewish Christians were moved by the Spirit to adopt an amazingly positive attitude to the Gentiles, whom they had previously despised. In Paul's language uncircumcised believers became 'heirs together' with Jews, members of the same body, sharers in the covenants of promise made to Israel.

God does not categorise people according to their religious labels. Even the distinction between Jew and Gentile was abolished in Christ and is no longer fundamental to God's dealings with humanity, because he treats all his creatures on the same basis.

Everyone has spiritual potential, not just Jews and disciples of Christ, for the following reasons.

First, people of all races are created by God in his image. However much this image has been distorted by human pride and evil, it has not been destroyed. All nations are descended from the one man Adam, who was made in the likeness of God (Acts 17:26). That privilege was not reserved for Israel. Furthermore, Christ restores men and women to their true identity and by God's grace overturns the legacy of sin and death left by Adam (Rom. 5:12-21). All nations are dependent on the grace of God for their divine destiny. This is not something that any can pursue as a right, or regard as their inalienable possession. All are dependent on the creator for fulfilment of their potential.

Second, the light of Christ shines on everyone. Christ is the light not of Israel only but primarily of the world. His light has shone on all since creation, but most especially through his incarnation. Christ reveals the nature of God: *No-one has ever seen God, but God the One and Only, who is at the Father's side, has made him known* (John 1:18). He also reveals the full extent of human capabilities and in himself is the example of what any person can become, for the Jew first and also for the Gentile (Eph. 4:13).

Third, the Holy Spirit is omnipresent. From the beginning of time the Spirit has been active throughout the created order. The Spirit is present everywhere and through the Spirit, the Father and the Son are at work in every human being. It is possible that the Spirit affects not only individuals but also the cultures they belong to. He introduces the receptive to the things of Christ, though they have never heard of him.

Fourth, all have conscience and therefore the capacity to know good and evil, right and wrong. Paul makes much of this in Romans 2, pointing out that though Jews despised other races because they did not have the Torah, nevertheless they often did what was right because the law was in their hearts through conscience.

What then is God's view of Muslims and Hindus, Buddhists and Sikhs? The question is wrongly worded. God does not label them according to their religion. He knows and loves them as his creatures. So how should Christians approach Muslims, Hindus, Buddhists and Sikhs? They should see them as human beings made in the image of God, one in the human race, and love them as brothers and sisters in the human family under God. We create problems for ourselves when we pigeonhole people according to a religious label.

Spiritual Achievement

Outside of Israel there is not only divine potential, but also spiritual achievement. Jesus recognised this when he met the Capernaum centurion and marvelled at his faith. Here was a hard-bitten soldier, not a learned philosopher or an ascetic holy man, a man you would not expect to rise to the heights of faith. But Jesus' commendation of him deserves pondering: *I tell you the truth, I have not found anyone in Israel with such great faith* (Matt. 8:10). In Israel Jesus had in fact met a great deal of unbelief, scepticism and downright hostility to the word of God from his own people, including the most religious. True, there were some who had shown faith in him, but none so much as this Roman officer. As was noted earlier in the discussion of the centurion's example, Jesus was not only impressed by the officer's faith in his ability to heal, but much more by the man's recognition of his divine authority. It took his disciples a long time to realise what this foreigner grasped in an instant.

This led Jesus on to remark that the centurion was no isolated exception; there will be many Gentiles from east and west who will take their places in the kingdom of heaven, presumably through a faith like his. The New Testament gives us other examples of people who were not Jews, who showed unusual spiritual insight, humility and faith. We have noted what the Gospels say about the Syro-Phoenician woman and the centurion, who was on duty at the crucifixion. Nothing is more impressive than the achievement of the Magi, wise men from far beyond Israel's eastern border. They acknowledged the one God, received messages from him, obeyed the directions God gave them and worshipped Jesus long before his people knew about him. Many Christians do not believe that people of other faiths can believe in the one true God and trust in him. But the Bible shows that God can communicate with such people and lead them to worship his Son.

There are God-fearers in all religions. They are distinguished by trust in the one creator God alone. They show their faith in action, for example by prayer and almsgiving. The New Testament cites three Old Testament examples of such God-fearing people. Jesus commended the Queen of Sheba and seemed to suggest that at the Day of Judgment she will be acquitted, because she travelled far to listen to the wisdom God gave Solomon. He also referred to the citizens of Nineveh, who repented at the preaching of Jonah. In this case a whole Gentile community turned to God, not only one or two individuals. The prophet did not believe they would repent and was offended when God forgave them (some Christians down the centuries have been guilty of similar attitudes towards other religious communities). The third example is the most extraordinary, the person of Melchizedek. This Canaanite priest king was not a Hebrew, nor related to Abraham, nor was he a member of the people of God, but he is likened to Christ. As noted earlier he symbolises the possibility of a person from another religion knowing God intimately and playing an important role in God's work apart from his chosen people. Unlike priests of the Baal worship common in Palestine, he is called 'priest of God Most High'. We assume that like Abraham he had been born into a polytheist society, but had come to put his faith in the one God who is above all gods. God chose to reveal himself to Abraham and to use him for his purposes, but he was not alone. Melchizedek was another, and we should not assume that there were no others who had come to believe in the one true God. Similarly in the centuries since Christ, we should expect God-fearers to have put their faith in the creator alone and found acceptance with him.

There is no reason why Christians should deny the spiritual achievements of the world's religions. Spiritual capacity is God-given. Despite human limitations and the distortions caused by sin, the Bible does acknowledge that there have been some exceptional men of faith outside God's covenant people. Whatever is true and good is from the creator and whatever is of pure faith is of God.

Chapter Six

God's Treatment of Religions

What is the verdict of the New Testament on the world's religions?
Are they valued or condemned? Does God use them in any way?
Are their insights fulfilled by Christ and given permanent significance?

Judged but not condemned

THE NEW TESTAMENT DOES NOT CONDEMN ANY RELIGION.
It does not reject any community, because of its religion. It does not
threaten the followers of any religion with hell fire. Rather it reverses the
Jewish prejudice against non-Jews, as people without hope and deprived
of God's law, and says that they have equal access to God's mercy with
God's chosen people. This does not mean that there is no criticism or
judgment of devotees of other religions, but judgment is based on what
people do, not on their religion or religious community. Practices which
are rejected include idolatry, polytheism, superstition, spiritism and the
commercialisation of religion, whatever the faith of the people involved.

In the four instances reported in Acts of encounters with Gentile
religions, the absence of condemnation is striking. Paul could have
indulged in sweeping generalisations rejecting the followers of the
religions he met, but he did not. A review of these four instances will
help to underline this point.

At Lystra, Paul and Barnabas nowhere condemned the people or the
priest of Zeus, despite the shock of being worshipped as Hermes and

Zeus. Instead the apostles urged the Lystrans to put their faith in the 'living God', whom the people knew about from the evidence of creation and providence. Their ignorance of the one true God is excused, because in the past God permitted all the nations to worship in their own ways. The fact that these polytheists had spiritual perception is recognised by the faith of the cripple, who was healed, and in the reaction of the crowd, who attributed the healing to divine power. At the same time the apostles openly called on the crowd 'to turn from these worthless things,' that is from the worship of many gods (Acts 14:8-18).

At Philippi Paul met a slave girl with a spirit of divination, who was being exploited for money by her owners. Such practices were common then and still are common in many parts of the world. Note that Paul did not use the occasion to launch an attack on the cult of Apollo and the Delphic oracle, or on Greek religion in general, despite being disturbed by the daily attentions of the girl. In fact he did not blame anyone for the girl's behaviour, but liberated her from the spirit that possessed her in the name of Jesus. Although her owners seized Paul and Silas and accused them of 'advocating customs unlawful for us Romans to accept or practise', they could not say that the apostles had denigrated their religious practices. But it is true that the account implies that Paul was critical of superstition, demonic influences and the exploitation of a girl prone to trance states for the sake of money (Acts 16:16-21).

At Athens Paul did not condemn the Stoics or the Epicureans. Despite being distressed by the plethora of idols at every turn in the city, he did not attack the religious sects or the priests in Athens. On the contrary he found common ground with the philosophers at the Areopagus and quoted from two of their poets to underline his point. He went out of his way, as he had done at Lystra, to exonerate his hearers for their ignorance of God's law and God's nature, saying that in the past God had overlooked such lack of knowledge in the Greek world. Now the creator is ready to judge people justly according to the revelation of the risen Christ. What Paul does criticise are the notions that the Lord of all the universe can be housed in man-made temples, worshipped as an image of gold or silver or stone, and served with food as if he needed anything. But in this Paul was not alone, for the Epicureans also rejected idol worship (Acts 17:16-34).

At Ephesus the town clerk of the city publicly acknowledged that Paul and his followers had not spoken ill of their goddess, Artemis, and had not robbed their temples. For a devout Jew like Paul the cult of the mother goddess would have been anathema. But he says nothing about this or against the local deity, concentrating instead on presenting the word of the Lord. On the other hand there is direct or implied criticism of sorcery, image worship and the commercialisation of religion (Acts 19:18-41).

Much missionary literature of the last two centuries has contained direct attacks on specific religions and condemnation of those who believe in them. Public preaching to people of other faiths has also contained generalised attacks on all non-Christian religions. By contrast the New Testament is courteous and restrained and does not indulge in sweeping judgements on other faiths or their followers. God views people with love and does not reject them, despite rebuking error and warning of judgement to come.

God's Use of Religion

Does God use the world's religions in any way, if so how? The New Testament is more positive than some might think, and less affirming than others might wish.

- The New Testament assumes that the religious language used by the peoples of the then known world witnessed to their knowledge about God, prayer, worship, forgiveness, sacrifice, ethics and much more. When Gentiles talked about such matters they shared some common spiritual understanding with their Jewish neighbours. Where did this knowledge come from? The most obvious source was the religions of the people of the Middle East and the Mediterranean basin. The religions were the purveyors of knowledge concerning the universe and God.

- A specific example of the significance of religious language is the use of the title 'Most High God' as a description of the supreme being. This was the title used by the slave girl with a spirit of divination in Acts 16:17. Although a Gentile herself, she used a description that had proved acceptable to both Jews and Greeks, providing them with a common denominator in referring to the deity. Jewish usage derived from the Hebrew *El Elyon*. It was by this name that Melchizedek blessed Abraham, for, he said, he is creator of heaven and earth (Gen. 14:18-20). On the Greek side the words indicated the high God, who is above all gods. Most languages do have a name for this supreme God, however many gods may be worshipped, showing that religions do recognise the difference.

- In Acts 17 Paul appeals to the common quest of human beings to seek for God until they find him. This search has been one of the mainsprings, which inspire the practice of religion. It was so in Athens in Paul's day, and it is so now. The account in Acts 17 shows just how much time and effort the Athenians gave to discussing religious ideas. This discussion dominated their agenda and made them open to discuss with Paul the message that he brought concerning Christ. Paul was not being wholly critical when he observed: *Men of Athens! I see that in every way you are very religious* (v. 22). Their desire to worship even the unknown God gave Paul an opportunity to proclaim the Lord of heaven and earth to them.

- It is significant that John finds in the Greek philosophical term, *logos*, a vehicle for conveying enhanced understanding of Christ as the eternal Word. Though we may agree that John did not accept the Platonic understanding of this term and gave it a Jewish and Christian orientation, it still remains true that he found in this Greek concept an ideal way of conveying the relationship of God and Christ. Later, this affirmation of Greek religious thought was to have surprising consequences. In the second century Christian apologists claimed that Plato and Socrates were proto-Christians, believers before their time, and therefore accepted by God.

- Nowadays we are used to distinguishing between culture and religious truth, and between what is believed about God and the way he is worshipped. Such a distinction between the fundamentals of the faith and the way God is worshipped and obeyed in different cultures was not unknown to the early church. The remarkable judgment given by James at the Jerusalem Council in Acts 15 recognised that Gentile Christians should be freed from the obligation of living like Jewish Christians. The converse of this is that Gentile religious cultural practices could be acceptable provided converts did not compromise essentials such as abstaining from idolatry and sexual immorality.

- A remarkable example of the extent to which God might go in using the skills acquired by non-Jewish religions occurs in the story of the Magi. As noted before, despite the warnings against astrology in the Old Testament, the Magi's knowledge of the stars was put to good use by God. God spoke to them through the stars, which they observed every day. God not only drew their attention to an unusual star, but also used their knowledge to convey to them that this star indicated the birth of one born to be king of the Jews. This was an exceptional case, but nevertheless it does show that God may use the knowledge of other religions to guide their devotees to himself and to the worship of Christ. It also shows that God is able to communicate directly with the devotees of other religions without using Jews or Christians, and that they are able to respond with faith and obedience, worship and sacrifice.

- Finally we may consider whether the New Testament supports the idea that Gentile religions are fulfilled by Christ. This is a complex question, which has been explored in many books. The idea that the gospel fulfils the truths and aspirations of other religions has been put forward in modern times. In the biblical context Christ fulfils the prophecies of the Old Testament, but does Christ also fulfil the desires of other religions? From the biblical point of view God revealed himself to Israel at many times and through various ways; the same cannot be said of Gentile religions. So if Christ is a fulfilment of the truth in religions outside Israel, it is because the truth has come to them through creation, conscience and other means. Acts 17 implies that Paul saw Christ as meeting some of the aspirations of Stoic and Epicurean religion rather than fulfilling their scriptures, creeds or philosophy.

God can use the truth that religions contain. But he does not need to. He can speak directly to people through his Spirit, who is active everywhere and in everyone. His preferred method is to speak through the revelation of Christ, his Word.

The Temporality of Religions

Religions are not eternal. They are temporary expressions of humanity's longing for the infinite. They are shadows of the real. In Christ the real has come and he contests the claims of religions for permanence, including Christianity.

In the past God has spoken to people at different times through different ways and messengers, but now he has spoken to the world through his Son. Since the person of his Son and the sacrifice of his Son are so much superior to anything that went before, the old has been superseded. There is no value in continuing with the old now that something much better has been given to humanity. That is the argument of the writer to the Hebrews. He applied this logic to Judaism and argued that since Christ has come even the Law of Moses and the worship of the holy Temple are outdated. If this is true of the law and sacrifices given by God to his people, how much more must it be true of the worship of other religions.

The New Testament sees the coming of Christ, both as Messiah and Son of God, as bringing in a new age. God has never done such a thing before, nor is there anything comparable in human religion. The new order supersedes everything that went before it. This does not however mean that what was true in the past has been abolished, destroyed or rejected. The writer to the Hebrews pictures the sacrificial system given by God in the past as but a shadow of the reality for which it stood; that reality was revealed by Christ. The law was good but it was not permanent and it was not the ultimate reality. This is not so much abolition by supersession as fulfilment. So Jesus emphasised in the Sermon on the Mount that he had not come to abolish the law but to fulfil it.

By analogy other religions are also superseded by Christ, but again not in the sense of rejecting what is of God in them, but in the sense of fulfilling the truth that they anticipated and pointed forward to. Paul explained to the people of Lystra that in the past God had allowed nations to go their own ways and worship as they felt best. Now that had changed, because of the descent from heaven of God himself in real human form. The shadow has passed the new has come.

Religions continue, both Jewish and Gentile, but the true worshipper whom the Father seeks must look beyond the outward forms to the inner reality and see that what humanity has longed for is to be found in Christ.

Chapter Seven

God's Way of Salvation

The New Testament is unequivocal in its affirmation of Christ as the Saviour of the world, the Lord of all and the way to the Father.

How does this relate to the world as we know it with its many sages and systems of belief? Can there be any justification in believing that there is only one way to God, which makes sense to people who are not Christians, even if they do not accept it?

The Way of Faith

THERE IS A PATH TO GOD, WHICH IS AND ALWAYS HAS BEEN open to people of all religions. It is available to all, whoever they are, wherever they live, whatever their race. It depends not on human achievement but upon God's grace. That is the way of faith.

The New Testament shows that the way of salvation is the way of faith, as exemplified by Abraham. Paul's exposition of this theme in Romans 4 emphasizes that Abraham was accepted by God on the basis of faith before he was circumcised, long before the law was given and without reference to his good deeds. Abraham believed that God would do what he promised and trusted God to forgive his sins and treat him as righteous.

Abraham's example is relevant for people of all races and religions, because he was born in a polytheist family and was not brought up as a Jew. Paul calls him 'the father of all who believe', both Jews and Gentiles, the father not of one nation only but of people of many nations.

Scripture shows that the way of faith has always been open to people of all religions, who come to put their whole trust in the Most High God, by whatever name they call him. It is universal, because the evidence about God from creation is there for all to see. It is available to all, because acceptance by God does not depend on special privileges, such as being born a Jew, or on exceptional knowledge or mystical experience. And the way of faith is acceptable to God, because it does not depend on human achievement but upon his grace.

That Abraham was no isolated exception and that people have come to know God by faith is suggested by other examples in the Old Testament. In the New Testament Jesus commenting on the faith of the centurion said that many who belong to other religions will be saved and enter the kingdom by faith in God, whilst many who are born Jews and have the privilege of knowing the scriptures will be rejected.

What is this faith, which God values and desires? It is not religiosity or zealous devotion to a religion, nor is it orthodoxy of belief or theological insight, nor is it confidence in the supernatural. According to Scripture what God is looking for is a person whose trust is focused on him alone with an undivided heart. The object of faith must be the one and only creator God, the Supreme Being, the Lord of heaven and earth. The measure of faith must be total. God can tolerate no rivals and will accept only undivided loyalty and trust. The evidence of this faith is that it acts in obedience and reliance upon God and his revelation. The reason why God approved of Abraham was that he believed God's promise of a child and acted accordingly. Faith that obeys God is the only faith that works.

Faith relies on some knowledge of God and of what he has revealed, but it is not the content of this knowledge which is vital, but the total reliance of the believer on God himself. The Bible consistently expects people to believe in God, even if they are not part of Israel. Paul elaborated on this in Romans, showing that human beings should obey God, because they know of him through creation and know what they should do through conscience. At the same time it is true that the Gentiles who show faith in God in the Bible are those who received a specific revelation from God. For example Naaman was told to bathe in the Jordan, Job encountered God, the Capernaum centurion met Jesus.

How can we relate this faith principle to world religions today? Muslims believe as rigorously as Jews in monotheism, that God is one and there is no other. That sets Muslims in the right direction. But as Jews and Christians have discovered, God requires much more. Only when we have lost all reliance on our own good deeds, our prayers and our religion, and cast ourselves solely on his grace does he draw near. Hindus traditionally believe in many gods, but they also believe in the Supreme Being (*Brahman*), the one without a second (*advaita*). There have been outstanding devotees of the *bhakti* tradition, who have expressed that love for God alone, which sounds like the faith of Abraham. One such devotee was Guru Nanak, the founder of Sikhism. His love for God and reliance on the grace of God for salvation are impressive. God alone knows the ones whom he accepts as men and women of faith, but the standard he is looking for is evident, that is total dependence on himself alone. History and experience suggest that only rare souls have found the way of faith and even they have longed to know the one they yearned for.

The Way of Christ

Christ is the personification of the way of faith. He is the way to the Father. By faith in him the believer comes to God, for Christ and the Father are one. Through Christ the way of faith is made available to all. What was possible but difficult for Abraham, Christ has simplified.

The way of faith sounds simple. In practice it has been anything but simple. Human beings have usually believed there must be a God (or gods) and atheists have been rare. But to know how to approach this God who is so silent and invisible has always been the problem. It has been easier to define God by negatives than to find anything positive to say about the great Unknown. This is why Christians believe the coming of Christ to have been of such cosmic significance. Unless God speaks we are all in the dark; unless God appears in a form we can understand we cannot know him. So the Logos was made flesh and dwelt among us. The Word was not only spoken but was also made visible. Christ has done even more than this, because he has made the way of faith attractive to millions through the revelation of the love of God. He has dispelled ignorance, and has also liberated humanity from the evil, which makes us prefer darkness to light. He has made God's way appealing and intelligible to the masses. What was an esoteric mystery he has transformed into common knowledge.

Christ makes God accessible to all. The New Testament views this in different forms.

God is no longer unknowable, because of ignorance. Thanks to the incarnation of the Word in the person of Jesus, he has been disclosed in human form. The God of the philosophers is an abstraction or a negation. The supreme being in the Upanishads can only be defined by negatives. It is 'not this, not that'. Most forms of Hinduism teach that the ultimate Being is unknowable. Even orthodox Islam teaches that believers cannot know God in himself, but can only know the will of God. Christ made the way to the Father simple and personal. In him the way becomes a person to follow and a guide to accompany.

God is no longer unapproachable, because of sin. Thanks to the sacrifice of Christ on the cross believers can enter into the holy presence of the Almighty. Imperfection has always been recognised as an obstacle between man and God. Hinduism describes this as *karma*, the ineradicable deposit of our deeds, which follows us in this life and through each transmigration. The human soul senses that only perfection is good enough for God and every blemish separates the devotee from his or her Lord. To get round this insuperable obstacle Hindu tradition posits that through thousands of lives and mega-cycles of time souls will be purified without defining exactly how this will take place. Islam teaches that a person's good deeds should outweigh their bad deeds on the day of judgement. In the context of the universal consciousness of human unworthiness before God, the cross of Christ is of cosmic significance. There the evil of the world, whatever its name, was placed upon Christ, who suffered its destructive consequences and liberated us from all sin.

God is no longer unattainable, because of human mortality. Thanks to the resurrection of Christ, death has been overcome and eternal life is God's gift to man. Every religion seeks to find an answer to the problems of suffering and death. This is particularly true of Buddhism, but Buddhism is not alone in its preoccupation with pain. Death is the final insult after a pilgrimage through a world of woe. For religions that believe in transmigration rebirth is not an answer to death but a repetition of its agonies. The resurrection of Christ turns death into a gateway to new life; destruction is destroyed. Suffering remains but it is no longer pointless. The way of the cross sanctifies the hardships of pilgrimage not only as the way of purification but as the way that leads to eternal life.

Christ gave the way of faith a human face. He revealed the name as well as the character of God, as Father. God-fearers have always longed to know how to approach their invisible creator. Christ made the hidden one visible. So he became the way, through which anyone may come to the Father.

One Way - many approaches

Christianity is avowedly universalist. From a creed that was limited to one race Christ created a faith for the whole world. The old distinction between Jew and Gentile was abolished. The new means of salvation was equally open to both. The manner of entering the new faith was radically different from anything that had been practised before. Unlike Judaism and many surrounding religions the new way could not be entered by birth according to the religion of the parents. Entry was to depend on individual choice. Since entry into the kingdom of God is not governed by the accidents of physical birth and is not limited to any racial group but is open to all, it may be entered by anyone from any race or religion. Human beings need no longer be restricted to the religion of their forbears.

Christianity is the only world religion, which is both international and not territorially based. As an international community it is available for all to join. It therefore clashes with the majority of religions, which are entered by birth and are part of a person's birthright. Christianity gives everyone the freedom to choose their religion, including the freedom to cease to be a Christian. This separates it from Islam, which seeks converts but refuses to give its members the freedom to leave as well as to join. Christianity gives freedom of choice, because God gives humanity freedom of choice.

God's way depends on freedom of choice, particularly in matters of faith, though religions have challenged this freedom. Most religions demand that their adherents by birth should never leave the religious community of their parents. Christianity believes that no one is born into a religion, but all are born the children of God. So no one is born a Muslim, a Hindu, a Buddhist or a Christian, for all are created by God and belong to him. God's invitation to his creatures through Christ is one to which all are invited to respond irrespective of their religion. God exercises no coercion or intimidation or compulsion in persuading his subjects to join his kingdom. He does not take back the freedom he has given us.

What many regard as the scandal of conversion is in fact the sign of a universal faith, which can be entered by the exercise of individual choice. Conversion is commonly used as a term to describe a change of religion or religious community. However from a Christian viewpoint conversion is not a change of religion, but a change of the inner person. It may subsequently result in a change in a person's religious affiliation, but that is not the heart of the matter. What is essential is the right of the individual to move in the direction God is calling them.

Why then should there be only one way? The New Testament knows only one God and acknowledges only one mediator and contemplates only one unrepeatable sacrifice for the sake of the world. The logic of belief in one God is that only his way is valid. God is one, therefore the path is one. Where there is belief in many gods, there are many ways; and where there is speculation about the supreme reality, there are many attempts to discover the truth. But when the truth is revealed and God provides the way the options narrow down to acceptance or rejection.

However there are many approaches to the one way. God leads people along different paths to bring them to the beginning of his way of salvation. In Bunyan's *Pilgrim's Progress* Pilgrim stumbled along many by-ways and over many hurdles before he finally arrived at the wicket gate that led to the cross. Every pilgrim must traverse their own individual route to the wicket gate. The experience of Christ's followers down the centuries has revealed an almost infinite variety of ways in which God has led people to discover Christ. There is no uniformity in the patterns of conversion. People have come out of every religious community, including Christendom, into the kingdom of God. They have come through every conceivable means. The variety of approach roads balances the insistence on receiving the grace of God by one way through Christ.

The way is free, because all is of grace. Therefore there are no preconditions to be met, no limitations to be overcome, no tests to be passed. The offer of salvation is unconditional. The gospel is for all.

Chapter Eight

God's Standards for Christian Mission

Christian mission to the world is often accused of standing for imperialism, the use of force or deception, and the domination of those who are being evangelised. If there is any substance in these accusations it could only be because the church has been unfaithful to the spirit of Christ. Christ's own mission to the world was characterised by humility as opposed to pride, self-giving in contrast to manipulation by inducements, and vulnerability rather than reliance on power and protected status.

Respect & humility

ONE OF THE MAIN OBJECTIONS TO THE CHRISTIAN APPROACH to other faiths has been the air of superiority, which Christians have often adopted. In the past they have talked of the 'heathen' living in darkness and bowing down to gods of wood and stone. Today churchgoers are more likely to realise that Hindus, Buddhists and Muslims are deeply religious. Far from living in darkness, their neighbours of other faiths appear to be more devout than they are and to have many admirable qualities. Nevertheless the impression persists that Christians think they are better than others.

Given that the New Testament views Christ as the way to the Father, the Saviour of the world and the Lord of all is it inevitable that Christians will appear to look down on other faiths? Christians have often been guilty of making a false assumption. They have confused the superiority of Christ with their own superiority. Christ's disciples did not make this error in the first century, perhaps because they were few in number and usually a tiny minority. They were taught to respect other cultures and other people, whatever their opinions, and to hold to Christ with humility, knowing they were in no way more deserving of God's mercy than those from whom they differed.

We have already seen that Peter instructed his readers to *show proper respect to everyone* (1 Pet. 2:17). It should be natural for believers in Christ to treat others with respect, because of the high regard that Scripture has for humanity. We know that everyone is made in the image of God for fellowship with God and to inherit an eternal destiny. All of us are loved by God, whatever our religion. He has no favourites and treats all as equals. Christ's own example teaches us to give special attention to the marginalised and to those whom society looks down on. No one is inferior in his sight. The respect we show to others should not depend on their looks, language, clothing or education. God does not label people according to their religion, nationality, race, language or education and nor should we.

The New Testament does not advocate respect for a person's views and opinions but for the person herself or himself. In this it differs from the current secular viewpoint, where individuals are said to be entitled to their opinions whatever they are and these opinions should be respected. Christ does not respect our opinions, which are often misguided due to lack of knowledge or to prejudice or plain sinfulness. But he does respect us as individuals. He gives us freedom to make mistakes and does not override that freedom. It is tempting for his followers to be less tolerant and to wish that people had less liberty to say what they like. The fact that some people have strongly held opinions, which are contrary to ours, and may reject or attack us, should not lessen our respect for them, because we are to see them as God sees them. What should save us from being impatient and wiser than God is a proper sense of humility born of knowing our own ignorance and fallibility.

Respect for the individual is an accepted standard in secular, democratic society. But humility is not prized to the same extent. This, however, is required of believers, because of Christ's example. He combined his extraordinary claims with the lowliness of a servant. If he could combine his claims with humility, so can his followers. In fact it should be easier for us to do this, because we know that we need God's mercy more than those who have had fewer privileges. To those who have been given much, of them will much be required.

How does Christ's example affect the way Christians treat people of other faiths? It should eliminate attacks on people, whether physical or verbal. It should also eliminate attacks on religions. The New Testament does not attack any religion. This does not mean there is a total absence of criticism. Idolatry, immorality, superstition and the prostitution of religion for money are all decried. But in the New Testament there are no sweeping dismissals of any religion, no attempts to denigrate any faith, no personal abuse and no threats against any religious community.

On the other hand the New Testament does not accept the notion that all religions are equal or equally valid or equally ways to God (or the ultimate reality). There can be no equality between the way of salvation God has provided in Christ and the ways of human religion. Nevertheless God allows human beings to go their own ways, to devise their own religious practices and to choose whether to search for God or not. The Father waits patiently for his creatures to turn to him. He has opened a way in Christ for people of all nations, languages and religions to come to him and enter his kingdom. This is the day of grace; the day of judgement is yet to come. It follows that where Christians are in a majority they are not to treat people of other faiths as second class citizens. Dhimmi status may be the norm in Islam, whereby non-Muslims are second class citizens, but it is not acceptable in a Christian society, where all are equals before God.

Self-giving

The pattern for all Christians is Christ. Christ fulfilled his mission to the world by giving himself completely for the sake of humanity. In doing so he redefined love, not as an emotion, but as an act of self sacrifice for the benefit of all, including his enemies, whatever their race or religion. That kind of love is what Christians owe to people of other faiths.

Reflecting on the example of Christ, John writes: *This is love: not that we loved God, but that he loved us and sent his Son as an atoning sacrifice for our sins. Dear friends, since God so loved us, we also ought to love one another*

(1 John 4:10-12). It is possible that John was thinking particularly of the need for believers to love each other in the family of Christ. That love, which is received and reciprocated in the family of God, is indeed very precious. But Christians have often been guilty of restricting their love in a way that Christ did not. We are to love our neighbours *as ourselves*, whether they respond to that love or not. Christ specifically taught his followers not to limit their love to those they knew and liked but to show love in action to strangers and enemies as well. It should be our joy that we give ourselves to our neighbours, who are Hindus, Muslims, Sikhs or Buddhists. We have much in common with them, most of all a shared humanity and a common creator.

The hall-mark of Christ's self-giving is that it is for all regardless of race or religion, poverty or wealth, status or the lack of it. Mission hospitals have usually been set up to benefit all, even though that vision may have been lost in the passage of time. Christian relief and development agencies are committed to serving people of all the religious communities where they work. They are also inspired by the conviction that love must be seen in action, just as it was in the life and works of Jesus. This compassion is specially concerned for the oppressed, the marginalised and the disadvantaged.

One of the criticisms levelled at missionaries is that they have given things to induce people of other faith communities to become Christians. For example, they have given economic benefits or educational advantages or medical services, so that the beneficiaries would convert. It is true that missions have set up schools, hospitals and development programmes. These were inspired by Christ, who healed the sick, fed the hungry and taught the illiterate. But Christ went further than this by renouncing his privileges and possessions, in order to give his life on a cross for the liberation of humanity. Paul understanding the depth of this divine agape, warned that without self-giving love no amount of religious fervour and humanitarian service would be of any value. So it is true that those who run mission hospitals and schools and aid agencies without giving themselves to those they serve, regardless of their response, fall short of Christ's standards. Nelson Mandela speaking at a conference in Zimbabwe in 2002 told the delegates that, despite all the criticism of missionaries, without them he would not have been standing there. 'They gave us education … they supported us … and (he added) they loved us.' Those last three words say more than anything else.

If Christians had always loved their opponents, the course of world history would have been very different. It is easy to look back on the errors of the past and to blame others, e.g. those who fought the crusades. What of the present? How are Christians showing love and solidarity with Muslims in the west post September 11th? How are believers reacting to the persecution of Christians in India by some Hindu extremists? It is all too easy to isolate ourselves from people of other faiths and to criticize those who threaten us. What Christ requires of his followers is that they should go out of their way to meet people who are not part of their circle and give themselves to those who belong to religious communities other than their own.

Vulnerability

Christians are called to witness for Christ. To those who are being evangelised this may sound threatening, especially if the witness is publicised through the lavish use of power and money. When people feel overwhelmed by human pressure to accept the Christian message, they will resent the pressure even if they are unable to resist it. In contrast to high pressure salesmanship, the pattern of authentic Christian witness follows the way of the cross. That is to say evangelism which is carried out from a position of power and at a safe distance is not Christ-like. Jesus became vulnerable when he became man. This vulnerability was the other side of neighbourliness. He could not share our sorrows and carry our iniquities from outer space. He could only come alongside his creatures by becoming one of them. By becoming one of us he shared our fate, except that his fate was worse because he died on a cross in our place. Incarnation made suffering inevitable. It also made mission possible.

Just as Jesus did not preach from a place of power and security, so he calls his followers to be open and vulnerable to rejection by those who hear their testimony. This was so for the apostles. Paul abandoned the position of rank and prestige in Judaism for the life of an itinerant preacher subject to violent opposition and arbitrary imprisonment. He commended himself to his hearers by being willing to suffer for them.

This did not convince his opponents, but it made him an authentic disciple of the crucified Messiah.

Today mission that is carried out by the power of wealth and protected by position or status lays itself open to the charge of imperialism. But where Christians are willing to suffer for their faith they earn the right to share in Christ's mission to the world. They may be rejected, but their message can be received openly, because it comes without any taint of pressure and without giving any ground for the charge of domination.

The value of vulnerability is a reflection of the colonial era, when western missionaries came to Africa and Asia with money to build institutions and with the prestige of belonging to the dominant west. Although they were often opposed and hindered by colonial governments anxious to preserve their commercial interests, they appeared to local people to preach from a position of power. This fuelled to some degree the charge that missionaries have used economic inducements or undue influence to persuade vulnerable groups to change their religion. As a result Christians have to go out of their way to share the gospel in lowliness and to accept opposition and persecution as tests of their genuineness.

Christians who suffer for their faith do earn the right to speak, and this right to speak is one they have long realised has to be worked for not assumed. In every continent the church continues to grow where the message is spread by the vulnerable ones who suffer. China is an obvious example, where many who have been imprisoned have spread the faith in prison and outside, toughened and emboldened by the hardships Christ has inspired them to endure. The church in Nepal is another modern example – there pastors and converts went willingly to prison till the law was changed to allow conversions.

The vulnerability of believers does not always produce a harvest, nor is there any guarantee that a persecuted preacher will gain a hearing. But where Christians are willing to be open to challenge, and where they witness in lowliness and do not hide from persecution, there their motives for mission are purified. In such situations, as Paul says, the gospel can be preached in demonstration of the power of God without any reliance on human power or wisdom. The complaint that mission depends on undue influence falls to the ground, for the preacher holds no influence other than truth and love.

Authentic witness follows the way of the cross. Just as Jesus did not preach from a place of power and security, so he calls his followers to be open and vulnerable to rejection by those who hear their testimony. Those who suffer for their faith earn the right to share in Christ's mission to the world.

But there is another sort of vulnerability, which Christians often ignore in this secular age when the opinions of others seem more important than the verdict of God. Christians are also vulnerable to God's demands and are called to be totally open to his commands. He has called the church to proclaim the good news and instructed Christ's followers to be witnesses to him. Christians can no more hide from God's calling to mission than Adam and Eve could hide from his voice calling in the garden of Eden. Nor can they shelter behind the fig leaves of their excuses, pretending that the world of competing religions makes it impossible to share the creator's message.

The church cannot avoid the clear command of Christ to make disciples of all nations. The mandate is unambiguous and matches the international character of God's kingdom, which exists for all peoples. It also corresponds to the reality that no other faith offers what Christ has achieved by the cross, resurrection and Pentecost.

Love for God and for their neighbours requires disciples to share what God has done for them. The task is to find a way of sharing God's gospel with humility and love in our multi-faith world. The early church showed the way; their successors have to follow that lead. There can be no escaping the brickbats and opprobrium that rain down on those who point to Christ as the way to the Father. Did he not say, *Take up your cross and follow me*? But did he not also say, *If anyone is ashamed of me and my words ... the Son of Man will be ashamed of him when he comes in his Father's glory*?

Christ's followers cannot escape vulnerability. Either they are true to Christ and dismissed by the world or true to the world and rejected by Christ.

Chapter Nine

Concluding Postscript:
Christian Relations with Other Faiths

The Modern Debate

IN THE PAST TWO CENTURIES MANY ATTEMPTS HAVE BEEN made to define what should be a proper Christian approach to other religions. In a recent book Terrance Tiessen has classified these assessments of religions from a Christian basis under five categories.

The no-agreement approach. This views other religions as wholly false. They are considered to be the product of demonic deception or the constructs of purely human thought and aspiration, and therefore essentially different from the revelation of God in Christianity. This negative assessment can be found in the post-apostolic period in some writers, such as Tertullian, and was the common approach of Protestant missionaries in the colonial period. Hendrik Kraemer provided a sophisticated theological restatement of this position.

The common faith approach. In complete contrast the common faith approach sees all religions as being many paths to the same ultimate end. No religion has an exclusive claim to the truth; all share a common core. Christianity is not superior but compatible with other faiths. This view is congenial to Asian traditions such as Hinduism, Buddhism and Sikhism, and to some Asian theologians, such as Raimon Panikkar and Stanley Samartha. In the west John Hick and Paul Knitter are well-known advocates of this approach.

The fulfilment or common ground approach. Proponents of this approach see religions as preparations for the gospel. Christ fulfils the truth in religions and brings them to perfection. This category covers a wide range of ideas from JN Farquahar's view of Christianity as 'The Crown of Hinduism' to Karl Rahner's description of devotees of other faiths as 'anonymous Christians'.

The different ends approach. Here is a view which takes off in protest against Farquahar's theory, on the grounds that religions ask and answer different questions, certainly different questions from those with which the gospel is chiefly concerned. Religions are not many ways to one end but ways to different ends. Each religion has its own ultimate objective. Each way has a destination in view, but as the ways are different so are the destinations. John Cobb and Mark Heim are proponents of this approach. Heim suggests that people may "establish a primary religious relationship to something other than the religious ultimate, or because there are distinctly different ways to relate to that ultimate, or for both reasons", they adopt a variety of religious ends. Christianity's distinctive goal is salvation, but other religious traditions may be committed to other goals and to the distinctive truth in their belief systems.

The point of contact approach. This perspective denies that all religions are paths to the same ultimate goal, but affirms that though they have fundamental differences, they may also contain elements which they share in common with Christianity. It also denies that Christ fulfils, perfects and uses religions as coherent systems. However it does affirm that there are elements in religions which are true and valuable. It is these elements, and not the religion as a system, which may be reinterpreted and deemed fulfilled in Christ. There are therefore 'points of contact' between Christians and people of other traditions. At the personal level God may be savingly at work in individuals within different religions by his grace. Jesus Christ is God's means of salvation, but this does not mean that he cannot save devotees in other religions, particularly those who put their faith in God as they understand him. God is drawing all people ultimately to Christ by every mode of his self revelation. Tiessen himself advocates this approach.

What light does our survey of the New Testament attitude to the world's religions shed on these five approaches?

Surprisingly the New Testament does not agree with those who advocate the no-agreement view. As we have seen Paul does find common ground with the Stoics and Epicureans in Athens. He is able to find quotations from their writings which support the revelation of God, which he put before his Athenian audience. His theological understanding, as outlined in Romans, relies on the belief that everyone should have some knowledge about God, whatever their religion. So in his encounter with the devotees of Zeus in Lystra, he reminds them that the evidence of creation and providence should help them to put their faith in the living God. As we have seen above in the section on God's use of religion, God is able to use the truth in religions to point devotees to himself, as for example he did in the story of the Magi and even in the life of a polytheist like Melchizedek. The New Testament does not attack any religion and refuses to condemn religions as wholly false, though it does condemn errors such as idolatry.

There is no suggestion that religions are alternative ways to God. The idea that all faiths are ways to the same end is foreign to the New Testament. Christ is the way to God and the saviour of the world. It is God who saves not religion. If there is a common core it is the common core of human identity made in the image of God, together with the evidence of a world created by God. In contrast to other ways Christ does claim to have exclusive knowledge of the truth.

The fulfilment theory is less easy to dismiss, though the New Testament does not explicitly use this terminology. The model of fulfilment is there in that Christ is a fulfilment of Old Testament prophecy. The writer to Hebrews elaborates on the way in which Christ's sacrifice fulfils the type of sacrifice given in the Mosaic covenant. However to extend the fulfilment paradigm to other religions is not so straightforward, and is not something which the writer to Hebrews or Paul or any other New Testament author attempts. This theory has foundered not so much on biblical evidence as on the practical reality that other faiths ask different questions and have different aspirations. As a disciple of Christ from a Hindu family, put it: the gospel not only does not fulfil Hindu aspirations it actually kills some of Hinduism's deepest desires.

This leaves the last two approaches for consideration. The different ends approach is based on empirical evidence. As we have seen the New

Testament does not discuss the nature of other religions or their ends and objectives. It is difficult to say whether the apostolic writers would agree or disagree with this approach.

Of the five approaches listed above, the nearest to the New Testament evidence is the 'point of contact' approach. The New Testament affirms that the followers of Gentile religions do have some knowledge of truth which God has revealed. The grace of God is at work outside Israel and outside the church. God is at work in followers of other ways and other gods. So though Christ is God's way of salvation, this does not mean that he cannot save people who do not know the gospel.

We conclude that the New Testament does not fit exactly into any of the five categories of Christian assessment of religions listed by Tiessen. This alone should give cause for further thought on this most contentious issue.

A Model for Christian relationships with people of other faiths

At the practical level of everyday life in our multi-faith world the question is: How are Christians expected to relate to Muslims, Hindus, Sikhs, Buddhists, Jews and followers of other religions?

When the church has been in charge, it has often failed to tolerate diversity of opinion and practice. Has Christ a better way? Are there relevant guidelines for a tolerant society in the New Testament?

The New Testament does contain guidelines for human relationships, and these are grounded in the nature of God, as revealed by Christ.

- God has created human beings in his own image and therefore all are of equal value in his sight. Muslims, Jews and Christians are all agreed on this fundamental point.

- God is love and his love embraces all human beings. His love is not confined to a chosen few, but extends to all whether they are believers or unbelievers, rich or poor, educated or illiterate. His love knows no class distinctions or racial and religious boundaries.

From this starting point we can identify three keys for harmonious human relationships.

The first is respect for everyone. God respects us and values us, so Christians should be able to adopt the same attitude to others. We can make a start by not labelling people according to their religion. God does not view people as Muslims, Hindus, Buddhists and so on, but as persons whom he has made. By viewing people according to their religious label, we tend to classify them impersonally and lump them all together, as if they were all the same. Muslims are no more identical than Christians. We will find it much easier to respect people by getting to know them. By getting closer to people it is possible to begin to break down the instinctive division between 'them' and 'us'. This does not mean that we disregard a person's religion, just that we need to find out what they actually believe and stand for. Respect is not the same as agreement. God respects our freedom to do and think and say what he does not agree with. We need to be strong enough and wise enough to do the same. The right to freedom of speech has arisen, because of respect for the individual's conscience and the Christian belief in a person's right to act according to their inner convictions.

The second is tolerance. The idea of toleration in the English language is associated with toleration of religious differences, and the Act of Toleration in the 18th century allowed religious freedom to Dissenting Protestants in England. This is relevant to our present discussion of relations between people of different faiths. What we are concerned about is differences of belief and opinion. Just as we expect Christians to have freedom to practice and propagate their faith, so we believe that others should have the same freedom. Disagreements with our neighbours of other faiths can easily irritate us. What does tolerance mean in these situations? As we have seen the New Testament does not attack any religion, but this does not mean there is an absence of criticism of practices which are said to be wrong, such as idolatry. We have freedom of speech, but not the freedom to belittle any faith, or to threaten any religious community, or to engage in personal abuse.

Christ's teaching and example challenge the quality of our tolerance. Applying the Sermon on the Mount to this topic, we can see that Jesus taught non-judgmental tolerance, pro-active tolerance and inclusive tolerance. He was non-judgmental in the sense that he taught us not to condemn or pass judgment on others. In some regards western society has adopted a non-judgmental stance, in others it is fiercely dismissive. It is the attitude of superiority from which we look down on others and are dismissive of people who belong to other faiths, that is wrong, not the spirit of discernment. Pro-active tolerance is implied in the Golden Rule. Doing to others what you would want them to do to you involves putting yourself in their shoes and trying to see life from their viewpoint. Inclusive tolerance can be seen in what Jesus said about loving our enemies. After the terrorist attacks by Muslims in New York, Mumbai and London it is easy to indulge in Islamophobia. Jesus calls on us to counter such instinctive hostility by imitating God's inclusive attitude. God is merciful to all; human mercy is all too often selective.

The third is love in action. In response to God's love Christians are expected to show love in practice in our multi-faith society. The New Testament repeatedly teaches that the quality of love required of those who follow Christ is not sentiment but self-giving action for the sake of others. Nowhere should this be more obvious than when Christians are under attack. The apostles not only taught that there should be no retaliation and no armed resistance, but also that there should be no attempt to take revenge. Instead of revenge love calls for reconciliation, that is reconciliation between enemies. This most costly act of love led Christ to the Cross, and his example calls his followers to act as peacemakers with their enemies. Instead of the pursuit of revenge disciples are called on to bless their persecutors and to be generous to them in their hour of need.

When the Christian approach to people of other faiths is based on respect, toleration and love, then it becomes much easier to deal with the differences of belief that divide us. We have a working model for a harmonious society, which is stronger and more inclusive than the secular model.

Summing up

Our survey of the New Testament approach to religions reveals the following significant points.

God deals with human beings without regard to their religious affiliation. He does not look at people through the kaleidoscope of religions. He does not label people according to their religion. He approaches his creatures directly, using the knowledge they have of the truth and awakening their desire to know him. Through his Spirit he is able to reach everyone everywhere and to communicate with them individually in the core of their being. God is for the whole world, not just for Jews and Christians.

The apostolic writers are overwhelmed by the inclusive appeal of Christ to the nations, whom they had previously dismissed as beyond the pail. The gospel is good news, because it is for everyone and comes as a free gift of God's grace. Christ has embraced everyone on the cross and created a new humanity out of the old hostilities. Therefore God is impartial in his dealings with all and not prejudiced in favour of the Jews, even though Jesus is the Messiah of the Jews and the Jewish king.

There is no reason why the followers of Christ should reject the spiritual achievements of religious leaders who do not know Christ, because God has given them spiritual capacity. They can distinguish good from evil and they are able to do what is right. Religions do contain and convey some truths that are compatible with the gospel.

What God is looking for is faith and obedience. He is not always disappointed. There are God-fearers in other religious traditions.

The New Testament reveals Jesus as God's way for humanity. He is the Word of God incarnate and the Light of the world. By his sacrifice on the cross, God has opened the door for all to receive salvation. Now that Christ has come there is no need for other ways. All are invited to respond to the invitation to the heavenly banquet.

Select Bibliography

Anderson, Norman, *Christianity and World Religions*, Leicester, 1984.

Bosch, D.J., *Transforming Mission: Paradigm Shifts in Theology of Mission*, New York, 1991.

Chakkarai, V., *Jesus the Avatar*, Madras, 1932.

Clarke A.D. & Winter B.W. (ed.), *One God, One Lord in a World of Religious Pluralism*, Cambridge, 1991.

Coward, H.G. (ed.), *Modern Indian Responses to Religious Pluralism*, Albany, 1987.

Cragg, Kenneth, *The Christ and the Faiths*, London, 1986.

Devanandan, P.D., *Preparation for Dialogue*, Bangalore, 1961.

D'Costa, Gavin, *The Meeting of Religions and the Trinity*, New York, 2000.

Fernando, Ajith, *The Christian's Attitude Toward World Religions*, Mumbai, 1988.

Glaser, Ida, *The Bible and Other Faiths*, Leicester, 2005.

Gnanakan, Ken, *Proclaiming Christ in a Pluralistic Context*, Bangalore, 2000.

Jathanna, O.V., *The Decisiveness of the Christ-Event and the Universality of Christianity in a World of Religious Plurality*, Berne, 1981.

Jeremias, J., *The Central Message of the New Testament*, London, 1965.

Kim, Sebastian C.H., *In Search of Identity: Debates on Conversion in India*, New Delhi & Oxford, 2003.

Kalapatti, J., *Dr. Radhakrishnan and Christianity: An Introduction to Hindu-Christian Apologetics*, Delhi, 2002.

Marshall, Howard, *Jesus the Saviour*, London, 1990.

Nazir-Ali, Michael, *The Unique and Universal Christ: Jesus in a Plural World*, Hyderabad, 2008.

Newbigin, Lesslie, *The Gospel in a Pluralist Society*, London, 1989.

Pinnock, Clark H., *A Wideness in God's Mercy*, Grand Rapids, 1992.

Ramachandra, Vinoth, *Faiths in Conflict*, Leicester, 1999.

Sanders, John, *No Other Name*, Grand Rapids, 1992.

Stott, John R.W., *Issues Facing Christians Today*, Grand Rapids, 1984.

Terrance L. Tiessen, *Who Can Be Saved?: Reassessing Salvation in Christ and World Religions*, Downers Grove & Leicester, 2004.

Thomas, M.M., *The Acknowledged Christ of the Indian Renaissance*, London, 1972.

Yong, Amos, *Beyond the Impasse: Toward a Pneumatological Theology of Religions*, Grand Rapids, 2003.

Zaehner, R.C., *Mysticism Sacred and Profane: An Inquiry into Some Varieties of Praeternatural Experience*, Oxford, 1957.

New Testament Index

Titus

Titus 2:10   154
Titus 2:11   102
Titus 3:1   150
Titus 3:1, 2   142
Titus 3:3   142

Philemon

Philemon 16   145

Hebrews

Heb. 1:1-3   103
Heb. 7:1-3   41
Heb. 7:1-22   131
Heb. 7 - 10   pages   **79-80**
Heb. 8:13   109
Heb. 10:19-22   103
Heb. 10:26-29   103
Heb. 10:32ff.   162
Heb. 10:33   159
Heb. 10:34   159
Heb. 11:4-7   130
Heb. 11:6   132
Heb. 12:14   143
Heb. 13:3   162
Heb. 13:16   141
Heb. 13:20   79

James

James 1:2   160
James 1:3f.   161
James 2:8   141
James 2:13   141
James 4:4   146

1 Peter

1 Pet. 2:9,10   156
1 Pet. 2:11; 4:3   146
1 Pet. 2:12   142
1 Pet. 2:13-17   150
1 Pet. 2:17   188
1 Pet. 2:21   159
1 Pet. 2:21ff.   162
1 Pet. 2:21-24   162
1 Pet. 2:23   163
1 Pet. 3:9   142

1 Pet. 3:9, 16   159
1 Pet. 3:14   159
1 Pet. 3:15   154
1 Pet. 3:18ff.   162
1 Pet. 4:12   160
1 Pet. 4:14   159
1 Pet. 4:16   159

2 Peter

2 Pet. 1:19-21   63

1 John

1 John 2:15ff.   146
1 John 3:18   141
1 John 4:8   140
1 John 4:10-12   190
1 John 4:16   140
1 John 5:19-21   20

Revelation

Rev. 2:9   150
Rev. 2:10   159
Rev. 3:9   150
Rev. 6:9   156
Rev. 7:9   116
Rev. 9:20   19
Rev. 12:11   159
Rev. 13   152
Rev. 13:7-17 pages   **22-23**
Rev. 13:8   131
Rev. 13:15-17   152, 159
Rev. 15:2   24
Rev. 17:9   22
Rev. 19:20   23
Rev. 21:26   116
Rev. 22:13, 16   163

About the Author

Basil was born in England but grew up in China, where he lived for nine years up to the age of 11. His parents were based in west China in the ancient city of Langzhong, which was steeped in Confucian learning and Chinese Buddhism. He went to the CIM (China Inland Mission) school at Chefoo on the sea, east of Beijing. School was interrupted by the outbreak of the Pacific War with Japan in 1941. Then for three years he was in Japanese prison camps for British, US and other foreigners. Basil's family were shipped back to Britain in 1945.

After school in England Basil spent a year of national service in Kuala Lumpur, and visited Singapore, Malaysia and Thailand. He then went on to study history and theology for five years at Cambridge. There he joined the student Christian Union and received God's call to mission. After being ordained as a minister in the Church of England, God guided him to India with Interserve (then BMMF).

To prepare for mission in India Basil went to BHU (Banaras Hindu University) in 1963 to study Indian philosophy and live in a student hostel. In 1964 Shirley and Basil were married in`Mussoorie. They joined the staff of the UESI in 1965 and moved to Delhi two years later when PT Chandapilla asked them to work with him there. His four years in Varanasi gave him a lifelong interest in Hinduism and seeing Jesus from a Hindu viewpoint.

All their four children were born in India, in UP, Delhi or Punjab. In 1983 they returned to England for the sake of their further education. After 30 years in Asia Basil was not about to turn his back on India. They settled in Leicester, because it had the largest Hindu population of any city in UK with 50,000 Gujarati refugees from East Africa. There they also met Jains for the first time and entered into dialogue with Muslims. Surprisingly Basil learnt more about Sikhs and Sikhism in England than he had learnt in India. He met Hakim Singh Rahi, poet and evangelist, and edited his book, *Sri Guru Granth Sahib Discovered*, which was published in Delhi by Motilal Banarsidass in 1999. Guru Nanak's devotion to the one and only true God is impressive.

On retirement Basil settled in Cambridge and began research to find out what the New Testament really has to say about the Christian approach to man's religions. That study gave rise to this book.

primalogue
Publishing & Media

Primalogue is a new generation publisher, focusing on quality, competence and value for money. We offer you our rich experience in the publishing industry and associated fields to provide you excellent products and services that are innovative and relevant.

Primalogue offers a wide range of services in printing and publishing.

Publishing

Primalogue helps you to publish your work with high quality under expert supervision. Our team comprises of experts in publishing, media, arts and Information technology and can offer you solutions best-suited to your needs. Please contact us if you would like to publish your works through Primalogue.

Publishing Services

Primalogue offers comprehensive solutions to organizations and individuals in printing and publishing. We manage a competent team to provide you the complete spectrum of services including editing, proof-reading, design, layout , printing, publishing and print management.

Consulting

We offer consulting services to organizations, writers, media houses. Our team comes with a rich experience in publishing, arts, media and technology. We can help you identify your publishing & media requirements and guide you in developing solutions.

Primalogue Publishing Media Pvt. Ltd.
#32 II Cross, Hutchins Road
Bangalore, 560084 India
Phone: +91- 80 - 41251811
Mobile: +91- 80 - 99801 39622

Email: enquiry@primalogue.com
Website: www.primalogue.com